CONSTITUTIONAL DIALOGUES IN COMPARATIVE PERSPECTIVE

Constitutional Dialogues in Comparative Perspective

Edited by

Sally J. Kenney
Associate Professor of Public Policy and Law
Humphrey Institute of Public Affairs
University of Minnesota

William M. Reisinger
Professor of Political Science
University of Iowa

and

John C. Reitz
Professor of Law
University of Iowa

Foreword by J. H. H. Weiler

First published in Great Britain 1999 by
MACMILLAN PRESS LTD
Houndmills, Basingstoke, Hampshire RG21 6XS and London
Companies and representatives throughout the world

A catalogue record for this book is available from the British Library.

ISBN 0–333–73690–7

First published in the United States of America 1999 by
ST. MARTIN'S PRESS, INC.,
Scholarly and Reference Division,
175 Fifth Avenue, New York, N.Y. 10010

ISBN 0–312–21767–6

Library of Congress Cataloging-in-Publication Data
Constitutional dialogues in comparative perspective / edited by Sally
J. Kenney, William M. Reisinger, John C. Reitz ; foreword by J.H.H.
Weiler.
    p.   cm.
Includes bibliographical references and index.
ISBN 0–312–21767–6 (cloth)
1. Constitutional law—Europe.   2. Judicial review—Europe.
I. Kenney, Sally Jane.   II. Reisinger, William M. (William Mark),
1957–   . III. Reitz, John C.
KJC4445.C665   1998
342.4—dc21   98–28240
                                                                                CIP

This book is printed on paper suitable for recycling and made from fully managed and
sustained forest sources.

10   9   8   7   6   5   4   3   2   1
08   07   06   05   04   03   02   01   00   99

Printed and bound in Great Britain by Antony Rowe Ltd, Chippenham, Wiltshire

We dedicate this book
to Madame Advocate General Simone Rozès
to John R. and Patricia A. Reitz
to Kathy and Mark

Contents

Notes on the Contributors   ix

Foreword by J.H.H. Weiler   xi

Acknowledgments   xviii

List of Abbreviations   xix

1 Introduction: Constitutional Dialogues in Comparative
   Perspective   1
   Sally J. Kenney, William M. Reisinger and John C. Reitz

2 Constitutional Dialogues: Protecting Rights in France,
   Germany, Italy and Spain   8
   Alec Stone Sweet

3 Experimental Constitutionalism: A Comparative Analysis
   of the Institutional Bases of Rights Enforcement in
   Post-Communist Hungary   42
   Jeffrey Seitzer

4 Political Economy and Abstract Review in Germany,
   France and the United States   62
   John C. Reitz

5 A Comparative Study of the Constitutional Protection of
   Hate Speech in Canada and the United States: A Search
   for Explanations   89
   William G. Buss

6 Intercultural Citizenship: Statutory Interpretation and
   Belonging in Britain   119
   Susan Sterett

7 The Judges of the Court of Justice of the European
   Communities   143
   Sally J. Kenney

8   Legal Orientations and the Rule of Law in Post-Soviet
    Russia   172
    William M. Reisinger

9   The Success of Judicial Review   193
    Martin Shapiro

Cases and Official Documents Cited   220

Books, Articles and Chapters Cited   227

Index   249

Notes on the Contributors

William G. Buss is the O.K. Patton Professor of Law at the University of Iowa. His teaching and scholarly interests are in constitutional law and education law. His most recent publications are 'Separation of Powers, Federalism, and the Demise of the Religious Freedom Restoration Act', in the *Iowa Law Review* and 'Intelligence Testing and Judicial Policy Making for Special Education', in *Psychology, Public Policy and Law*. He has taught at Durham University, Durham, England (1982–83) and Victoria University, Wellington, New Zealand (1994).

Sally J. Kenney is Associate Professor of Public Policy and Law at the Humphrey Institute of Public Affairs at the University of Minnesota where she also directs the Center on Women and Public Policy. She is the author of *For Whose Protection? Reproductive Hazards and Exclusionary Policies in the United States and Britain*.

William M. Reisinger is Professor of Political Science, University of Iowa. His research focuses on democratization in the former communist states and post-Soviet public opinion. He is the author of numerous articles and chapters, and also of *Energy and the Soviet Bloc: Alliance Politics since Stalin*. He is co-author of *Can Democracy Take Root in Post-Soviet Russia?*

John C. Reitz is Professor of Law at the University of Iowa College of Law and a specialist in the comparative study of legal systems. After earning a BA in German language and literature at Harvard College and a JD from the University of Michigan Law School, Reitz practiced law for eight years in Washington, DC, before joining the law faculty at Iowa. His teaching and research interests include comparative law, comparative economic regulation, the law of the European Union, administrative law, and contracts and commercial law. During 1989–90, he held scholarships from Fulbright and the German Marshall Fund of the United States to conduct research at the University of Muenster, Germany. He has lectured at the Universities of Muenster and Freiburg in Germany, the Moscow Linguistics University in the Russian Federation, and the University of Law and Political Science and People's University in Beijing, China.

Jeffrey Seitzer is Visiting Assistant Professor of Political Science at Indiana University Northwest. He is author of *Constitutional Democracy and the State: An Institutional Approach to Comparative Constitutionalism* and a number of articles and chapters on law and institutions in Germany, Hungary, and the United States.

Martin Shapiro is Professor of Law at the University of California, Berkeley. He has written numerous books and articles on American and comparative law and politics, including *Courts: A Comparative and Political Analysis* and the review of 'Public Law and Judicial Politics' in Ada W. Finifter (ed.), *Political Science: The State of the Discipline*, 2nd edn.

Susan Sterett is Associate Professor of Political Science at the University of Denver. Her research interests include administrative law, immigration and European rights, and the early twentieth-century American social welfare state. She is the author of *Creating Constitutionalism*.

Alec Stone Sweet is Professor of Political Science in the School of Social Sciences, University of California, Irvine. He is the author of *The Birth of Judicial Politics in France* and *Governing with Judges: Constitutional Politics in Western Europe*, and co-editor of 'The New Constitutional Politics of Europe', a special issue of *Comparative Political Studies* (1994). His present research focuses on the emergence and evolution of judicial systems in international society.

Foreword

This book is among the most remarkable of its kind to be published to date. It is a reflection of the best in a new scholarly approach to legal Europe, and it has some unique features which position it on a pedestal all its own.

What is 'its kind'? It is about Europe; it is about courts in Europe, or rather the 'judicial branch' since it resolutely views courts as an integral part of government and governance; and it is about the way in which non-doctrinal approaches to law may illuminate legal norms and legal institutions.

Though this is not the case today, twenty years ago or so the mere fact of putting out a book of the kind I have just described would have been remarkable.

Europe as an object of inquiry for political scientists enjoyed an early classical period in which the likes of Haas, Deutsch, Schmitter, Lindberg and Scheingold laid a most sophisticated foundation of integration theory. But, as the Continent seemingly refused to follow the plans of its visionaries and as facts seemed to get in the way of theory, spill-over became spill-out and integration studies went into a medieval period of hibernation, to be salvaged by a renaissance only in the late 1980s in the heydays leading to the Single Market. I say 'seemingly' since that very period of political (and theoretical) hibernation saw the most dramatic developments in legal integration; indeed it was the 'Heroic Period' of constitutionalization and judicial empowerment. Part of the failure of the political science community was its temporary blindness to the unusual character and unusual importance of courts, legal institutions and legal culture to the emerging European polity. European law was unthinkingly associated with discredited international law, its constitutional features not visible to the political scientists.

The legal community did of course pay huge attention to the dramatic legal developments. But lawyers, too, had their blind spots. Twenty years ago it would have been relatively novel, and hence remarkable, to find a book such as this one dealing with European law and legal institutions in the same broad manner and with the same methodological perspectives as the contributors to this book do; it would have been equally remarkable to find a group of (mostly) political scientists with the interest, factual knowledge and expertise to contribute to such a book; and it would, perhaps, have been remarkable that a distinguished Research Center in an American University would dedicate its resources to the comparative study of the judicial process in Europe from a non-doctrinal perspective, although, let us admit it, even more remarkable if it were a university in Europe!

For those too young (or, like me, too old and hence forgetful) to remember the landscape of European legal scholarship two or three decades ago, the following words could serve as a good refresher. They are the words of Martin Shapiro commenting in the late 1970s on what was, on its own terms, a very fine piece of scholarship on the European Court of Justice of the European Community. It was, he said:

> Constitutional law without politics . . . [presenting] the European Community as a juristic idea; the written constitution as a sacred text; the professional commentary as a legal truth; the case law as the inevitable working out of the correct implications of the constitutional text and the [European Court of Justice] as the disembodied voice of right reason and constitutional theology (Shapiro 1980, 537–8).

Much has changed since then. To be sure, fine doctrinal scholarship has, thankfully, not disappeared. It is not simply legitimate but inevitable and indispensable. *La Doctrine,* let us not conveniently forget, is the vernacular of the broadest judicial and legal conversation. The Talmud, strictly speaking, is mostly a Rabbinical commentary on the sacred Text of the Pentateuch. And yet, inevitably and indispensably, exegetic and homiletic Rabbinical commentary becomes part of the living text itself. This is no different in more modern legal traditions.

Where European legal scholarship has changed in the last generation, by way of self-generation as well as direct importation and osmosis from other branches of law, from other disciplines and from other jurisdictions, is in the drawing of the boundaries of legal discourse and its purposes. This change has not only taken a generation to establish itself but has also been generational.

It is a new generation of academic scholars, in Europe and the USA, which has not simply expanded the reach of the inquiry beyond doctrine. These scholars have gone even beyond the 'Law and . . .' approach, be it Law and Economics, Law and Society et cetera. This new generation does not distinguish between, on the one hand, 'pure' law pieces and, on the other hand, other pieces enriched by the insights of, say, the political scientist or economist or legal sociologist. Instead, European Law has become according to this approach a discourse in which those insights are integral. The new 'pure law' is one in which doctrine, as a matter of course, is situated in its broader economic, political and social context. That is the norm. Alongside this expanded discourse there is no longer 'Law and . . .'; there is, instead 'Law without . . .'.

In another change, the 'sacred' nature of law has come to be treated far more gingerly. Exegesis and homiletics may be acknowledged as part of the living text but, learning from a realist lesson made explicit both in Scandinavia and the USA, the notion of judicial 'neutrality' is dealt with in a far more nuanced way. Ideology and differing hermeneutic sensibilities are acknowledged as inevitable. After all, when an omniscient God gave his Nomos to Moses at Sinai and intended it to live for eternity, are we really to assume that he did not understand that it would be shaped and reshaped in the hands of its frail and sinful human custodians? And could any terrestrial constitution maker believe otherwise?

Being a latecomer to this insight, new European legal scholarship seems thankfully to be escaping some of the tedious rage which results from it and which affects other legal fields. It is always worth remembering that just as a court is an institution, the output of which is partly shaped by the sensibilities of its frail and sinful human members, so is the output of scholarship about courts. Indeed, scholars, being more self-aware, might be even more adept than courts in concealing their own sensibilities. Still, in the burgeoning European critical scholarship, whilst *politesse* is always preferable to invective, deference to courts and colleagues has happily diminished and is continuing to diminish, and normative criticism has become far more common.

The most telling development in my eyes to a changing legal landscape is the as yet slow realization in European law circles that the broader legal discourse does not only enhance our understanding of the role and impact of legal institutions and judicial processes in society which are the classical interest of the social sciences, but that it enriches the quality of the legal profession, be it in litigation, other aspects of practice, the legislative process and more. The skilled and experienced legal practitioner is always a legal realist, often without even realizing it. Without batting an eye, he or she will tell a young colleague in the course of preparing a brief or oral argument: 'Good point, but no chance before *this* judge' and then explain why; the explanation will have little to do with 'the law' and everything to do with the judge. Likewise, without giving it much thought or finding it exceptional, a Member of Parliament will request the parliamentary draftsman: 'Please make this judge-proof' and the latter will not need an explanation why, although he or she might realize how difficult a challenge that request may be! The new broad discourse of law is, in some respects, no more that an attempt to study in a more methodical and rigorous way these intuitions. This, too, should provide a lesson in humility to those who don't do but do teach: the explication of intuition is a messy business. Even today, a goodly chunk of the most successful entrepreneurs never went to business school.

This generational transformation in the discourse of European law, to which this book makes so important a contribution, is far from complete and not without a controversial (not to say fractious) fallout. Part of the controversy is the usual hurly-burly of academia. But there are three additional, attitudinal dimensions, which explain the resistance to the new winds and give the controversy, at times, an exceedingly sharp edge.

One I have already mentioned: a generation of scholars is made, in some respects, to feel obsolete. People who write their work with fountain pens do not, at times, take kindly to computers. The reactions range from oblivion, to amusement, adaptation, but also annoyance and hostility. The hostility typically takes two variants: 'What's new? We knew this all along' and/or 'This is not law' or 'This is bad law.' This last charge is often justified. There are plenty of articles written with all the jargon of political and social science which, however, cannot conceal a weak grasp of European law and add little to existing learning. Examples abound in the seemingly endless number of student-edited American international and comparative law reviews. Talking in a new language about European legal integration is no substitute for having something new or interesting to say.

This is also the cue to a second factor aggravating some of the reactions to the transformed discourse. One should not fear to speak its name: it is the Americanization of the broader discourse of European law. It is not surprising that this creates some negative reactions in Europe. There is often a brashness and measure of hegemonic *chutzpah* to the American tone resulting from a *'been there – done that'* attitude. It is a confidence that comes from a much longer experience with federalism, with constitutionalism, with judicial review, with a social and political science which has taken courts seriously and a legal profession and academy which lost its innocence earlier and feels far more comfortable with an expanded legal discourse. There is, thus, often a distinct 'ugly American' tone in writing coming from this side of the Atlantic. The truth is that in many respects Americans have not 'been there' and have not 'done that'. The European experience in integration, in constitutionalism and in judicial review is in large measure distinctly un-American, deriving from and developing with a different telos and ethos. There are few things more annoying than the encounter with sloppy comparative Euro-American analysis, clumsily grafting on to European institutions and processes insights deriving from a very different American political culture.

For their part, there is at times something equally ugly in European attitudes and resentments: an anti-Americanism which derives from a similarly annoying sense of cultural and intellectual superiority which occasionally is only a thin guise to a sense of inferiority in the face of American legal and political scholarship.

Finally, in explaining the difficult transition to a new European legal discourse one additional factor should be mentioned. In the dialogue(s) about constitutional dialogue, we should not forget the uneasy dialogue – if that is what it may be called – between political science and lawyers. Often it is less of a dialogue and more a series of cross-purpose monologues. Political scientists and lawyers have learnt enough of each other's language to carry on a conversation, of sorts. And there may even be, like the English spoken in European institutions, a new kind of language or dialect for carrying on this conversation. The word *discourse* has an honorable place in that new dialect.

But am I exaggerating in suggesting that there is, too, an unmistakable streak of mutual contempt in the on-going dialogue between political scientist and academic lawyers? In dealing with lawyers the political scientist often goes into anthropology mode. When political scientists talk among themselves the lawyer often becomes a primitive subject (or object) which has to be observed, at times humored, and even listened to carefully. But the lawyers' explanation of what they are about is but another datum to be integrated in the altogether deeper political analysis. At times one cannot blame the politologists for taking this approach on seeing the oblivion of so many lawyers to the broader significance of their practices and discipline. For their part, the lawyers (some at least) will listen, or appear to be listening, with equal care to their political science colleagues. But among themselves they too shrug their shoulders. Here are some of the lawyers' plaints about political scientists: 'They just do not know law – the

ostensible object of their inquiry.' 'They always focus on a handful of
famous cases and often get them wrong.' 'Their understanding of law
is always derivative – something they picked up from this or that legal
scholar; ironically, they do not understand the indeterminacy of legal
scholarship.' There is, let us admit it, some truth in these plaints,
though I doubt whether these grains of truth are the real explanation
for the resistance that the transformed discourse of legal Europe
encounters.

It is in this scholarly landscape, no longer pristine, that this new
book appears. One of its virtues is the skillful manner in which it
avoids many of the pitfalls of narrative and dialogue I have just mentioned. In tone, content and erudition it is exemplary. That alone is
worth a great deal.

What makes it so remarkable, however, is both scope and execution.

First, its definition of *Europe* is bold and operates at many levels:
the book deals with individual states, it deals with transnational
Europe in its two principal guises of European Community and
Council of Europe and (wholly appropriately given the theme of constitutionalism and judicial review) the book also deals with the new
Central and Eastern European jurisdictions. Just as America is not
the USA, Europe is not the European Union, a lesson fully driven
home in this volume.

Its definition of the legal landscape is also bold. Law does not mean
courts and 'courts' do not simply mean 'Supreme Courts'. Despite its
focus on the judicial process, the book draws a very wide canvass of
the legal landscape and its actors including in the legal conversation
all manner of courts and all shape of players.

There is a second sense in which the volume transcends not only
the old but also much of the new genre of European law scholarship.
It is not confined to structure and process – government and governance – the darlings of so much of the European integration literature. Some of its studies focus on substantive rights such as freedom of
expression and show the complex and normatively ambivalent faces of
constitutionalism and integration. Where it does focus on governance,
it manages to illuminate areas which have to date remained in the
shade such as the process, indeed phenomenon, of judicial appointments to the European Court.

A third virtue is its methodological richness, which is shortchanged
by the bland catchphrase, political science. In truth it is the broad
range of social sciences which inform the various contributions as well
as that delicate interface between legal theory and political science.

Perhaps the greatest contribution of the entire volume, aptly the subject of its remarkable concluding chapter, a contribution which transcends even its 'European' orientation, is in provoking us to a deeper understanding of the phenomenology of courts, judicial review and constitutionalism in contexts which are different from the well-established and well-known Western liberal nation-state.

In this sense the literature has been greatly enriched by this volume and for that, all contributors should be congratulated.

J.H.H. WEILER
Manley Hudson Professor and Jean Monnet Chair, Harvard University,
and Co-Director, Academy of European Law,
European University Institute, Florence

Acknowledgments

The editors' interest in this project arose while participating in the University of Iowa's Comparative Law and Politics study group. We would like to thank Gerhard Loewenberg, Geoffrey Palmer and the others who have taken part in this study group and thereby helped improve our understanding of the literature. In particular, Professor Peter Shane, later Dean of the College of Law at the University of Pittsburgh, deserves special credit for spearheading the study group for several years.

The authors first had the opportunity to discuss these issues in depth and to present their research while spending the month of June 1995 together at a seminar hosted by the University of Iowa's Obermann Center for Advanced Studies. Although most of the chapters were substantially reworked after the seminar, the lengthy period that the authors spent together during the seminar helped each of us refine our ideas and deepen our familiarity with each other's work. We are extremely indebted to Dr C. Esco Obermann and the late Avalon L. Obermann, whose generosity makes the Center's annual faculty seminars possible. We thank the Center's director, Dr Jay Semel, for his help in planning and conducting the conference and subsequent follow-up. Thanks also go to Lorna Olson, Annie Wilcox and the rest of the Center's staff, who worked hard to support our work, before, during and after the seminar.

We thank also Professors Kenneth Holland and Eric Heinze, who participated in the June 1995 seminar but whose contributions do not appear in this volume. They greatly enriched our discussions and writings. Finally, we would like to express our appreciation to Professor Joseph Weiler, who spent several days with us during the seminar, and Professor Martin Shapiro, who kindly agreed to participate in the seminar 'on paper' by reading all of the chapters and contributing one of his own.

List of Abbreviations

CERD	International Convention on the Elimination of all Forms of Racial Discrimination
CDU	Christian Democratic Union
CSU	Christian Social Union
ECHR	European Court of Human Rights
ECJ	European Court of Justice
EU	European Union
FDP	Free Democratic Party
FPRLR	Fundamental Principles of the Laws of the Republic
GFCC	German Federal Constitutional Court
ICC	Italian Constitutional Court
SCT	Spanish Constitutional Tribunal
SGIs	Strict Guidelines of Interpretation
SPD	German Social Democratic Party

1 Introduction: Constitutional Dialogues in Comparative Perspective

Sally J. Kenney, William M. Reisinger and John C. Reitz

Today, at the end of the twentieth century, it is scarcely possible to recount, much less understand, the major political and social developments in industrial societies without attention to legal norms, courts and judges. The number of countries with judicial review of legislation jumped sharply in the aftermath of the Second World War and again following the end of communist rule in Eastern Europe and the Soviet Union. Judicial review of administrative acts is also being significantly strengthened in many countries that long rejected or restricted it. Especially in Western Europe, transnational courts add another dimension of legal norms that can influence social life. Increasingly, scholars are coming to view courts as political actors and to argue that judges, their modes of arguing, the type of evidence they require, even their partisan policy preferences, influence lawmakers and administrative agencies.

These developments stand out in part because courts have long justified their rather unique powers on the grounds that their officers and procedures are impartial, apolitical (in the partisan sense) and largely constrained by the letter of legislation, a written constitution or, sometimes, precedent. This image of courts as 'above politics' predominates even in the US (see, for instance, Shapiro 1995, 57–8), where scholars have long reflected on the activism of courts, especially that of the US Supreme Court. Thus, even in countries that are accustomed to granting great power to their courts, the prospect of *gouvernement des juges* is obscured by the traditional understanding of courts as apolitical.

The urge to classify legal processes as separate from politics contributed to important disciplinary trends within the fields of political science and legal studies. Political science has long recognized courts and constitutions as important but, historically, has studied both little differently than would legal academics–emphasizing formal institutions, doctrine, and normative theory. Over the last 30 years, however, political scientists devoted to studying law and courts have produced fewer such analyses in favor of investigations of courts as political institutions (broadening the focus beyond constitutional courts) and of law as a political arena that can be studied with the same approaches used to study legislative and executive processes.

The legal community has, of course, lavished great attention on legal doctrine, especially that produced by courts. This is not to say that legal scholarship has completely ignored politics and political institutions. At least since the Legal Realists, the claim that law constrains the judges' decisions in ways that eliminate the influence of their own policy preferences has been subjected to strong criticism within the legal community. More recently, critical legal theorists have challenged even more frontally the distinction between law and politics, arguing that judges should be seen as a distinctive category of politicians whose decisions are guided by their own social and political judgments, whether or not they are aware of the basis for their decisions (Kairys 1990). But while it should be apparent that lawyers can no longer ignore the political dimensions of legal doctrine, much legal commentary remains pre-eminently doctrinal.

The problematic nature of the traditional disjunction between the political science and the legal academic approaches to studying law is highlighted when the focus is shifted from one's own country to comparative studies of different political-legal systems. It is mostly the work of those taking a comparative view that has convinced specialists in legislative behavior, administrative law, constitutional law, and judicial politics that these seemingly separate specialties are closely linked (e.g., Shapiro 1981; Schmidhauser 1987; Cappelletti 1989; Holland 1991; Kenney 1992; Stone 1992; Shapiro and Stone 1994; Tate and Vallinder 1995; Jacob *et al*. 1996). In particular, scholars studying the role of the courts in the various recent transitions toward democracy and the rule of law have highlighted the political dimensions of the role played by law and the courts (e.g., Greenberg, Katz, Oliviero and Wheatley 1993; Stotzky 1993).

The literature cited in the foregoing paragraph, almost exclusively by political scientists, testifies to the revival of interest, at least among political scientists, in studying the courts' political role. The writers of this volume see themselves as building on that literature to foster study of the political roles of courts and legal doctrine in ways that get beyond the traditional political science/law divide. To a greater extent than in any of that literature, however, the studies in this book are both comparative and interdisciplinary. The first four of the following chapters in this volume are expressly comparative in the sense of using developments in more than one country or between a transnational court and several countries to highlight the intersection of law and politics. The next three (Chapters 6, 7 and 8) focus on a single country or supranational court, but provide some comparative context for understanding the issues and also benefit from the comparative framework provided by the earlier chapters. We are, in addition, an interdisciplinary group. Although political scientists dominate and only two out of the eight authors are academic lawyers (Reitz and Buss), one of the political scientists (Shapiro) teaches on a law faculty, another (Sterett) has interdisciplinary training in law, and they and two others (Stone and Kenney) have already devoted considerable scholarship to legal topics. Moreover, the chapters that follow result from substantial interaction among all the authors, as described in the acknowledgments, so that each had the opportunity for the kind of extended exposure to the thinking of the other discipline that is so critical for successful cross-disciplinary work.

In this volume, we largely restrict our geographic focus to Europe, although the issues and methodologies treated herein deserve extension elsewhere. Europe is a natural site for investigating legal and political issues in new ways. While sharing many aspects of their political and legal heritages, the various European societies are diverse. This diversity extends to the configuration of institutions, legal traditions, the broader political economy and social structure. For many European countries, democracy and legality have 'consolidated', that is, have become taken as a given by all powerful actors. In others, steps to establish both democratic governance and the rule of law have only recently been taken. Even in the countries with long-established legal systems, the post-war era has seen critical institutional changes; foremost among them has been the introduction of judicial review of legislation. Finally, at least in the West, supranational economic and social integration has meant the rise of supranational judicial review in the form of the European Court of Justice (ECJ) and the quite different form of international judicial review by the European Court of Human Rights (ECHR). Significant cross-national diversity therefore characterizes the evolution in European court roles. This diversity makes Europe an especially promising area for approaches that are explicitly comparative and interdisciplinary.

4 *Introduction*

We can usefully group the 'sites' for studying law and politics in Europe into three categories: Western Europe, Central and Eastern Europe, and transnational courts. All three have seen exciting new developments in the post-war era. In the court systems of Western Europe, the process of change that is attracting scholarly attention is evolutionary, though highly significant. Elites in each country have struggled over how to redefine roles and responsibilities among institutions in response to changing realities. In the formerly communist societies of Eastern Europe, a quite different task faces political and legislative elites: how best to establish the appropriate roles and responsibilities for courts, legislatures, presidents, bureaucracies and other institutions. These leaders are trying, moreover, to establish effective balances of power in great haste, aware that their choices will influence the success of economic marketization and political democratization. On the transnational level, the ECJ and the ECHR have assumed a prominent role in European life as a result of the explosion of cross-border trade, finance, communication and travel in the post-war era and the resulting demand for cross-national coordination and the broadening of individual rights. The very successes of these courts have raised the question about the political role they play.

The chapters that follow take on issues arising in all three sites. The authors bring doctrinal, behavioral, institutional and historical methods to bear on these issues. The essays in this volume thus go beyond introducing the reader to many facets of comparative law and politics in Europe. They also introduce the reader to an array of approaches available to bridge the divide between political science and law.

While none of the essays that follow resolves the tension between the inside (law) and the outside (political science) view of law – nor could they – taken as a whole, the essays in this book suggest a framework for bridging that divide. In one way or another, the approach taken in each of the following chapters can be encompassed within the framework set out in the next two chapters, which conceptualize the political role of the courts as being exercised in dialogue with various other political actors, their 'interlocutors' (cf. Weiler 1994). The courts' side of the dialogue is expressed in their published opinions. Politicians and mass publics may respond in more complex ways through various kinds of political behavior, but the framework of dialogue permits bringing the doctrinal level of court behavior into direct relationship with the political behavior of other parts of the polity. It focuses attention on the way in which political behavior and doctrine respond to each other (Fisher 1988).

Chapter 2, Alec Stone's essay on 'constitutional dialogues', serves as an excellent introduction to the European style of constitutional review through specialized judicial bodies known as constitutional courts. Focusing on France, Germany, Italy and Spain, Stone asks how these constitutional courts interact with, on the one hand, the legislative branch and, on the other, the regular courts of the country. Based on analysis of a number of celebrated cases in each of these countries, he argues that the dialogues that result from the interaction force the constitutional courts to act like legislators and the legislators and non-constitutional courts to engage in constitutional adjudication.

In the next chapter, Jeffrey Seitzer takes this concern for dialogue between constitutional court, legislature and regular courts to Eastern Europe by comparing Germany and Hungary. Seitzer explores the consequences for the constitutional dialogues of the structural and procedural differences in constitutional review in the two countries and suggests specific institutional changes that might enhance the Hungarian system's capacity for self-criticism and self-correction.

In Chapter 4, John Reitz's contribution brings the focus back to Western Europe. Reitz attempts to use the 'new institutionalist' literature of political science to define the political economies of Germany, France and the USA, respectively, for the purpose of explaining why the mechanism of abstract review initiated by governmental officials makes sense in Germany and France, but not in the USA. His study thus seeks to provide an understanding rooted in political and economic ideology and structure for a procedural device that the chapters by Stone and Seitzer have shown to have great significance for the nature of the constitutional dialogues between constitutional court, legislature, and regular courts in Europe, though it is firmly rejected in the USA. To the extent that Reitz's method uncovers unarticulated policy bases for legal doctrine, it also offers a way to make the legal dialogues in one country intelligible to those coming from another country.

Chapter 5 by William Buss expands the geographic scope westward by comparing Canada and the USA, as well as Germany, Denmark and the ECHR, and extends the approach illustrated by Reitz's chapter from procedural to substantive law by treating the issue of the constitutionality of laws designed to restrict hate speech. Like Reitz, Buss considers whether explanations for the apparent differences he observes could be based on the political and social factors in each country. Buss thus also aims to assist in the translation of constitutional dialogues from one legal system to another. His rather more critical treatment of that kind of explanation/translation implicitly comments on Reitz's methodology, as well as on his own.

Susan Sterett, the author of Chapter 6, expands the scope of the book by focusing on Britain, a country that lacks both a written constitution and – leaving aside questions of European Community law – judicial review of legislation. Based on analysis of the interaction between courts and administration with respect to immigration policy, she argues that, even in the absence of formal constitutional litigation, courts play a role in shaping state policymaking. Immigration law is a branch of administrative law, but this kind of dialogue, establishing the role of the courts *vis-à-vis* that of the other branches of government, is necessarily constitutional. Sterett's point also seems generalizable beyond public law: in order to account adequately for judicial behavior, we should conceive of the courts as in dialogue with the other branches of government in all areas of the law. Sterett's essay thus suggests that the utility of the concept of judicial dialogues is not limited to constitutional review. Courts are political animals, whatever they do, and therefore an analysis of their behavior has to include consideration of the dialogue between courts and politicians of the political branches and a wide range of other 'interlocutors'.

The next chapter, by Sally Kenney, introduces the ECJ. In the case of this supranational court, the complexity of its constitutional dialogues is enhanced by the number of European institutions which share in legislative power at the level of the European Union (EU). Although Weiler (1994) has convincingly argued that the dialogue of greatest importance to the ECJ is with national courts and member states, the Court has also been the arbiter of institutional disputes among the EU institutions. As Kenney observes, the European Parliament's claim to a greater role in selecting members of the Court is an attempt to increase its own power and stature and to make judicial appointments federal rather than intergovernmental: that is, no longer solely within the discretion of member state governments. Surprisingly, in view of the acknowledged political role the ECJ has been playing, Kenney is one of the first to investigate who judges are and how they are selected.

In Chapter 8, William Reisinger takes us in yet another methodological direction while also taking us further east to the Russian Federation. His concern is with the transition from a regime that denied the autonomy of law and used courts in a crudely instrumental manner to a regime in which courts might possibly function in dialogue with other branches of government. In order to learn how

Russia is progressing in this transition, Reisinger argues that it is necessary to measure how the orientations toward law are changing among all segments of the Russian populace. His concern is thus not limited to the dialogue between courts and other branches of government, but with the broader discourse about law within various societal groups, including judges, lawyers, legal scholars, journalists and political elites. His chapter argues for the use of content analysis as a way of assessing whether legal orientations are changing in the direction of stronger support for the rule of law. The chapter also reports on the results of a pilot project he carried out on articles and books from Russian legal literature during the periods immediately before, during, and after the fall of communism in Russia.

Reisinger moves the focus from the dialogues between courts and other branches of government to the broader societal discourses about law because he believes this broader discourse to be critical for maintaining the basic legitimacy of courts despite their political roles which tend to undermine that legitimacy, especially if too openly acknowledged. It is precisely to the fundamental question of political legitimacy – though once again focused on the issue of judicial review – that the final chapter by Martin Shapiro turns. Shapiro seeks to evaluate the various hypotheses for explaining why judicial review has been developed in some countries but not others. He is thus seeking to explain the basis for the legitimacy of the dialogues the rest of the chapters study. His wide-ranging essay covers all the courts and countries treated in the other chapters and thus provides a fitting conclusion to the book.

2 Constitutional Dialogues: Protecting Human Rights in France, Germany, Italy and Spain
Alec Stone Sweet

As European systems of constitutional justice have matured, the interdependence of lawmaking and constitutional interpretation has tightened, blurring boundaries allegedly separating judging and legislating, often to the point of irrelevance. This interdependence became increasingly obvious once scholars began focusing attention on the impact of constitutional jurisprudence on public policy (Shapiro and Stone 1994). This line of research documents the capacity of constitutional courts to shape, pre-empt and even dominate legislative processes. In its most extreme formulation (my own), European constitutional courts are explicitly conceptualized as adjunct – or 'specialized' – legislative chambers, engaged in continuous, highly-structured dialogues with governments and parliamentarians in the making of public policy (Stone 1992, 1994).

This chapter examines the reverse side of the same coin. As the coin turns over, the relative importance of *constitutional politics conceived as legislative process* gives way to the relative importance of *constitutional politics as judicial process*. The construction of constitutional law is driven by ongoing interactions – constitutional dialogues – between constitutional courts, the legislature, and the judiciary. Mainstream European legal scholarship, which rarely moves beyond the textual analysis of constitutional provisions and case law, misses much of what is most important about the new constitutionalism in Europe: namely, its profoundly participatory nature. The chapter is divided into four parts. I begin with a brief introduction to systems of constitutional justice in France, Germany, Italy and Spain. Of crucial importance are mechanisms for the protection of human rights. I then turn to two sets of constitutional dialogues, between constitutional courts and parliamentarians, and between constitutional courts and judicial authorities, about the nature, content, and application of rights. As constitutional courts have consolidated their positions as the supreme interpreters of the constitution, the role and function of parliamentarians and of ordinary (that is, non-constitutional) judges have been transformed. Most important, legislators and judges behave as constitutional adjudicators, and therefore as adjunct builders of the constitutional law.

THE EUROPEAN MODEL OF CONSTITUTIONAL REVIEW

European constitutional courts (what will be called the Kelsenian Court below) make up an institutional 'family' to the extent that they share common attributes distinguishing them from institutions that exercise constitutional review elsewhere. By constitutional review, I mean the authority of an institution to invalidate laws, administrative decisions and judicial rulings on the grounds that these acts violate constitutional norms. The contrast between European and American 'models' of review is the standard reference point.[1] In American judicial review, 'any judge of any court, in any case, at any time, at the behest of any litigating party, has the power to declare a law unconstitutional' (Shapiro and Stone 1994). Although formulated broadly, the power is in practice conditioned by a number of doctrines designed to distinguish 'the judicial function' (*the settlement of legal disputes*) from 'the political function' (*legislating*). Most important, judicial review powers are said to be exercised only to the extent that they are necessary to settle a concrete 'case or controversy'. It can then be further said that the power of judicial review is not wished for, in and of itself, but at times *must* be exercised in order to resolve a pending legal conflict. Advisory opinions on constitutionality are necessarily precluded as a judicial usurpation of the legislative function. American separation of powers notions – which rest on the formal equality of the executive, legislative, and judicial branches of government – both enable and restrict judicial review.

In Europe, constitutional review of legislation by the judiciary is formally prohibited, and this prohibition is the very core of separation of powers doctrines. According to these doctrines, American-style judicial review is attacked as a *confusion* of powers enabling the judiciary to participate in the political function. Thus whereas the American judiciary is responsible for defending the integrity of a hierarchy of legal norms, the apex of which is the constitution, the European judiciary, according to the traditional orthodoxy,[2] is charged with defending a normative hierarchy, the apex of which is the statute.

A problem is posed. Who will defend the constitutional law, arguably the law most in need of protecting, if not the judiciary? The problem became acute following the collapse of authoritarian regimes – after the Second World War in Germany and Italy, the late 1970s and early 1980s on the Iberian Peninsula, and post-1989 in Central and Eastern Europe – which provided critical moments of democratization and constitutional reconstruction. It turns out that specialized constitutional courts, the prototype of which had been invented by Hans Kelsen for the Austrian Second Republic, provided the common solution. Primarily because it enables the effective exercise of constitutional review while preserving traditional separation of powers doctrines, the Kelsenian constitutional court, and not American judicial review, diffused throughout Europe.

The European model of review can be broken down into four constituent components. First, constitutional courts possess a monopoly on the power to review the constitutionality of statute, and other judicial bodies remain precluded from engaging in such review. Second, the jurisdiction of constitutional courts is formally restricted to the settling of constitutional disputes. Unlike the US Supreme Court, constitutional courts do not preside over judicial disputes, or litigation, which remains the purview of the judiciary. Instead, specifically designated authorities refer specific questions about constitutional interpretation to constitutional judges for answers. Third, constitutional courts have links with, but are formally detached from, the judiciary and legislature. They occupy their own 'constitutional' space, a space neither clearly 'judicial' (the resolution of particular legal disputes by a judge) nor 'political' (the elaboration of general legal rules by a legislator). Fourth, constitutional courts possess abstract review powers (in American terms, the power to issue *binding* advisory opinions on the constitutionality of statutes) in order to eliminate unconstitutional legislation and practices *before* they can do harm. Thus, in the European model, the judiciary remains bound by the supremacy of statute, while constitutional courts preserve the supremacy of the constitution.

Kelsen's court had to be modified in one absolutely crucial respect. Kelsen had argued that constitutional courts should be denied jurisdiction over constitutional rights, to ensure that judicial and legislative functions would remain as separate as possible. If constitutional judges were allowed 'to refer to [rights], invoking the ideals of equity, justice, liberty, equality, morality, etc.', the argument went, they would inevitably subvert and even replace the legislator (Kelsen 1928). Kelsen's admonition was easily swept aside in the race to legitimize new regimes by entrenching constitutional rights. For the reasons already stated, the burden of protecting these rights was thrust upon contemporary Kelsenian courts, rather than on ordinary judges. In consequence, as Kelsen predicted, constitutional courts have developed into powerful policymakers.

Jurisdiction

Table 2.1 simplifies and summarizes constitutional review mechanisms in France, Germany, Italy and Spain, as review is exercised by the French Constitutional Council (hereafter cited as the Council), the German Federal Constitutional Court (hereafter cited as the GFCC), the Italian Constitutional Court (hereafter cited as the ICC), and the Spanish Constitutional Tribunal (hereafter cited as the SCT).[3] There exist three main types of review processes: abstract review, concrete review, and the constitutional complaint procedure. Abstract review is called *abstract* because it takes place in the absence of a concrete case or controversy. Concrete review is called *concrete* because the review of legislation is a stage in formal litigation originating in the judiciary. Constitutional complaints, as they are known in Germany – *amparos* in Spanish – are petitions from individuals who (1) allege that their constitutional rights have been violated by a public authority, and (2) request redress from the constitutional court for this violation.

   Abstract review processes result in decisions on the constitutionality of legislation recently adopted but not yet in force (France), or recently promulgated (Germany, Italy, Spain). Abstract review is initiated by elected politicians.[4] Executives and legislators (France, Germany, Spain) and federated member-states or regional governments (Germany, Italy, Spain) may, within prescribed time limits, attack legislation as unconstitutional before the constitutional court. Such attacks are made in writing, in documents known as referrals or petitions. Unlike other maneuvers available to parliamentarians, referrals cannot be quashed by majority vote. The act of referral can effectively suspend the legal force of the referred law (France, Germany in some cases, Italy) pending a ruling, or permit the law to be applied until a ruling, which must take place within prescribed time limits (Germany in some cases, Spain). Once a referral has been made, constitutional courts are then required to render a decision.

Table 2.1 European Constitutional Courts and the Constitutional Review of Legislation

	France	*Germany*	*Italy*	*Spain*
Constitutional Court	Constitutional Council (Council)	Federal Constitutional Court (GFCC)	Italian Constitutional Court (ICC)	Spanish Constitutional Tribunal (SCT)
Year Created/Began Operations	1958/1959	1949/1951	1948/1956	1978/1981
Abstract review	Yes	Yes	Yes	Yes
Authority to initiate abstract review of legislation	President Pres. of Assembly Pres. of Senate *Since 1974:* 60 Assembly deputies 60 Senators	Federal government Länder governments 1/3 Bundestag	National government (against regional laws) Regional governments (against national laws)	Prime Minister Pres. of Parliament 50 Deputies 50 Senators Executives of autonomous regions Ombudsman ('Defender of the People')
Laws referred	National legislation	Federal or Länder (federated member state) legislation	National and regional legislation	National and regional legislation

Table 2.1 *Continued*

	France	Germany	Italy	Spain
Laws must be referred	Within 15 days following adoption by parliament	Within 30 days following adoption by Federal or Länder parliament	Within 30 days following adoption by regional or national government	Within 90 days following adoption by parliament or regional government
Effect of referral	Suspends promulgation pending a ruling. Council must rule within 30-day limit	Suspends application of the law pending ruling	Suspends application of the law pending ruling	Referral has no legal effect on the law. STC must rule within 30-day limit
Concrete review	No	Yes	Yes	Yes
Authority to initiate concrete review of legislation		Judiciary Individuals (after judicial remedies exhausted)	Judiciary	Judiciary Ombudsman Individuals (after judicial remedies exhausted)

Concrete review is initiated by the judiciary (Germany, Italy, Spain) in the course of litigation in the courts. The general rule is that the judges must refer such questions if two conditions are fulfilled: (1) the question of constitutionality is material to the case (that is, who wins and who loses critically depends on the answer to the question); and (2) the constitutionality of the relevant act or rule is in reasonable doubt. The referral suspends the litigation pending a ruling. The constitutional court then renders a judgment, which is sent back to the referring court for implementation. The judiciary is constitutionally obligated to apply faithfully the constitutional court's decisions. Individuals (Germany, Spain) and an ombudsman (Spain) have the right to refer constitutional complaints directly to constitutional courts, once judicial remedies have been exhausted.

RIGHTS, NORMATIVE HIERARCHIES AND CONSTITUTIONAL DECISIONMAKING

The normative structure of the constitution is the formal hierarchical relationship established by the language of the constitution (1) between any given constitutional provision and the rest of the constitution, and (2) between the constitutional law and other legal orders (that is, the private law, the various code laws). Whether this normative structure has an existence apart from how it is authoritatively interpreted by constitutional judges is a complicated question. Although I proceed from the standpoint that constitutional *meaning* is continually being (re)constituted by adjudication, constitutional *language* and constitutional *meaning* nevertheless remain analytically distinct. The language of any constitutional provision is a site of contestation about meaning, and that contestation drives constitutional development.

Placing ourselves in the position of the constitutional judge may simplify matters, if only initially. They are obliged to resolve legal controversies about rights which are inherently controversies about the meaning and applicability of rights; they are also required to defend their decisions in a published jurisprudence. In their rulings, European judges present their decisionmaking as if it were a distinct two-stage process. First, the content and meaning of the relevant constitutional law are determined. Second, the specific controversy at hand is resolved by applying that law. The judges are telling us that, after carefully considering the language and architecture of the constitution, they are in a position to decide a particular case. In fact, as we shall see, the two stages are tightly interdependent, taking place more or less simultaneously within linked processes of interpretation. This simple truth turns out to be critical to our understanding of constitutional politics. In any event, because constitutional interpretation lies at the core of constitutional politics, and because constitutional language shapes constitutional interpretation, students of constitutional politics have little choice but to take the normative structure seriously.

The Direct Effect of Constitutional Rights

When the framers of the German, Italian and Spanish constitutions established an institution to enforce the supremacy of the constitution, they initiated a revolutionary transformation of their legal and political systems. In France, a comparable transformation was accomplished after 1971, when the French Council began to incorporate a set of historical rights texts into the 1958 constitution. Prior to this revolution, only the legislature could determine if and how rights were to be respected. In the jargon of European law, constitutional rights had no 'direct effect', because they did not confer on legal subjects judicially enforceable rights. Litigants could invoke 'public liberties' in court and judges could apply them, but only after such liberties had been codified in statutes: that is, only after legislatures had commanded judges to enforce them. Thus, rights entered into the public law indirectly by virtue of a legislative act, rather than directly by virtue of their higher law status. Today, the positive source of individual rights is the constitution.

Table 2.2 lists those constitutional rights and duties *expressly* contained in the German, Italian and Spanish constitutions and in texts incorporated into the French constitution by the Council (leaving out the myriad rights generated by case law). European constitutions proclaim the classic liberal or negative rights well known in the USA, but also a host of collective and positive rights. They also enumerate the responsibilities of citizens to their state and of the state to the citizenry. Finally, constitutions make the protection of rights a participatory process. Not only do they provide for the protection of constitutional rights by constitutional courts, but they also at times command legislatures to create the conditions necessary for the enjoyment of some rights and to promote, encourage and protect others.

Table 2.2   Rights and Responsibilities Proclaimed by European
Constitutions

Right or freedom	France	Germany	Italy	Spain
Human dignity		X		
Life		X		X
Equality before the law	X	X	X	X
Equal rights for men and women	X	X	X	X
Religion	X	X	X	X
Conscientious objection to military service			X	X
Security	X		X	X
Privacy	Y	X	X	X
Personal honor		X		X
Inviolability of home and person	Y	X	X	X
Movement and travel	Y	X	X	X
Spoken and written expression	X	X	X	X
Marriage and family	Y	X	X	X
Freely develop one's personality	X	X		X
Asylum for persecuted non-nationals	X	X	X	
Adequate health care	X		X	
Concerning association and political participation				
Political participation	X	X	X	X
Vote and run for elected office	X	X	X	X
Petition		X	X	X
Personal beliefs, ideology	X	X	X	X
Resist political oppression	X	X		
Assembly	X	X	X	X
Association	X	X	X	X
Concerning the economic system				
Private property	X	X	X	X
Inheritance		X	X	X
Private enterprise	Y	X	X	X
Work	X	X	X	X
Choose occupation		X	X	X
Adequate pay			X	X
Adequate housing			X	X
Equal pay for men and women			X	
Form and join unions	X	X	X	X
Workers' participation in management	X		X	
Strike	X	X	X	X
Unemployment compensation	X		X	X
Old age pensions	X		X	X

Table 2.2   Continued

Right or freedom	France	Germany	Italy	Spain
Vocational training			X	X
Leisure and vacations	X		X	X
Concerning the educational system				
Public education	X	X	X	X
Religious education	Y	X		X
Participate in school management				X
Teaching and research	Y	X	X	X
Private schooling	Y	X	X	
Concerning the judicial and penal system				
Access to the courts and judicial				
protection	Y	X	X	X
Remedies for judicial malfeasance			X	X
Legal defense	Y		X	X
Public trial				X
Speedy trial				X
Refusal to self-incriminate				X
Immunity from				
retroactive application of the laws	X	X	X	X
Habeas corpus		X		X
Presumption of innocence	X		X	X
Immunity from double jeopardy		X		
Rehabilitation while incarcerated			X	X
Social security benefits while incarcerated				X
Death penalty constitutionally abolished		X	X	X

Duties	France	Germany	Italy	Spain
Of citizens				
Military service		X	X	X
Pay taxes	X		X	X
Work			X	X
Financially support, educate their children			X	X
Vote			X	
Of the state				
Guarantee media pluralism	X	Y	Y	X
Protect the family and children	X	X	X	X
Facilitate social and economic progress			X	X
Regulates property rights in public good			X	
Provide equitable distribution of resources				X

Table 2.2   Continued

Duties	France	Germany	Italy	Spain
Provide public health care	X		X	X
Pursue full employment				X
Provide unemployment compensation	X		X	X
Guarantee safety of working conditions			X	X
Protect public health	X		X	X
Guarantee leisure or vacation time	X		X	X
Promote culture and science	X		X	X
Protect the environment			X	X
Provide old age pensions	X		X	X
Protect handicapped			X	X
Protect consumers				X
Protect linguistic minorities			X	
Provide public education	X	X	X	X
Nationalize industries	X			

Note: X indicates a right or duty established by the written constitutional law; Y indicates a right established pursuant to the case law of the French Council.

Normative Hierarchies

The constitutional law establishes hierarchies of norms and these hierarchies condition constitutional interpretation. The direct effect of constitutional rights, for example, establishes a simple hierarchical relationship between constitutional text and statute: any law that violates rights provisions is an invalid law, *ab initio*, because rights are higher law. Intraconstitutional hierarchies are more complicated, but the normative structure implies a privileged status for rights provisions. In Germany, Italy and Spain, the text proclaims human rights before it establishes state institutions and distributes governmental functions and in consequence rights are considered to possess not only independent juridical existence but perhaps even 'supraconstitutional' status. This privileged status is reinforced by rules governing constitutional amendment: in Germany, Italy and Spain, constitutional law treats rights provisions as rigid and immutable and non-rights provisions as flexible.[5]

Far and away the most complicated hierarchical problem faced by constitutional courts appears when two or more constitutional provisions, possessed of equivalent hierarchical status, conflict with one another in a particular case. Even a cursory glance at the list in Table 2.2 suggests the broad range of such potential problems. In a dispute about abortion law, does the right to life trump a women's right to freely develop her personality? In a libel dispute, should the press' freedom of expression or should an individual's right to personal honor be given primacy? In a dispute about expropriation, how much guidance does the constitution give judges when, on the one hand, the right to property is proclaimed while, on the other, property is to be used for the good of the community? One could go on and on. What is clear is that this type of problem is both inevitable and impossible to resolve definitively (although the law may often appear to be settled by judicial decisions). Not surprisingly, such intraconstitutional tensions are the great source of constitutional decisionmaking and development.

Constitutional Decisionmaking

By constitutional decisionmaking, I mean the act of determining the meaning of a given constitutional provision (or set of provisions) in order to resolve a dispute about the nature of an infraconstitutional norm (or act). Every act of constitutional review is an act of constitutional decisionmaking. In deciding, a constitutional court simultaneously makes policy *and* constructs the constitution. The policymaking function of constitutional case law is clearly revealed when we focus attention on the outcome of a given dispute in terms of the disputants involved. The resolution of the dispute establishes the law governing that dispute. The constitutional development function of the case law is most evident when we attend to the court's reasoning, or justification, for why an infraconstitutional norm (or act) is or is not constitutional. Authoritative interpretation of a constitutional text produces powerful prospective effects on future policymaking and dispute resolution. It legitimates some policy routes and delegitimates others and signals to Parliament, the judiciary and to future litigants that some lines of constitutional contestation have been closed off or narrowed, while others have been opened up.

The constitutional law, in contrast to all other domains of law in civil law countries, is fundamentally a judge-made law. This is a hugely important consequence of the dynamics of constitutional politics. Because meaningful distinctions between constitutional case law and the constitutional law have become increasingly irrelevant, constitutional review processes function as permanently constituted fora for the ongoing revision of the constitutional text.

Constitutional Rights and Decisionmaking

The language of constitutional rights effectively delegates enormous discretionary authority to constitutional courts. Although a few rights are expressed in absolutist terms – the most important being 'equality before the law' provisions, found in all four countries and 'human dignity' in Germany – the great majority of rights are expressly limited. Put bluntly, constitutions generate infraconstitutional tensions that in turn generate constitutional decisionmaking processes. To illustrate, here are a handful of expressly 'limited' rights:

> In Spain, Article 20.1.a proclaims the right to free expression, which Article 20.4 then 'delimits' with reference to 'other rights, including personal honor and privacy'. Article 33.1 declares the right to private property, while Article 33.3 provides for the restriction of property rights for 'public benefit', as determined by statute.

> In Italy, Article 14.1 states that the 'personal domicile is inviolable', save for searches and seizures done 'in cases and in a manner laid down by statute in conformity with ... personal freedom' (Article 14.2). Article 21.1 announces that 'the press shall not be subjected to any authority of censorship', while Article 21.6 provides that 'printed publications ... contrary to morality are forbidden' and Article 21.7 states that Parliament possesses the responsibility to 'prevent and repress all [such] violations'.

> In Germany, article 2.1 states that 'everyone shall have the right to the free development of her personality in so far as she does not violate the rights of others or offend the constitutional order or moral code'. Article 10.1 proclaims that the 'privacy of posts and telecommunications shall be inviolable', while Article 10.2 states that 'this right may be restricted only pursuant to statute'.

> In France, Article 11 of the 1789 Declaration of the Rights of Man declares that 'every citizen may ... speak, write and print freely, but is responsible for the abuse of this liberty in circumstances determined by statute'. The 1946 social and economic principles of the 1946 include the proclamation that 'the right to strike is exercised according to the laws that regulate it'.

In broad language, then, European constitutions require lawmakers to respect constitutional rights *and* to regulate how rights are to be enjoyed and exercised. Although expressed in disparate provisions, this latter competence is usually conceived holistically, as a coherent set of 'constitutional interests' (sometimes called 'constitutional values') possessed by government: to provide for public order, to protect public morality, to secure the public weal. The formal structures of European constitutions order parliaments and judges to resolve conflicts between constitutionally-protected interests of government and constitutional rights in any given case, but gives little indication of exactly how to do so. Instead, the structure invites complex processes of 'balancing': contestation and decisionmaking about the proper, relational limits of constitutional rights and interests.

As the next two sections of this chapter demonstrate, the dogma that constitutional courts 'function' to protect constitutional rights misleads,[6] unless we mean by this no more than that these courts, *in conjunction with the legislature and the judiciary*, resolve rights disputes by (1) balancing constitutional rights against other rights and (2) balancing constitutional rights against the constitutional interests of government. What constitutional courts are doing most of the time is working to reconcile tensions within the constitution itself. European courts and legal scholarship have generated an ever-growing set of doctrines to explain and to synthesize this work.[7] Virtually all are elaborations on a common sequence: interpretation, balancing, proportionality. Constitutional judges first seek to interpret away intraconstitutional conflicts on the theory that the constitution is a body of harmonious norms. If they are not able to do so, they resort to balancing tests, which themselves are subject to proportionality tests. Stated simply, in resolving a conflict between two rights – or between a right and an interest – the right or interest that gives way must be preserved as far as is possible. Thus, every statutory restriction of the exercise or full enjoyment of a right is constitutional only to the extent that the limitation established is 'reasonable': that is, the limitation is derived from an identifiable constitutional interest and does not reduce the enjoyment of the right more than is necessary to secure that interest. In fact, such doctrines do little more than admit, albeit in a convoluted manner, the following: that protecting constitutional rights is tough work; that constitutional judges must possess and use wide discretion in order for them to do their job properly; and that no firm and fast rules for balancing can be articulated. I do not mean that courts do not seek to generate such rules (courts do), or that decisional outcomes are random (they are not). The meaning of proportionality doctrines and balancing tests is more profound. They signal to us that constitutional courts do not protect rights without becoming deeply involved in the facts: that is, in the policymaking component of the case at hand.

Finally, constitutional courts have further enhanced their own discretionary powers by interpreting certain constitutional provisions as open-ended invitations to generate 'new', unenumerated rights. The Spanish Court, for example, 'insists on the necessity of a systematic and teleological constitutional interpretation, rather than strictly literal',[8] especially with reference to the 'finality' of Article 1. Article 1 states that 'Spain ... considers liberty, justice, equality and political pluralism as the foremost values of its legal order.' Thus not only does the SCT possess jurisdiction over the most extensive list of rights in Western Europe, but all other constitutional provisions are to be interpreted in light of the objectives of liberty, justice and equality. The German constitution enumerates a relatively short list of rights, but the Court compensates for this by treating Article 1 ('human dignity shall be inviolable') as open-ended and Article 2.1 (the right to freely develop one's personality) as denoting 'nearly anything the individual might wish to do' (GFCC 1957). The Italian Court has recently repudiated the theory that Article 2 – 'the Republic guarantees the inviolable rights of man' – refers only to those rights enumerated in subsequent articles. Beginning in the late 1970s, the ICC began elaborating a 'transcendental' or 'metajuridical' conception of Article 2, in order to ground a 'dynamic theory of constitutional rights' (Seventh Conference of European Constitutional Courts 1991, 161–78). In 1988, the ICC explicitly declared that Article 2 constituted an 'open norm' (ICC 1988b) which allows the Court to recognize rights somehow 'forgotten' by the framers (Panthoreau 1990). The right to marry, to be born, to sexual liberty, to privacy have all been generated by Article 2 case law. Finally, the French bill of rights, entirely the product of case law, is composed of the following: the 1789 declaration of the rights of man, the social and economic principles listed in the preamble to the 1946 constitution; and the mentioned but (left unenumerated) 'fundamental principles of the laws of the Republic' (FPRLR).[9] The French Council has discovered that the FPRLR contains such rights as personal liberty and inviolability, freedom of teaching, freedom of research, the right to a legal defense and the principle of judicial independence; it has also elevated to constitutional status of certain 'general principles of law', including the continuity of public service and the separation of powers.

PARLIAMENTS AND CONSTITUTIONAL ADJUDICATION

Whenever legislators engage in constitutional decisionmaking, they behave as constitutional judges. Today, governments and parliaments do so all of the time and for three mutually reinforcing reasons. First, the constitution commands legislators to protect rights and establishes the parameters (normative structure) in which decisions about constitutionality are to be made. Second, the adjudication of rights by parliamentarians is a facet of the struggle among political parties to control constitutional development and policy outcomes. Most of the important ideological conflicts that divide parliaments can be expressed as conflicts about the nature and application of rights, precisely because rights provisions reflect, rather than harmonize, the opposed visions of society held by the parties at the time the constitution was negotiated. In this struggle, each party seeks to implement its own version of a right, or of a proper balance between two rights and (the same thing) each seeks to fix relatively enduring, substantive rules of policymaking binding future legislative processes.

Third, the existence of constitutional review mechanisms gives agency to constitutional commands to protect and to balance rights and gives urgency to ideological conflicts about rights. Simplifying a complicated politics, opposition parties provoke constitutional debate in order to win, in constitutional review processes, what they could never win in 'normal' legislative processes: an amendment or veto of unwanted legislation. The government and its majority have a powerful interest in engaging the opposition in constitutional deliberation in order to avoid censure at the hands of the constitutional court. As important, each side seeks to construct constitutional law, fully aware of the prospective, symbolic effects of this construction on the legitimacy of its party program and social vision. This behavior is inherently 'judicial'; it constitutes a 'legal level' within a multitiered system of constitutional adjudication. It can be understood in rationalist (functional and instrumental) terms: parties anticipate the attitude of the constitutional court in order to gain reward or avoid punishment. It can also be understood as the progressive constitution of a new discursive field: an institutionally-bounded process by which the norms and vocabulary of constitutional law are elaborated and then absorbed into the norms and language of policymaking.

The discussion below, organized with reference to mode of review, focuses on the reciprocal impact of constitutional review and legislative process. The politics of abstract review tend to recast the legislative process into one of constitutional adjudication. Concrete review processes (which involve interactions between Parliament, the judiciary and the constitutional court) and the constitutional complaint procedure (which adds individuals to the mix) serve to transfer the constitutional court's concerns for the policy effects of existing legislation to Parliament, and to prompt implementation of the court's decisionmaking. I make these distinctions, which are far more relative than stated here, to focus analytical attention on what are separate adjudicatory activities.

Abstract Review

We observe parliaments behaving as constitutional judges most clearly when we pay attention to the politics of abstract review. The risk, or explicit threat, of an abstract review referral by the opposition, for example, triggers constitutional deliberations. These deliberations result in reasoned judgments about how best to protect rights, and about how best to balance rights with constitutional interests. Lawmakers not only deliberate constitutional law, but defend their decisions as judges do, with reference to legal materials. Put in the language of judicial process, we can say that when parliaments engage in constitutional decisionmaking, they behave as constitutional review bodies of first instance, over which constitutional courts exercise appellate control.

The French case provides the ideal laboratory for research on the impact of abstract review, since abstract review is the sole mode of review that exists. It bears emphasis that the Council has only been able to construct French constitutional law, now a huge and imposing edifice, because parliamentarians themselves struggle to construct the constitution. Parliament is the sole source of the Council's caseload, and without a caseload, the Council would not be worthy of study. But caseload there is. Since 1974, when the constitution was revised to permit any 60 deputies or 60 senators to petition the Council, opposition parliamentarians have referred every budget and nearly every other important or controversial bill adopted (since 1981, the Council has reviewed more than 30 per cent of all domestic legislation). Rights provisions are the primary source of law invoked in referral, and by the Council in its rulings of unconstitutionality.[10] Referrals have been remarkably successful: since 1981, 57 per cent of all referrals resulted in at least partial annulment by the Council. French rights politics are therefore a species of legislative politics.

That French lawmakers behave as judges of the constitution can be empirically observed and evaluated. The constitution requires that every bill drafted by the Government be submitted to its legal advisor, the Conseil d'État (Council of State), which reviews the legislation for 'legality'. By the mid-1980s (when referrals became more or less systematic and predictable), the Conseil d'État had recognized the identity of legality and constitutionality, assuming the responsibility to evaluate inconsistencies between draft bills and the constitutional text and to warn ministers of potential constitutional risks (Stone 1989). Once a bill has been submitted to Parliament, formalized rituals organize constitutional deliberations. The major parties employ constitutional counsel, usually high profile university law professors, who advise them on how to attack or defend bills in debates and help them to draft Council referrals. Once introduced, any deputy or senator can raise a point of parliamentary procedure known as a motion of unconstitutionality (*motion d'irrecevabilité*). These motions, often written in the stylized form of a French judicial decision (and published in the debates), shut down legislative discussion pending a formal debate and ruling on the bill's constitutionality by the full chamber. Parliamentarians support their positions by citing constitutional texts, legal scholarship and the Council's existing case law. If the motion passes, the bill is declared unconstitutional and it is killed.

Motions of unconstitutionality are today a regular part of legislative life. In the 1981–7 period, the National Assembly alone debated and voted on 94 such motions, a figure to be compared with 93 Council decisions. Subject to strict party discipline, the motions are virtually never adopted. Their importance, however, is to set the stage for the constitutional politics to come. As bills wind their way through the legislative process, opposition parties unpack their constitutional arguments again and may even threaten referral to the Council in order to force or cajole the Government and its majority to accept their amendments. Dozens of bills have been amended as a result of such constitutional debate.

In Germany and Spain, a similar politics exists. The more important the bill being discussed, the greater the chance that debates will become exercises in constitutional decisionmaking. In Spain, the documentation distributed along with proposed legislation to parliamentarians includes a specific chapter devoted to the SCT's relevant case law and the major parties employ law professors to help them attack or defend proposals. In Germany, '[g]overnments and politicians continually threaten to drag their political opponents to Karlsruhe – the location of the court' and these threats trigger lengthy processes of constitutional debate and decisionmaking. Parliamentary committees regularly invite leading constitutional experts, including former constitutional judges, to testify on constitutional aspects of current legislation and to predict future court decisions. Most important, German (Landfried 1984, 1992; Kommers 1994) and Spanish[11] parliamentarians, like their French counterparts, debate and make reasoned decisions about the constitutionality of legislation. If compromises do not succeed in pacifying conflict, Parliament's deliberations are transferred to constitutional courts for a final hearing.

Parliament and Constitutional Decisionmaking

It would be a mistake to dismiss parliamentary adjudication of rights as inherently less meaningful or less 'judicial' than the deliberations of a constitutional court. Parliament and the court are doing more or less the same thing, speaking in more or less the same language and working through more or less the same normative materials. This should come as no surprise, since each institution makes up the targeted audience for the other; that is, each institution seeks to persuade the other institution that, by a virtuous process of principled reasoning, it has correctly interpreted the constitutional law. That parliamentary majorities and constitutional courts often disagree about how to apply the constitutional law to resolve legislative conflicts should signal to us not that parliament erred, but that the number of potentially persuasive, reasoned positions on the constitutionality of any given bill is greater than one.

When the court annuls a bill, it substitutes its own reading of rights, and its own policy goals, for those of the parliamentary majority. Oppositions only activate the court because they are hoping that the court will obstruct and/or shape policy innovation, and perhaps even freeze constitutional interpretation. Among dozens of French, German and Spanish examples available, the fate of affirmative action in France in 1982 suffices to illustrate the point (Stone 1992). After its victory in the 1981 elections, the French Socialist government sought: (1) to promote equality in political participation and representation by establishing a proportional representation electoral system for local and national elections; and (2) to enhance the status of women by, among other things, encouraging their participation in elections. Its first attempt to make good on the pledge targeted certain local elections. The final bill stipulated that communal electoral lists could not include 'more than 75 per cent candidates of the same sex'. The Right attacked the reform as an 'unconstitutional, demagogic, and dangerous' discrimination against men, and referred the bill to the Council, which annulled the provision, relying on Article 6 of the 1789 declaration of the rights of man, an equal treatment under the law provision. The decision (Council 1982) ignored altogether the constitutional command contained in the 1946 social principles, cited constantly by the Left during the legislative debates, according to which Parliament shall guarantee that women possess the same rights as men. As an act of policymaking, the Council had vetoed an important provision of the 1982 electoral law. But the Council had also constructed the constitution: the ruling is today read as prohibiting affirmative action, not just in electoral matters, but in all matters of public policy.

In cases like these, it is nonsense to suppose that the constitutional court functions as some kind of bulwark against the tyranny of majority rule. In fact, the Socialists sought to promote the rights of an underrepresented category of citizens, by activating a constitutional provision that had been all but ignored up to that point in time. The Council blocked this effort, on the basis of the parliamentary opposition's reading of the right to equality. This part of the outcome raises another general point. In exercising review of prior parliamentary acts of constitutional decisionmaking, the constitutional court rarely if ever protects rights that would otherwise be ignored by Parliament. Instead, the court is faced with making a legislative choice about how best to protect rights from what is in effect a 'menu' of policy options, elaborated in parliamentary debates about the constitutionality of a bill in question. Constitutional judges, more often than not, choose from this menu precisely because parliamentarians, more often than not, zero in on the salient constitutional issues and debate them intensely.

When parliaments balance constitutional rights and constitutional interests, 'judicial' and 'legislative' behaviors blend: each constitutes the primary activity of the other; they cannot be dissociated. Just as legislators often consciously work to protect and to strengthen the exercise of rights, they also engage in balancing, on their own, without prior prompting from constitutional judges. The evidence of such behavior is published, in parliamentary debates and in the internal structure of the statute itself. When it receives an abstract review referral, oppositions are in effect requesting an appellate ruling on a point of constitutional law and a final legislative 'reading' of the bill. The court cannot do one without doing the other any more than parliaments can. The German abortion decision of 1993 illustrate these points, in somewhat spectacular fashion.

In 1975, the German Court annulled an attempt on the part of the Social-Liberal (SPD-FDP) coalition to decriminalize abortion, declaring that the foetus possessed constitutional rights, including the 'right to life' mentioned in Article 2 of the constitution (GFCC 1975). In June 1992, the Bundestag voted again to decriminalize abortion. To protect the woman's right to choice and 'free development of personality' (also contained in Article 2), the law legalized abortion in the first 12 weeks, after counseling. But the bill also sought to protect the foetus's constitutional rights, and to enhance the baby's well-being if brought to term. Legislators maintained criminal penalties for terminating pregnancies beyond the 12-week limit, subject to certain (mostly medical) exceptions. In addition, the bill included comprehensive, wide-ranging provisions designed to make it easier for poorer women to choose not to terminate their pregnancies. Thus the 'Law to Assist Pregnant Women and Families' provided child care for pre-school children, the construction of more low income family housing, free contraception for individuals 21 years old and under, and the establishment of a widely available network of counseling offices. It was referred to the Court by the state of Bavaria and 248 Christian Democrats of the Bundestag.

The Court annulled the law (GFCC 1993), essentially holding to its 1975 ruling: the state's obligation to protect embryonic life means that abortion cannot be formally legalized, even in the first trimester, but that abortions performed for medical, eugenic, social and criminal reasons could go unpunished. The social hardship standard, however, was tightened and recast as 'unreasonable burden': abortions would be tolerated by the criminal law if carrying a baby to term would impose 'heavy and unusual burdens' going well beyond 'reasonable sacrifice'. The Court made it clear that such tolerance could only be sustained to the extent that the state actively sought to discourage women from choosing to terminate. The Court then laid down detailed instructions for redrafting the counseling requirement, and among these were that: the sole purpose of counseling is to make 'women aware of the unborn's own right to life' and to 'encourage' them to 'accept their tasks as mothers'; counselors must employ 'scientifically developed 'conflict counseling' that requires a 'woman to reveal her motives', because 'an uninvolved "it is up to you" demeanor is unacceptable'; and counseling facilities must be separated from facilities providing abortions. Although the Court praised the legislature for working to enhance housing and child care for low-income families, it ruled that neither public nor private health insurance could be used to pay for abortions. The legislature implemented the Court's preferred policy choice in a corrective revision exercise.

Concrete Review and Constitutional Complaints

We cannot begin to understand European systems of protecting rights if we do not pay attention to parliamentary decisionmaking, both before and after the constitutional court decides. The German abortion cases – no more than many other examples – show just how seriously parliament can take its responsibility to protect rights and to engage in balancing prior to the intervention of constitutional judges. They also illustrate how, subsequent to certain kinds of constitutional decisions, legislators function as agents of the constitutional law by implementing the court's preferred policies. Concrete review and constitutional complaint processes organize the protection of rights outside parliamentary space. But because these processes necessarily provoke constitutional decisionmaking, that decisionmaking regularly leads to legislative implementation of constitutional case law. A few examples will make the point.

Unlike their French, German, and Spanish counterparts, Italian parliamentarians are not authorized to refer laws to the ICC, yet Italian lawmakers nonetheless interact with constitutional judges.[12] Since 1980, few issues of social policy have been as controversial as the distribution of retirement pensions and other social welfare benefits (Giorgis, Grosso and Luther 1995). In particular, the ICC has been bombarded with judicial referrals claiming that the myriad formulas for calculating cost of living adjustments, both within the public sector and between the public and private sectors, violate the principle of non-discrimination derived from equality provisions. Until 1988, the Court largely deferred to parliamentary discretion, ruling that differences in work and in labor-management relations may be presumed to justify differences in treatment. In 1988, the Court declared that differences of treatment had become intolerable, and invited the legislature to enact legislation to harmonize the pensions regime across categories (ICC 1988a). Five years later, fed up, the Court ruled that the absence of such harmonization itself constituted a violation of the rights of employees to equal treatment. It justified its change of heart as follows:

> [The ICC] can neither continue rendering decisions of inadmissibility [of concrete review referrals] in respect of legislative discretion, nor continue admonishing [Parliament to act]. Factually, irrational and discriminatory regulations, explicitly denounced in judgment 220/1988 have not only persisted but have become worse .... To simply call again for the legislature to intervene – after having waited so long, in vain – would appear ... as an abdication of the functions of the Constitutional Court, and a protection of legislative inertia rather than a protection of legislative discretion. (ICC 1993)

The Court then (1) specified how harmonization must proceed to satisfy constitutional requirements of non-discrimination and proportionality, (2) ordered Parliament to right the situation, in the next budget law at the latest, and (3) threatened to 'right the situation' itself if the legislature did not act (by, presumably, empowering the judiciary to award damages in future cases). In the January 1994 budget law Parliament did act, explicitly acknowledging the ICC's prompting.

Although the traditional scholarly position is that abstract review is inherently more 'political'[13] and 'legislative' than other modes of review, constitutional litigation by non-state actors is not necessarily less 'policy-interested' than petitions made by opposition politicians. The animus for many concrete review references and constitutional complaints is to encourage the court to annul controversial legislation or to establish rules constraining future legislative action. In 1969, for example, the German SPD-FDP coalition government took power promising to promote 'democracy and equality' in university governance by, among other things, diminishing the absolute authority of full professors on university governing councils, and expanding the authority of untenured professors, staff and students. Weary with the slow pace of federal legislation, the SPD-FDP controlled state of Lower Saxony adopted its own law, based on federal government drafts. The law was referred to the GFCC by 398 disgruntled professors in individual constitutional complaints. Relying on Article 5 of the constitution, which states simply that 'teaching shall be free', the Court annulled the law (GFCC 1973). Ruling that full professors must always prevail within university councils, the GFCC transformed the *federal* discussion in progress from a debate about the wisdom of the legislation into a debate about constitutional compliance. Under the watchful eye of the Right-wing CDU-CSU opposition, which supported the full professors and threatened referral if the coalition did not fully comply with the ruling, the GFCC's jurisprudence was copied into the federal law (see the discussion in Stone 1994).

In these examples, legislative compliance is facilitated by the clarity of the constitutional commands of the constitutional court, commands that (1) speak to Parliament directly and (2) are backed up by the threat of future censure.

THE JUDICIARY AND CONSTITUTIONAL ADJUDICATION

The development of constitutional review has gradually transformed the role and function of the ordinary law courts. This transformation has been labeled 'the constitutionalization of law' or the 'constitutionalization of the legal order'. By constitutionalization I mean the process by which: (1) constitutional norms come to constitute a source of law, capable of being invoked by litigators and applied by ordinary judges to resolve legal disputes; and (2) the procedures and adjudicatory techniques of constitutional decisionmaking are established as an important mode of judicial decisionmaking. Constitutionalization is in part the logical, legal consequence of the normative structure of the constitution, and especially of the direct effect of rights provisions, and in part the product of a complicated set of dialogues between constitutional courts and the judiciaries.

As constitutionalization has proceeded, the traditional conception of the legal system – that the various domains of law, such as public and private law, or civil and administrative law, were more or less autonomous realms, governed by different sources of law and different principles of adjudication – has given way to a view that constitutional law, as the ultimate source of legality, unifies these domains into a more or less coherent legal order. And the powerful, quasi-official myth of the judge as a slave of the codes, prohibited from interpreting and rewriting the laws, has been shattered. The very existence of constitutional review subverted the 'sacred' nature of statute within the legal order, and the practice of doing constitutional review socialized judges into a new role, that of protecting the legal order from statutes (and other legal acts) contaminated by unconstitutionality.

The discussion below seeks to account for important commonalities and difference among the cases. It bears emphasis in advance that comparative research on constitutionalization, or on the impact of constitutional review on the work of the judiciary, does not exist. There is also a startling scarcity of empirical work even at the national level that documents the relationship between ordinary and constitutional judges. What follows is therefore necessarily schematic, a first cut at comparative analysis. Generalizing across cases, the greater the level of constitutionalization, the more the distinction between constitutional jurisdiction and ordinary jurisdiction collapses. That is, as constitutionalization deepens, ordinary judges necessarily behave as constitutional judges: they engage in principled constitutional reasoning (decisionmaking), and resolve disputes by applying constitutional norms. Constitutional judges become more deeply involved in what is, theoretically, in the purview of the judiciary: they interpret the facts in a given dispute, and they review the relationship between these facts and the legality of infraconstitutional norms. Cross-national differences are closely tied to the existence or non-existence of particular modes of review. In Germany and Spain, where abstract review, concrete review and constitutional complaint procedures coexist, extensive constitutionalization has proceed quickly. In Italy, the absence of a constitutional complaint mechanism has reduced the capacity of the constitutional court to control judicial outcomes and, in consequence, the pace of constitutionalization has been much more gradual. In France, where promulgated statute remains sovereign and no formal links between ordinary and constitutional jurisdictions exist, a primitive form of constitutionalization can nevertheless be observed.

The Constitutionalization of Law in Germany, Italy and Spain

In traditional theory and practice, rights did not possess direct effect. They were instead viewed, and this was true in all four countries, as programmatic statements, at most expressing a set of guidelines for legislative protection of rights. In Germany, Italy and Spain, new constitutional laws proclaimed rights and provided a means of protecting them. Inevitably, the knotty problem of the scope of direct effect was posed. In these countries, no one in any position of authority has ever denied the juridical status of rights within the public law. By definition, rights are restrictions on the power of the state, designed to protect individuals in their relations with public authority. Not surprisingly, constitutionalization became visible almost immediately in the domains of tax and social security law, other forms of administrative law and criminal law. The juridical status of constitutional rights outside public law provided a tougher test for constitutionalization. In relationships between private persons (for example, employers with employees, associations with individuals, individuals with individuals), did the violation of constitutional rights provide the basis for legal actions and remedies in the courts? If so, would not ordinary judges be required to enforce and therefore interpret the constitution? Traditionalists said no to both, since (1) the private law (family law, contracts, torts, inheritance, and so on) constituted a sphere outside the reach of the state, and therefore outside the reach of the constitutional law, and (2) only the constitutional court possessed the power to interpret the constitution. Others disagreed, arguing that the constitution – of which rights are an integral part – comprises the source of all legality, including the legality of private relationships, and that all judges have a sacred duty to defend legality and therefore the higher law.

In Germany, Italy and Spain, both questions asked above have been answered in the affirmative. The German experience represents the paradigmatic case of constitutionalization, an experience on the whole reproduced in Spain. It can be summarized by the following sequence. Immediately following the founding of the Federal Republic, ordinary judges began to behave as constitutional judges, on their own, without prompting from the constitutional court (Quint 1989). The constitutional court legitimized this behavior in its review of the constitutionality of judicial decisions. The GFCC went even further, in effect ordering all judges to work to balance constitutional rights and interests in light of the sweeping proportionality tests described above, and announcing that it would use its constitutional complaint jurisdiction to review this balancing behavior on a case-by-case basis. Thus the GFCC required all judges to engage in exactly the same kind of constitutional decisionmaking in which the constitutional court engages. Such a requirement necessarily leads the constitutional court to become deeply involved in the work of the ordinary judges (fact finding, choice of law, and so on).

The resolution of conflicts between traditional rights enshrined in the Civil Code and the constitutional right to free speech served to formally constitutionalize German private law. The landmark constitutional decision involved the suit brought by the producer and distributor of the 1950 film, 'Immortal Beloved', against a minor bureaucrat in the Hamburg state government, Erich Lüth (GFCC 1958). Lüth had called on Germans to boycott the film as a protest against the easy rehabilitation of its director, Veit Harlan, an anti-Semitic filmmaker whose work for the Nazis had led a court to convict him for crimes against humanity. The producers based their action on s.826 of the Civil Code, which prohibits 'intentional injury against another person in a manner contrary to good morals'. The lower court found that Lüth's speech had indeed caused injury, and ordered him to desist. Lüth appealed directly to the Constitutional Court, which (extraordinarily) waived the usual requirement that remedies be exhausted. The GFCC found for Lüth, using its decision to clarify the relationship between constitutional and private law. Most important, the Court proclaimed that the 'value system' expressed by the constitution 'affects all spheres of law', and that therefore 'every provision of the private law must be compatible with this system of values, and every such provision must be interpreted in its spirit'. The Court then declared that 'the constitution requires the [ordinary] judge' to verify the conformity of the private law with basic rights, and at all times to interpret the former as if they were in harmony with the latter. In the private law, constitutional rights thus possess what in German legal parlance is called indirect effect, since the judge is obliged to (re)construct statutes in light of them. 'If he … ignores the influence of constitutional law', the Court ruled, 'he violates objective constitutional law'.

The GFCC also made it clear that no simple formula for accommodating the private law to constitutional rights exists, and indeed that accommodation could only be made in case-by-case acts of constitutional decisionmaking, itself structured by the requirements of balancing and proportionality. Because, in the Court's words, the Constitution 'desires' the establishment of 'an equilibrium … between the mutually contradictory and restrictive tendencies of the constitutional rights and the general laws' [for example, the Civil Code], judges must 'weigh the values to be protected against each other', and give precedence to the most important of the interests at stake in any given case while maintaining maximum integrity for the interest to be subordinated. These judicial obligations are reinforced by the threat of review, via the constitutional complaint procedure, of the ordinary court's decisionmaking. In the Lüth case, the GFCC examined the facts and then determined that Lüth's right to free speech outweighed damages suffered by the filmmakers. In subsequent cases also involving civil suits alleging damages caused by speech acts, the Court went on to develop multiple lines of jurisprudence, some favoring free speech, others favoring interests inherent in the Civil Code. Thus, in GFCC (1969), the Court quashed a Federal Supreme Court ruling to the effect that a call for a news vendor boycott of a pro-Communist weekly constituted protected speech. The Supreme Court had relied on the Lüth decision. Before finding for the Leftist weekly, the constitutional court walked through the case step-by-step, sifting through the facts and reconstituting its context. It concluded that: 'an assessment of the conduct of the defendant ... shows that the Federal Supreme Court went too far in its interpretation of the protective scope of the constitutional right to free expression of opinion'. In such instances, distinctions between the work of ordinary and constitutional judges are obliterated.

A constitutional court's capacity to facilitate constitutionalization and (the same thing) to control judicial outcomes depends significantly on the existence of the constitutional complaints procedure. In both Germany and Spain, virtually all such complaints attack the constitutionality of judicial decisions, effectively positioning the constitutional court as a super-appellate body. This is the German situation, post-Lüth. In Spain, in 1982, the Spanish Supreme Court (the high court of appeal for the entire judiciary) declared that the rights enumerated in the new constitution expressed a legislative program but not a set of juridical commands enforceable in the courts. The constitutional court annulled the high court's decision on *amparo* (a claim to the SCT, on the part of an individual, to the effect that the individual's constitutional right has been violated by a specific act of a public authority) asserting the constitution's binding normative status, a ruling accepted by the Supreme Court (SCT 1982). Without the *amparo* mechanism, the pace of constitutionalization in Spain would depend entirely on intrajudicial comity and cooperation. The *amparo* enables the constitutional court to impose its preferred solution, a wide-ranging set of doctrines establishing the direct and indirect effect of rights.

To take just one example, in 1987 a journalist working in the province of Soria published a satirical piece spoofing the foibles of a local mayor. Offended, the mayor sued, claiming a violation of his personal honor. The judge of second instance agreed with the mayor and ordered the journalist to pay a small fine. The journalist referred the matter to the constitutional court, which annulled the judge's decision on the grounds that the judge had not given enough weight to the journalist's right to free expression (SCT 1986). The judge of second instance deliberated again, but again found for the mayor, although he carefully cited the SCT's case law on free expression. A second *amparo* ensued, and the SCT again quashed the decision, this time insisting that only the journalist could win the case (SCT 1987). Like the German Court, the SCT has the capacity to reach deeply into the private law and to reshape it. The Court, in effect, 'teaches' ordinary judges how to behave as constitutional judges, a pedagogical role backed up by the ever-present threat of constitutional complaint.

The Italian case contrasts sharply with the German and Spanish cases. Constitutionalization has proceeded, but only by provoking a drawn-out 'war of judges' (Merryman and Vigoriti 1967; D'Amico 1990) that has finally ended in a relatively stable stalemate. The crucial issue to be resolved was the extent to which interpretations of the constitutional court were binding on ordinary judges. When the ICC was created, it was assumed – as in Germany and Spain – that ordinary judges retained substantial autonomy over dispute resolution, finding facts and applying the law, whereas constitutional judges answered questions about the constitutional interpretation. As should by now be clear, it is impossible for constitutional judges to review the constitutionality of statutes without invading the domain of the legislator and of the ordinary judge. In Germany and Spain, the authority of the constitutional court's interpretations is ultimately secured by the constitutional complaint. In Italy, the constitutional court's position can be guaranteed only by annulling legislation, and even then not always completely.

The fate of Article 392 of the Code of Judicial Procedure provides a classic example. In 1955, the Code was comprehensively revised in order to remove its fascist elements and to harmonize it with constitutional rights. Accordingly, Article 304 established the right to counsel at various stages of judicial investigation and during hearings, in line with Article 24 of the new constitution. Article 392, however, denied the right to counsel at early stages of judicial proceedings wherein no investigation or evidence-gathering was necessary (for example, when the proof of the crime was not in question). In 1965, after a lower court judge referred a challenge to Article 392 to the ICC, the Constitutional Court declared that Article 304 governs all judicial proceedings, including those covered by Article 392 (ICC 1965a). Thus the ICC chose not to annul Article 392, presumably out of deference to the legislature, and instead ordered the ordinary courts to simply ignore it. Two months later, the Supreme Court of Cassation, citing relevant legislative debates, declared that it was not bound by the ICC's ruling, but only legislative intent. Given no choice, the ICC annulled the offending provision from the code two months later, blaming the Supreme Court's refusal to accept its interpretive authority (ICC 1965b). The Constitutional Court's position had been won, but only at the price of bringing the legislature into the equation. Further, in a series of subsequent skirmishes on the effect of the annulment, the Supreme Court rejected the ICC's position that the annulment of Article 392 had retroactive effect (to the date of promulgation), ruling instead that the provision was void from the date of the ICC's decision.

In the end, the ICC and the Supreme Court have been able to forge a kind of truce, in the form of two related doctrines, both of which had fully emerged by the early 1980s. The ICC articulated (and has since reaffirmed many times) the 'doctrine of the living law', according to which the Supreme Court possesses the power to make rules binding on the judiciary through its authoritative interpretation of statute (ICC 1984; and see Zagrebelsky 1987; Pizzorusso 1989). Although the ICC reserves the power to review this judicial lawmaking, it nonetheless recognizes (and constitutionalizes) the Supreme Court's interpretive autonomy. The Supreme Court, for its part, has agreed in principle to accept the ICC's reasoning as binding. The practical effect of these doctrines is to require each court, within concrete review processes, to engage the work of the other. Ordinary judges behave as constitutional judges when they decide how to frame and then ask constitutional questions of constitutional judges. Constitutional judges take into account how the living law accommodates the constitutional law, in its reception of these questions and in the answers given.

France: Constitutionalization without Concrete Review?

The Council's case law has given the 1958 constitution a *judicial* agency that French constitutions have never before possessed. Most important, the Council's incorporation of a bill of rights made it possible for the ordinary courts to apply the constitution to resolve litigation before them. In so doing, ordinary judges necessarily behave as constitutional judges. Further, the Council has ordered the judiciary to enforce what are known as 'strict guidelines of interpretation' (SGIs), decisions declaring that certain statutory provisions can only be applied by the administration and by judges as interpreted by the Council or be unconstitutional.

The establishment of judicially-enforceable rights has recast the traditional function of civil courts to enforce the codes and apply the laws. It has led the Supreme Court (Cassation) to engage in principled construction of statutes, what that Court calls the 'constitutional correction of legal norms'. According to the tenets of this doctrine, judges are obliged to interpret all legal norms, including legislation, as if they were in harmony with constitutional rights. When legislation and the constitution conflict, judges openly rewrite the former by binding acts of interpretation. After all, in the presence of a law deemed unconstitutional, all judges can do is correct the law by rewriting it, since a law once promulgated is immune to review. As a result, litigants are beginning to invoke constitutional rights in their arguments, backed up by the Advocate General. In 1988, for example, the Court heard a suit brought against a tire manufacturer by an employee who had been fired for having talked to a journalist about working conditions at the company. The Court found for the plaintiff, in effect incorporating the right to free expression into the Labor Code (cited in Cartier 1995). As important, the Advocate General had passionately pressed the argument that fundamental rights were both prior and superior to the codes, and therefore they must prevail in any conflict of norms in which they are involved. The task of the high administrative court, the Conseil d'État has been somewhat more incremental, although no less revolutionary. During the Fourth Republic, the Conseil d'État had succeeded in cataloguing, under the banner of 'general principles of law', a long list of restrictions on administrative action. Most of these principles, like 'individual liberty', 'equality before the law', 'freedom of conscience' and 'non-retroactivity', are in fact rights. In the 1980s, the Conseil d'État simply began to convert them into constitutional rights, a move that secures their permanence and higher law status (see Favoreu and Renoux 1995).

The status of SGIs is much more contested. In the 1980s, following the example of the Italian and German courts, the Constitutional Council began rendering SGIs as a means of softening its impact on the work of Parliament. The percentage of decisions containing SGIs has increased over time, in some years to as high as 60 per cent (slightly more than 70 have been rendered as of this writing). The Council has further declared, following jurisprudence dating from the early 1960s, that its reasoning (*les motifs*) is binding on all public authorities. SGIs raise the problem of judicial compliance with the Council's reasoning, and therefore of coordination between the Council and the judiciary, because SGIs are Council assertions that a given statutory provision can only have one precise meaning in order to be constitutionally valid. To simplify a complicated politics, the position of the Supreme Court is that 'there is no legal obligation to follow [SGIs]' (Poullain 1995). Some judges are even openly hostile to being placed under the tutelage of the Council.[14] The Conseil d'État likewise insists that it is not legally bound by the Council's reasoning; it has nevertheless incorporated SGIs and has even employed the language of the Council's case law in several of its decisions since 1988 (Favoreu and Renoux 1995). Without concrete review it is unlikely that this problem – if it is a problem – will be resolved in any definitive manner. More important, the Council, the Conseil d'État, and the Supreme Court are today consciously working to harmonize a coherent jurisprudence of rights in the interest of coherence and judicial security (predictability).

Prospects for Reform

In 1990, the Rocard government, with the full support of President Mitterrand and the President of the Council, formally proposed a constitutional amendment to establish limited concrete review. The change would have permitted litigants to challenge the constitutionality of legislation on the grounds that the legislation had violated their constitutional rights. Once requested, the high appellate courts – the Conseil d'État and the Court of Cassation – would decide if the challenge was serious and, if so, would refer the matter to the Council. The revision would have placed the Council in direct contact with litigation and with the citizenry, consolidating its 'judicial' status and its position as the defender of constitutional rights in France. The amendment was rejected by the Right-wing Senate.[15] A similar proposal was debated again in 1993, with the same result. The Right opposes the revision on the grounds that the Council already possesses too much power; it argues further that an expansion of the Council's rights jurisdiction would only be acceptable if the allegedly imprecise 1946 Preamble were to be replaced by a new bill of rights written and adopted by the representatives of the people. Neither the revision nor a new charter of rights has any chance of being adopted in the near future.

CONCLUSION

The normative structure of European constitutions and the way in which this structure has been developed by constitutional courts have recast the work of Parliament and the judiciary, reinforcing the centrality of constitutional decisionmaking as a *general* mode of governance. Government ministers and private law judges regularly behave as constitutional judges, and constitutional courts recognize, welcome, and even insist on this behavior. Constitutional courts rely heavily on the diffusion of a culture of constitutional adjudication: the provision of caseload conditions the construction of constitutional law, the legitimacy of which ultimately depends on subsequent implementation and diffusion. Most important, a huge range of outcomes – legislative, judicial, constitutional – can only be understood by taking into account the constitutional decisionmaking of those who are not formally constitutional judges. This chapter provides a framework for conceptualizing constitutional politics, conceived as the process by which the constitutional law is constructed. Given the paucity of research (both comparative and national) on the subject, the framework remains primitive. Nonetheless, only an analytical framework that focuses our attention on the interactions between constitutional courts and their institutional interlocutors can capture the essence of the new constitutionalism which today is pan-European, extending eastward deep into the former Soviet Union.

Notes

1. Of course, not all European polities possess constitutional courts or constitutional review (Great Britain and the Netherlands, for example), but nearly all European constitutional courts (an exception is the Greek Surpeme Court) conform to the main elements of the European model described here.
2. This orthodoxy is breaking down rapidly (see the fourth part of this chapter).
3. I have simplified the language commonly used to distinguish different modes of constitutional control. Constitutional courts also perform other functions not discussed, including: reviewing the constitutionality of international agreements, verifying compliance with electoral laws, settling disputes between national and subnational governmental entities.
4. The Spanish ombudsman, too, can initiate abstract review.
5. In Germany, constitutional rights provisions (Articles 1–20) are expressly frozen into place by Article 79.3, a perpetuity clause that forbids constitutional revision of rights texts. In Spain, Title X of the constitution establishes one procedure for a normal revision of the constitution, controlled by elected politicians, and another for revision of rights provisions, involving supramajorities of elected politicians plus a referendum.
6. The dogma is constantly reiterated (see, for example, Gusy 1985; Third International Colloquium 1991; Weber 1986).

7. The Seventh Conference of European Constitutional Courts (1991) was dedicated to the topic of constitutional rights.
8. This is broadly true of constitutional interpretation in all four cases.
9. For a history of the preamble and its incorporation, see Stone (1992, chs 1–4).
10. Rights provisions are the source of well over 90 per cent of all Council annulments.
11. Very little research on the Spanish Court has been produced in English, but see McGee (1987), and Stone (1995).
12. The standing orders of the Chamber of Deputies and of the Senate provide the terms of an ongoing, structured dialogue with the ICC. The Chamber's rules require that ICC's decisions on the constitutionality of legislation be transmitted to a Committee on Constitutional Affairs, which then examines the decision and recommends legislative action, if necessary. Recommendations are formally communicated to the Chamber, the Senate, the Government and the ICC.
13. Because it is initiated by politicians without reference to a 'case or controversy'. During the twentieth century, the academy's hostility to abstract review and to the Kelsenian Court has gradually been replaced by support (see Stone 1992, chs 1, 3, 9).
14. In August 1993, for example, the Professional Association of Judges issued a *communiqué* calling on judges and prosecutors to ignore SGIs, which they characterized as nothing but 'trivial gloss', *Le Monde*, 9 August, 1993.
15. The Senate possesses an absolute veto only with respect to constitutional changes.

3 Experimental Constitutionalism: A Comparative Analysis of The Institutional Bases of Rights Enforcement in Post-Communist Hungary

Jeffrey Seitzer[1]

Many Central and East European constitutions recognize a wide range of economic and social rights (Preuss 1995). Though the state provision of social welfare has widespread public support in the region (Schwartz 1992a), some commentators argue that the formerly communist countries should instead recognize a more limited range of traditional political and civil rights (Johnson 1995; Kommers and Thompson 1995). There are many causes of concern, but an especially prominent one is the possibility that the obstacles to full judicial enforcement of economic and social rights could produce cynicism about constitutionalism, which, in turn, could hinder the consolidation of democracy in the region (Sunstein 1992, 1993b).

While the viability of democratic institutions is admittedly important, such warnings often miss the mark in that they exhibit what Sokolewicz (1995) terms 'constitutional nominalism', or the confusion of terminology with actual conditions. Instead of basing sweeping prescriptive claims on analyses of constitutional provisions, he suggests, theorists should examine the practice of constitutionalism in the countries of Central and Eastern Europe as well as in the states which provide models for their constitutional systems.

It is in this spirit that I compare institutional relations over rights enforcement in post-communist Hungary and post-war Germany. The current Hungarian Constitution recognizes an unprecedented number of individual rights, which are directly enforceable by a constitutional court with extraordinarily expansive jurisdiction (see the first section below). Still, the Hungarian Constitutional Court does not dominate the political process in Hungary to the degree one would expect given these features of the Constitution. Though the Hungarian system is partly modeled on the German one, differences in state structure enable the Hungarian Parliament to respond to the Constitutional Court more readily and often with greater effectiveness than its German counterpart can to the GFCC (see the second section below).[2]

The ensuing analysis examines the impact of state structure, institutional design and procedural rules on relations between constitutional courts and the regular judiciary, not merely on those between the political branches and constitutional courts (Stone 1998). I argue that one divides authority not just to prevent the abuse of power, but also to encourage the consideration of different views on an issue (Sunstein 1993b; Holmes 1995), because this enhances the system's capacity for self-criticism and self-correction, but without undermining the system's ability to respond definitively to problems in the short term.[3] The fact that legislative discourse comes to resemble that of constitutional tribunals is a problem, because the Parliament does not have an independent voice in the 'constitutional dialogue' over constitutional questions. This concern also applies to the regular judiciary to a more limited degree, even in a country such as Hungary that formally excludes ordinary courts of law from constitutional adjudication (see the third section below).[4]

Finally, I suggest changes in the jurisdiction of the Hungarian Constitutional Court that would enhance the overall system's capacity for experimenting in this way with substantive understandings of rights and with institutional means for their enforcement.[5] It would do so, however, without altering the main contours of the Hungarian system of constitutional control or eschewing enforcement of certain categories of individual rights.[6]

Rights in the Communist Era

The current Constitution is really a series of amendments to the 1949 Constitution.[7] The 1989 reforms were meant to be provisional. In 1994, Parliament agreed to draft a new constitution, but there have been several stumbling blocks to its completion and promulgation.[8] The amendments were so sweeping, however, that one can treat the amended version as a completely new constitution.[9]

One of the most remarkable features of the current Constitution, the extraordinary number of directly enforceable rights it establishes, is a reaction to the abuses of the communist period, when legal rights were mere paper guarantees. Like its model, the 1936 Soviet Constitution, the 1949 Hungarian Constitution contained a variety of rights provisions, weighted primarily toward economic and social rights. The liberalization program beginning in the late 1960s led to a major expansion of the catalogue of rights in 1972, so that it included a wider range of political and civil rights. But there were no independent means of enforcing these rights. Until the 1980s, for example, even administrative actions were not subject to judicial review, and throughout the period the highly limited statutory protection of individual liberty was clearly subordinated to Communist Party control (Brunner 1981).

During this period, it fell to Parliament to ensure the constitutionality of state action. But the Parliament mostly sanctioned decisions made by Communist Party officials in the parliamentary executive organ, the Presidential Council, which was authorized to substitute decrees for statutes. So even if Parliament were willing to exercise genuine constitutional control, the Party could have easily circumvented these efforts (Lamm 1988, 116–24).

In the 1980s, the government sought to counter growing dissatisfaction with the regime by introducing important legal reforms. The cornerstone of the reforms was the establishment of the Constitutional Council, which could declare statutes and decrees unconstitutional and set a deadline for changes to be made. But this was of little practical significance, for the Council's decisions were merely recommendations to Parliament, which remained firmly under the control of the Communist Party (Lamm 1988, 76–96).

The current Constitution seeks to combine the communist tradition of state provision of social welfare with the Western emphasis on genuine constitutional control. Not only does it expand the range of individual protections significantly, but it also makes all rights, political and civil as well as economic and social ones, directly enforceable by the Constitutional Court (Halmai 1990; Pogany 1993). In what follows, I will consider the institutional features of the Constitutional Court more fully. Suffice it to say here that the establishment of such an institutionally well-equipped constitutional court reflects the intensely held belief that the protection of individual liberty and the guarantee of social welfare cannot be left to chance (Sajó 1995, 1996).[10]

Parliament and Rights Enforcement

Given the number and type of constitutional rights recognized by the Hungarian Constitution, it is not surprising that the tribunal charged with ensuring these guarantees, the Hungarian Constitutional Court, intervenes often into the political process in Hungary (Sajó 1995, 256–7). But the high profile of the Constitutional Court does not necessarily mean that it dominates Hungarian politics. A closer analysis of the actual interactions between the Constitutional Court and the legislative branch is necessary to determine whether the general concerns of commentators like Sunstein (1992, 1993a) about an excessive judicialization of politics applies in a meaningful way to Hungary.[11]

The appropriate starting point is the abstract norm control procedure, which empowers certain state officials to challenge the constitutionality of state action before it occurs. Because constitutional court jurisdiction is mandatory in a wide range of cases, constitutional courts often have no choice but to review state action, when a constitutional claim is properly before it. In this sense, constitutional courts are often forced into the role of republican schoolmaster, who hovers over state officials as though they were unruly students. With constitutional courts poised to strike at the first misstep, officials are encouraged to formulate policy with a view to the possible constitutional court reaction (Landfried 1984; Stone 1992, 1994, 1998).

Abstract review gives constitutional courts considerable leverage over the lawmaking process. It also makes the threat of a court challenge an effective legislative tactic, for parliamentary minorities can gain concessions from majorities concerned to avoid a possibly adverse court judgment. This is especially true in Hungary due to the Constitutional Court's expansive jurisdiction. German law permits the Federal Government, a state government, or one-third of the lower house of Parliament (the Bundestag) to challenge the constitutionality of federal or state law before it takes effect (Kommers 1989, 15). Hungarian law erects a somewhat lower hurdle, for it permits a standing parliamentary committee, 50 members of Parliament, or the Parliament itself to initiate a abstract norm control proceeding. The Hungarian Constitution also authorizes the President to lodge an abstract review petition. Finally, parliamentary challenges in Hungary may be registered before legislation is enacted, not merely before it is promulgated, as is the case in Germany (Brunner 1995, 27–8).

The Hungarian Constitutional Court could be involved directly in the earliest stages of the legislative process. The Court sought to preclude this possibility by establishing guidelines comparable to the US Supreme Court's ripeness doctrine (Klingsberg 1994, 323–5). The Hungarian Constitution still provides the Constitutional Court with greater potential leverage over the lawmaking process, since the Court can apply these rules in a flexible manner, perhaps intervening much earlier in the process than is possible in Germany with its more rigid jurisdictional rules. In the midst of a recent parliamentary debate, for example, the Court violated its own precedent when the President of the Court, László Sólyom, announced it would render a decision very quickly on a proposed government austerity package (Sajó 1996, 35).

Another important difference between the two constitutions is the extent to which they recognize governmental duties to provide services or to ensure social welfare and economic equality. The German Basic Law, for example, is weighted decidedly in favor of 'negative' rights, such as guarantees against arbitrary treatment by government. But the GFCC has read affirmative governmental duties into many negatively cast rights provisions, establishing a wider range of economic and social rights than the text of the Basic Law suggests. In the *Numerus Clausus Case I* (1972), for example, the GFCC ruled that restrictions on access of minimally qualified persons to university education could hinder the right to occupational freedom, so the state must seek to ensure that qualified applicants are not unnecessarily excluded from pursuing their chosen course of university study (Kommers 1989, 294–303). In most such cases, however, the Court does not specify precisely what the state must do to comply with the judgment, leaving the Parliament considerable discretion in fulfilling its duties (Currie 1994, 16–7).

The Hungarian Constitution contains a far more extensive set of economic and social guarantees than the German Basic Law, and it makes state neglect of its duties under the Basic Rights a cause of action before the Constitutional Court through an individual petition (Brunner 1995, 36–7). I will discuss Hungarian jurisdictional rules more fully in the next section. Here, it is merely necessary to stress the expansive nature of one type of individual petition. The 'popular complaint' provision is universal and abstract in that anyone may file an individual petition with the Constitutional Court, whether or not they themselves are in fact or even potentially harmed by the action. Individuals may also challenge alleged state neglect of its duties (Brunner 1995, 30).

Together, these features of the Hungarian Constitution give the Constitutional Court far greater potential authority to micro-manage

Hungarian politics. Not only is the universe of possible constitutional violations significantly larger, but the process of challenging state action *and* inaction is much more rapid. This potential for micro-management is illustrated clearly by a recent series of decisions on government efforts to scale back social spending. As noted, the Court announced during parliamentary debate on a major government austerity package that it would render a judgment very quickly, because it had received 'many complaints' (Sajó 1996, 35). Since there had been no parliamentary or presidential challenge to the proposed welfare bills, the Court was very probably referring to a popular complaint. Also, in striking down many provisions of the package, the Court made reference to general principles of law, such as 'legal certainty', to give flesh to the vaguely worded guarantee to 'social security'.

The Court's position calls to mind the American Supreme Court's 'New Property' decisions of the 1960s (Reich 1964). But the important difference, as András Sajó points out, is that the Hungarian decisions establish substantive, not procedural, standards. In other words, it is not merely a matter of ensuring notification and hearings before introducing changes in or cancellation of benefits; rather, changes in benefits may be a *per se* violation of legal certainty (Sajó 1996, 37–8).

The point here is not that the Hungarian decisions are illegitimate. Actually, I am not making an argument about the substantive or doctrinal legitimacy of the decisions at all. My concern is to emphasize that the Hungarian Constitutional Court tends to intervene earlier in the legislative process and set stricter limits on state action than does the GFCC.

Given these differences, one would expect the Hungarian legislature to be even more prone to pre-emptive self-defense than its German counterpart. Interestingly, though, the Hungarian Parliament seems more willing than the German Bundestag to assert its independence *vis-à-vis* the Constitutional Court. One of the great peculiarities of German constitutional politics, in fact, is the discrepancy between the range of discretion the GFCC grants the legislature and the latter's claims to be operating under compulsion from the former. Take, for example, the rightly famous *First Abortion Decision* (1975). The general perception of this case is that the GFCC forced a reluctant lower house, the Bundestag, to adopt a very restrictive abortion statute. Indeed, the Constitutional Court scuttled a hard-won political compromise, ruling that the state must take action to protect unborn life. The Court also established interim regulations which were 'in effect draft legislation' (Stone 1994, 454). The decision, however, gave Parliament more wiggle-room than generally thought, for, according to the Court, a range of measures could fulfill the state's duty. Possible actions include, but are not limited to, criminal sanctions. In the words of the Court:

> However, punishment should never be an end in itself. Basically, its use is subject to the decision of the legislature. Nothing prevents the legislature from expressing the constitutionally required disapprobation of abortion by means other than the threat of penal sanctions. What is determinative is whether the totality of those measures serving to protect prenatal life, whether classifiable as measures of private, public, or, more particularly, of social and criminal law, in fact guarantee protection commensurate with the importance of the legal interest to be safeguarded. (Kommers 1989, 353)

Parliament, however, opted for criminal penalties. According to the junior partner of the governing coalition at the time, the Free Democratic Party (FDP), the government might have enacted a less restrictive alternative. Then, in a subsequent case, the FDP argued, the GFCC might have ruled that the revised statute did not provide sufficient protection to unborn life, compelling the adoption of even more restrictive measures, such as criminal sanctions. But, as the FDP made clear, this would have placed the onus for the enactment of criminal penalties on the GFCC, not Parliament (Klug 1976).

While the German Bundestag and the GFCC do work together to formulate constitutional principle (Stone 1994, 1998), on contentious issues the GFCC usually plays the lead role by default. In other words, because the German Bundestag refuses to make full use of the discretion permitted it by the GFCC, the Bundestag's relations with the GFCC resemble call and response more than a genuine institutional dialogue between equal partners.

This is not the case with relations between the Hungarian Parliament and the Constitutional Court. The difference between the two sets of institutional relations is not due to greater self-restraint by the Hungarian Constitutional Court, but instead it is mostly attributable to the fact that the Hungarian Parliament does not quite as readily raise the white flag in conflicts with the Constitutional Court. Instead of engaging in 'auto-limitation', as the German Bundestag tends to do (Stone 1994, 447), the Hungarian Parliament crafts legislation which pushes the envelope of its permissable discretion.

The relative assertiveness of the Hungarian Parliament in its relations with the Constitutional Court is illustrated by the former's response to the latter's *Retroactive Justice* decisions (1993). In 1991, the Parliament passed legislation extending the statute of limitations for crimes committed during the 1956 Revolution, which the Constitutional Court promptly nullified. Because it establishes criminal penalities retroactively, the Court ruled, the law violates the principle of legal certainty (Brunner and Sólyom 1995, 511–19). In response to the Court ruling, the Parliament drafted a new law that justified criminal sanctions on international agreements covering war crimes and crimes against humanity, rather than simply the demands of justice (Morvai 1994). Casting its action as necessary to protect international human rights, the Parliament was able to gain Court approval of important parts of the revised legislation (Brunner and Sólyom 1995, 520–38).

The Parliament was even more successful in responding to the Court's decisions on the privatization of property. In the *First Compensation Case* (1990), the Court struck down the government's privatization program because it discriminated against those who did not have property confiscated in the communist era. The Court established an equal protection standard that required the government to show that any scheme which discriminated between owners and non-owners of property in fact benefited non-owners of property more than would a non-discriminatory scheme (Brunner and Sólyom 1995, 126–35). Because this exacting standard was practically impossible to satisfy, it proved an insurmountable barrier to privatization and provoked a very hostile public response. In the *Second* (1991) and *Third Compensation Cases* (1991), the Court backpedaled steadily, until it effectively accepted the government's initial position (Klingsberg 1993).

In these cases, the Hungarian Parliament achieved what Stephen Carter in the American context calls a 'forced reconsideration' of a court decision. In other words, the political branches craft legislation to provoke a court response. Often, this serves a merely symbolic function, for example, to placate a constituency angered by a court decision. But it also provides courts with an opportunity to rethink a decision and perhaps reach an outcome more acceptable to the political branches (Carter 1986).

In important respects, the Hungarian Constitution is modeled on the German Basic Law, so what explains the apparent differences in parliamentary assertiveness between the two systems? One possibility is the cumbersomeness of the legislative process. Testing the boundaries of parliamentary discretion risks another rebuke from the Court. The prospect of revisiting a contentious issue encourages parliamentary self-censorship to stave off another Court challenge, according to German legislative leaders, such as Herta Däubler-Gmelin (1993). In the long series of Party Finance Cases, for example, the Bundestag passed several revised statutes conforming quite closely to Court dictates, only to be forced by the Court to reconsider the issue (Currie 1994, 207–13). After one shift in Court position, Martin Hirsch of the Free Democrats expressed a widely held sentiment when he challenged the justices to write 'the law themselves' (*Frankfurter Allgemeine Zeitung*, 13 November, 1993, 3).

Of course, achieving passage of major legislation in the Hungarian Parliament is not a cakewalk either. Note, for example, the extensive legislative maneuvering required to pass the various property compensation bills (Comisso 1995). So after several of these statutes ran afoul of the Constitutional Court, why was the Hungarian Parliament willing to brush itself off and charge once more into the breach, seeking at least to preserve, if not extend, legislative discretion over the right to property?

While revising legislation is not a savory prospect in either system, important differences in state structure make this comparatively easier in Hungary. The first difference is the German federal system. While German federalism divides policymaking and administration between the national government and state governments, respectively, it also requires that statutes with a substantial impact on the states be approved by the states in the Federal Chamber, or Bundesrat, at the national level (Katzenstein 1987). More than half the proposed statutes must gain the approval of the Bundesrat. Because many controversial laws are watered down or filtered out in this way, there is a lesser need for parliamentary minorities at either the national or state level to embark on the 'road to Karlsruhe' in an attempt to block legislation. This partly accounts for the relatively small number of abstract norm control cases before the GFCC (Stone 1994, 450–1).

The other important consequence of the German federal system is that opposition to Constitutional Court judgments is often expressed at the state level. Recently, for example, the state of Bavaria defied the Constitutional Court by requiring the hanging of crucifixes in school classrooms (*New York Times*, 14 December, 1995 and *Der Spiegel*, 14 August, 1995). Opposition to the Constitutional Court also takes the form of variable implementation of Court decisions, as illustrated by decided differences in access to abortion between the northern and southern states in the last two decades (Klein-Schonnefeld 1994).

This is not to say that the Bundestag is completely passive its relations with the Constitutional Court. Parliamentarians regularly engage in more subtle, roundabout forms of circumventing Court judgments. Recent examples are offered by Finance Minister Theodor Waigel's child allowance plan and the controversy over parliamentary salaries and expenses (*Der Spiegel*, 2 October, 1995, 34). Stone (1994, 454) is right, however, that open defiance to the Constitutional Court in the Bundestag is rare.

Hungary, by contrast, is a unitary system with a one-house legislature (Agh 1995). Though the Constitution provides for local self-government, these local institutions have no authority over national-level policymaking and administration (Brunner and Sólyom 1995, 586–607), as do the German state governments. The fact that the national and local governments do not intermesh in Hungary makes it more difficult to engage in the sort of decentralized opposition to Constitutional Court judgments evident in Germany with its elaborate federal system. The streamlined character of the Hungarian state also encourages expression of disagreements with the Constitutional Court in the national Parliament, because the parliamentary maneuvering necessary to formulate a response to the Constitutional Court need not be coordinated with another forum.

There is a related structural difference that partly accounts for the relative assertiveness of the Hungarian Parliament. In formal terms, the Hungarian Parliament is elected by a system very similar to the German hybrid one. Of the 386 deputies in the Hungarian Parliament, 210 are selected by proportional representation and the remainder in single district elections. In practice, however, the results in the 1990 and 1994 elections were closer to those typical of the Westminster first-past-the-post model, because the strongest parties received a disproportionately large share of the delegates. In the 1990 election, the largest party received approximately an 18 per cent boost, whereas in the 1994 elections the popular vote winner received nearly a 20 per cent larger share of the seats in Parliament (Arato 1994, 26–7). This informal disproportionality makes it far easier to put together the legislative majorities necessary to challenge the Constitutional Court than might be the case if parliamentary representation more accurately reflected popular support for the parties, as it does to a limited degree in Germany.[12]

The structure of the Hungarian state encourages officials to press for changes in Court doctrine, because it establishes a much lower institutional threshold for the expression of opposition to the Court.

But this still does not account entirely for institutional relations over particular cases. For this, one must examine shifting political constellations.

We have seen that in response to an adverse Constitutional Court ruling, the German Bundestag established criminal penalties for certain abortion services, even though the Court opinion arguably did not require it to do so. According to a FDP minister at the time, Werner Maihofer, the *First Abortion Decision* (1975) came as a relief to Catholic members of the Social Democratic Party who voted for the initial reform bill only to maintain party discipline. The Court ruling provided them with a pretext to abandon party loyalty and vote for a restrictive provision more in line with their socially conservative outlook (Maihofer 1993).

The alignment of political support also partly accounts for institutional relations over constitutional principle in Hungary. In the *Compensation Cases* (1990–91), public support ran strongly in favor of the government. One counselor at the Constitutional Court conceded privately, for example, that the Court shifted its position on privatization because it feared 'a revolution' (Klingsberg 1993, 45). In the *Welfare Case* (1995), by contrast, the government austerity measures were quite unpopular (Sajó 1996, 40–1). By striking down the program the Court may have done the government a favor because it could bow to public pressure, all the while appearing to make a good faith effort to comply with requirements of international financial institutions.

Though the Hungarian Parliament responds readily and at times effectively to the Constitutional Court, I will close this section by suggesting a change in Hungarian Constitutional Court jurisdiction that would enable the Parliament to participate even more effectively in an institutional dialogue with the Court. Abstract norm control is a central component of both the German and Hungarian systems of constitutional control. But the Hungarian Constitution permits the review of legislation before it is enacted, whereas in Germany this is possible only in exceptional cases. Eliminating pre-enactment review in Hungary would enhance the dialogic character of Hungarian constitutional politics, while leaving abstract norm control intact. Because there would be more delay in the process of review, the Hungarian Parliament would have much-needed, though admittedly limited, breathing space. Parliament could complete legislation before the Constitutional Court intervenes. The extra time might also make it possible for Parliament to marshall support for a provision. Favorable public sentiment might encourage the Parliament to press for, and the Constitutional Court to engage in a reconsideration of Court doctrine, enhancing the system's capacity for self-diagnosis and self-correction.

Judicial Politics in Germany and Hungary

We have seen that prior to 1990, the Hungarian judiciary did not serve as a bulwark against arbitrary state action. In fact, it often aided and abetted state authority by interpreting the law in a way that reinforced the position of the Communist Party. In view of this history, it is not surprising that when Hungarians established a constitutional court, they rendered it formally independent of the traditional branches of government. In other words, the Constitutional Court is not a part of the regular judiciary, as is the Hungarian Supreme Court, which has the final say over legal disputes of a non-constitutional nature. Neither is the Constitutional Court part of the legislative branch, as was the Constitutional Council in the communist era. The Constitutional Court, rather, is an independent branch of government alongside the Parliament, the President and the Supreme Court, so only certain details of its jurisdiction and composition are subject to parliamentary control (Brunner 1992).

In granting independent constitutional status to a special constitutional court, Hungary follows a long-established trend in post-war Western Europe (Shapiro and Stone 1994). The Hungarian Constitutional Court also follows a basic pattern on the Continent in that it has a formal monopoly on constitutional questions. Unlike in the USA, where courts at all levels may render judgments regarding the constitutionality of state action, only the Constitutional Court may do so in Hungary. Under the concrete norm control procedure, more specifically, a court of ordinary law must refer a case to the Constitutional Court for resolution before proceeding, when it determines the case cannot be decided without resolving a constitutional question (Brunner 1995, 31–2).

By establishing separate courts for distinct areas of law, countries such as Hungary formally exclude the ordinary courts of law from constitutional adjudication. But matters are not so simple. The courts of ordinary law must engage in constitutional interpretation: for example, to determine whether a case raises a constitutional question that must be addressed by a constitutional court.

The role of the regular judiciary in constitutional adjudication, however, is potentially more significant than that of constitutional dispatcher. This is illustrated by German judicial politics. Many of the German Basic Rights contain legislative-reservation clauses, which provide the Federal Parliament with a role in the definition and enforcement of rights. The freedom of expression protected under Article 5, for example, 'find(s) (its) limits in the provisions of general statutes, in statutory provisions for the protection of youth, and in the right to respect for personal honor' (Currie 1994, 344). Unlike the negatively cast provisions of the US Bill of Rights, the German Constitution creates a presumption in favor of legislative restriction of individual rights, which means that conflicts between constitutional norms and those protected under ordinary law are built into the structure of the Basic Rights. In order to preserve as much of both the constitutional and non-constitutional norms as possible, the GFCC requires balancing of the constitutional and non-constitutional norms. There are no systematic studies of the relations between the Federal Constitutional Court and the regular judiciary in cases involving conflicts between constitutional and non-constitutional norms, so I cannot offer any firm conclusions. Nonetheless, the Constitutional Court often affirms the judgment of the court of ordinary law, even though the non-constitutional court resolved the conflict between constitutional and non-constitutional norms differently from how the Constitutional Court itself would have (Currie, 1994, 181–207; Quint 1989, esp. 302–12).

The decisions of ordinary courts have important implications for constitutional democracy. By insisting on the importance of non-constitutional norms in a particular instance, as the German Federal Supreme Court has done repeatedly in regard to property rights (Kommers 1989, 262–3), these courts compel the Federal Constitutional Court to reconsider or clarify its position. Moreover, when the Constitutional Court affirms their independent judgment, the non-constitutional courts reinforce the limited autonomy of ordinary law *vis-á-vis* constitutional law. Because it is easier to question and revise ordinary law, this makes it easier to experiment with different approaches to political and social issues than if these were treated as constitutional questions.

The Hungarian system has all the basic ingredients for such limited, informal constitutional adjudication by the regular judiciary. The Hungarian Basic Rights contain legislative-reservation clauses. There is also a large body of ordinary law enforceable by regular courts; and, with one important exception discussed below, the two systems of concrete norm control are quite similar.

There are indications that the traditionally passive Hungarian regular judiciary (Sajó 1993) is becoming more assertive. Take, for example, the ordinary court reaction to a 1991 Constitutional Court decision. Like most constitutional courts, the Hungarian Constitutional Court's primary responsibility is norm control. If a case involves a suspect norm, then it is set aside until the necessary change is made. The non-constitutional court then applies the revised norm to a particular case. Under certain circumstances, however, Article 43(4) of the Constitutional Court Act empowers the Constitutional Court to apply a revised norm itself (Brunner and Sólyom 1995, 626–7). But when the Court acted on this authority and set aside a non-constitutional court judgment in the *Paternity Case* (1991), ordinary court judges protested that they, and not the Constitutional Court, were responsible for applying law and regulations in particular cases. In response to these criticism, the Court now does not set aside judgments of non-constitutional courts (Sólyom 1995, 65–8). Perhaps in time the regular judiciary will discard its traditional passivity and make greater use of its limited institutional autonomy in constitutional questions. The instances of assertiveness by the German regular judiciary occurred over a much longer period of time, so it is too early to reach any general conclusions about the relative assertiveness of the Hungarian ordinary court.

Certain features of the Hungarian system of constitutional control, however, create institutional disincentives for the regular judiciary to participate more fully in a dialogue with the Constitutional Court. The key difference between the German and Hungarian systems of constitutional control with an impact on judicial politics involves the right to individual petition. An important post-war German innovation on the 'Austrian model' of constitutional control (Stone 1990, 82–4) was the right of individual petition to the Constitutional Court. By not limiting the system of constitutional control to state officials, the Germans introduced a 'democratic' element into post-war German constitutionalism. In fact, many believe that the right of individual petition, known as a 'constitutional complaint', played a very large role in winning acceptance for the new system among the general public (Gusy 1988).

The Hungarian Constitution follows the German model in this respect. Both systems place important restrictions on the constitutional complaint procedure. With some limited exceptions, for example, individuals may lodge a constitutional complaint only after all other judicial remedies have been exhausted and within a specified period (Gusy 1988, esp. 94–101; Brunner 1995, 34–6). The constitutional complaint procedure in both countries does not have the preventive character of abstract and concrete norm control. It is meant as a last resort for individuals with a grievance against the state.

In Hungary, there are other forms of individual petition besides the constitutional complaint. Under the Hungarian concrete norm control procedure, for example, the parties to a case may request review by the Constitutional Court. The German concrete norm control procedure, by contrast, permits only the judges of ordinary courts to refer a case to the GFCC.

This feature of Hungarian concrete review explains the relatively small number of concrete norm control cases initiated by ordinary court judges. From 1951–91, there were 2619 such cases before the GFCC (Stone 1994, 451), an average of approximately 65 cases a year, whereas in Hungary there were a total of 81 concrete norm control cases in the Court's first three years, which is an average of 27 cases a year. But the vast majority of these 81 cases were initiated by the parties to the case (Brunner 1995, 32).

It is difficult to draw firm conclusions from these statistics. We have seen that the regular judiciary in countries such as Germany and Hungary engage in constitutional interpretation, when they decide that a case does not raise a constitutional question. Perhaps the Hungarian ordinary courts are asserting their limited institutional autonomy by deciding that a case does not raise a constitutional question?

It is more likely, however, that the small number of referrals from non-constitutional courts in Hungary indicate that the regular judiciary has not completely abandoned its traditional passivity. Permitting parties to the case to initiate the concrete norm control procedure creates a disincentive for non-constitutional courts to engage in constitutional interpretation, for, much like parliamentary minorities and the abstract norm control procedure, parties to a case are likely to raise constitutional issues when it provides a tactical advantage. Because this relieves ordinary court judges of the responsibility for identifying and formulating constitutional questions, it tends to reinforce the traditional passivity of the Hungarian regular judiciary.

The popular complaint is another form of individual petition in Hungary, which is not available in Germany. The popular complaint differs from the constitutional complaint in that one may register a popular complaint even if one has not exhausted all judicial remedies. In Germany, the Constitutional Court can waive this requirement only if serious consequences would result, an exception rarely granted by the Court (Currie 1994, 164–6). Also, the Hungarian popular complaint procedure does not require that one have a personal stake in the issue, and neither does it place a time limit on the lodging of a petition (Brunner 1995, 30–1).

Individual petitions constitute a large percentage of the cases before both constitutional courts. Of the 6950 cases before the Constitutional Court between 1990–1993, for example, 5460, or 78.6 per cent, stemmed from individual petitions. Individual petitions form an even larger part of the German Constitutional Court's docket. Roughly 97 per cent of the 84 984 cases before the Court between 1951–1991 stemmed from individual petitions (Stone 1994, 451). Of the 5460 individual petitions in Hungary between 1990–1993, only 56 stemmed from constitutional complaints (Brunner 1995, 19), while all of the individual petitions in Germany are constitutional complaints.

To understand the implications of this difference, it is necessary to clarify the importance of time to the long-term viability of constitutional democracy. Continental systems of constitutional control seek to prevent unconstitutional action from ever taking place. This is, indeed, a worthy goal. But it is wrong to assume that constitutional courts will always be on the right side of an issue. Seen in this way, some delay in the system of constitutional control is useful. State officials, whether in political institutions or courts, seek to calculate how other institutions will respond to a proposed action. A delayed response often changes the incentive structure. In the time that it takes for an individual to seek relief before the ordinary courts of law, for example, there might have been changes in court composition or general societal outlook, which might produce a different result from that obtaining if the case were decided immediately. This possibility might encourage state officials, even ordinary court judges, to risk an independent judgment on constitutionality.

Differences in the institutional design of the two constitutional courts are also relevant. The GFCC has two chambers, each with eight members serving non-renewable 12-year terms. The justices are selected through a process involving both houses of Parliament to ensure as much as possible that each chamber represents the major political parties and regional interests. Originally, the two chambers were to address distinct types of constitutional questions. A major imbalance in the workload of the two Senates forced a change in the division of labor in 1956. Now, there is a more even distribution that does not conform neatly to form of petition. Cases are now directed to the two Senates according to the type of legal issue raised. The Plenum must still occasionally change the distribution to even out the workload (Kommers 1989, 19–21). While officially it should not matter which Senate hears a case, it is possible that the two Senates might reach a different decision on the same issue. This introduces an additional element of contingency into the process of constitutional control, which, for reasons outlined above, might encourage an ordinary court judge to risk an independent judgment.[13]

The Hungarian Court has 11 members, who are elected by a two-thirds majority of Parliament. Though the Hungarian Court has three chambers, most major cases must be decided by the full court with a quorum of eight (Brunner 1995, 21–4). This more unified structure does not afford the same limited possibility as under the German system that one's case will go to a different chamber which might decide the case differently. For ordinary court judges, this makes delay in the process of constitutional control even more important when calculating whether one should risk an independent judgment. This is because one must look to the possibility of changes in Constitutional Court composition or in Court outlook as possible sources of shifts in doctrine.

Of course, given the Constitutional Court's formal monopoly over constitutional questions, perhaps the ordinary courts of law should never think in these terms. But we have seen that even in a system like Hungary's the cause of constitutional democracy is better served when ordinary courts of law make occasional use of their limited institutional autonomy in constitutional questions. So the question is how to introduce more delay into the system of constitutional control? Obviously, eliminating abstract forms of review is the most effective means of slowing down the process. As noted, however, abstract norm control is one of the defining features of the German and Hungarian systems of constitutional control, so it is unrealistic and even improper to suggest that Hungary eliminate abstract forms of review.

Fortunately, such major surgery is not necessary. A more realistic alternative is to limit the right of individual petition to the constitutional complaint procedure.[14] Doing so would no longer make it possible for individuals to circumvent the regular judiciary entirely when they have a constitutional claim. Besides preventing judges from relying on individuals to raise constitutional questions, this jurisdictional change would give the regular judiciary some room to maneuver, because a decision about whether a case raises a constitutional question would not be subject to immediate review before the Constitutional Court; but it would not change the fact that the Constitutional Court renders definitive judgments on the constitutionality of state action. In this way, the Hungarian system of constitutional control could achieve a better balance between deliberation and decisiveness.

CONCLUSION

The relative success of a constitutional system should not be measured by whether non-elected officials play a prominent role in policy-making, or by whether particular branches make 'mistakes'. More important in the long term is the system's capacity for self-criticism and self-correction. This essential institutional elasticity is enhanced when different branches of government respond to (and occasionally even challenge) one another, because it helps the system identify problems and bring pressure to bear on responsible institutions, encouraging them to address the issue.

This suggests that when evaluating constitutional systems in Central and Eastern Europe, one should focus not on the range of rights contained in the constitutions, or even on high-profile constitutional court cases. Instead, one should look to the actual relations among levels and branches of government to determine the extent to which the system can reach definitive judgments on constitutionality in the short term that are subject to possible revision in the long term.

Overall, the Hungarian constitutional system exhibits a productive balance between deliberation and decisiveness. Nonetheless, changes in the jurisdiction of the Constitutional Court would encourage both the Parliament, and especially the regular judiciary, to participate more actively in Hungarian constitutional politics. These changes will not ensure that there will never be problems stemming from the Constitutional Court's efforts to enforce the unprecedented range of rights recognized by the Hungarian Constitution, but carefully crafted procedural changes could enhance the ability of the system to experiment with different solutions to these problems. In this way, the Hungarians can develop the appropriate mix of traditional and non-traditional rights and, in the process, solidify their democratic political culture.

Notes

1. I am grateful to Rainer Forst, Alex Kaufmann, Sally Kenney, Oliver Lepsius, Bill Reisinger, Janet Smith, and the other contributors for helpful advice and encouragement, as well as to the German Academic Exchange Service, the Obermann Center for Advanced Study at the University of Iowa, and the Max Planck Institute for European Legal History in Frankfurt am Main, Germany, for financial and institutional support.

2. Ideally, one would distinguish between the legislative and executive branches in each country and treat their relations with the respective constitutional courts separately. For purposes of exposition, when I speak of Parliament, I mean both the legislative and executive branches acting together. To avoid any confusion, I specify when a response to a constitutional court stems from a branch or level or government acting alone.

3. My argument is one of process, not substance. I am not concerned with the constitutionality, morality, or advisability of particular courses of action. In fact, I assume that all institutions will act in a way that is objectionable on one or all of these grounds at different points. My concern is the ability of other institutions to respond to these actions and bring about changes in the long-term.

4. The analysis of judicial politics in each country (see the third section) is more speculative than that of the relations between the respective parliaments and constitutional courts (see the second section). Relations between constitutional and ordinary courts is a neglected area of research (Stone 1998). My analysis of the limited empirical evidence and of the incentive structures facing ordinary court judges in their relations with constitutional courts is meant as a first step in a more systematic study of the question.

5. The emphasis on democracy as ongoing experimentation is inspired by John Dewey's (1954 [1927]) pragmatism. The use of comparative-institutional analysis to identify and evaluate possible alternatives emulates *The Federalist Papers* (Rossiter 1961) and Max Weber's (1979 [1919], 2: 1381–469) efforts to determine the unique needs and capacity of the German system in the aftermath of the First World War.

6. I recognize that this primarily American understanding of divided government is in tension with the more harmonious continental view reflected in the Hungarian Constitution. In suggesting changes in Constitutional Court jurisdiction, however, I do not require Hungarians to sacrifice comprehensive constitutional control or state duties to provide for public welfare. Rather, I am only encouraging tendencies already implicit in the Hungarian system. This distinguishes my reform proposals from those who suggest steering the formerly communist countries on to a more American path of development (Kommers and Thompson 1995).

7. An English language translation of the current Hungarian Constitution is available from the Hungary Homepage at http://www.centraleurope.com/ceo/hungary/hunhome.html.

8. One obstacle is disagreement over substantive provisions, such as the inclusion of a wider range of economic and social rights. Also, in order to lend the document more democratic legitimacy, opposition parties were granted disproportionately large representation on the drafting committee, giving small minorities a veto over proposed provisions (Arato 1996).

9. The scope of the changes in 1989–90 gave rise to the oft-repeated joke that the only thing remaining from the communist era document is the designation of Budapest as the Capital.

10. A similar belief motivated the establishment of many of the constitutional courts in Western Europe in the post-war era (Shapiro and Stone 1994 and Stone 1998).

11. In the third section, I distinguish between a 'judicialization of politics', on the one hand, and constitutional politics which is Constitutional Court-centered. This is necessary, we shall see, because the regular judiciary can serve as a limited counterbalance to constitutional courts.

12. As Arato (1994) points out, this informal disproportionality also facilitates the passage of constitutional amendments. Arato laments this because it prevents the consolidation of the system. Since citizens turn to democratically elected bodies for significant political and social change, frequent recourse to constitutional amendment procedure will hasten the development of a democratic political culture. On the importance of ongoing constitutional experimentation in the region generally, see Holmes (1993).

13. Recently, for example, there was an unprecedented public conflict between the two Senates of the GFCC. Each Senate had addressed an issue in separate opinions and disagreed over which decision was authoritative. The conflict should be resolved by a plenary session of the Court, but the Second Senate voted against calling a full session by a five to three margin. (*Frankfurter Allgemeine Zeitung*, 12 December 1997).

14. There are many advocates of such a change, including members of the Hungarian Constitutional Court (Brunner 1995, 31).

4 Political Economy and Abstract Review in Germany, France and the United States

John C. Reitz[1]

This chapter attempts to illustrate the value of the concept of 'political economy' – defined below with help from the 'new institutionalist' literature of political science as the combination of political and economic ideology and structure that characterizes a given country – to explain important differences among legal systems. As an example, this chapter deals with the device of abstract review – facial challenges to the constitutionality of legislation at the behest of certain official parties with automatic standing – which is rejected in the USA but enthusiastically accepted in Germany and France. The rationales given in all three systems suggest that there are good reasons for and against abstract review, but what counts as a weighty argument on one side of the Atlantic is dismissed as unimportant on the other. Conversations between lawyers from different systems usually stop here, often in mutual bafflement. Comparative analysis rarely gets much farther. This chapter argues that the differences make sense in view of the contrast between the state-centered political economies of the German and French states and the market-centered political economy of the USA.

The value of this approach lies first and foremost in its contribution to international understanding. By showing that many important differences in legal systems relate to fundamental distinctions among their respective political and economic systems, this approach enables lawyers from each side of the Atlantic to take seriously the other side's legal ideas, even if they are not moved to adopt them. It creates a 'sympathetic understanding' of the foreign legal system so that outsiders can see that the system merits the same respect and critical thinking that their own system does. It can also, of course, lead to a deeper understanding of one's own legal system.

The idea that political and economic factors influence law is hardly new (Weber 1954 [1925]; Cain and Hunt 1979 [excerpting Marx and Engels]; Constantinesco 1983, 362–84), but has not been explored very systematically, at least in the West.[2] Nevertheless, comparative studies of specific areas of law are increasingly pointing to features I would include in political economy to explain observed differences (Board 1973 [environmental law]; Brickman, Jasanoff and Ilgen 1985 [toxic chemical regulation]; Roe 1991 [corporate law]; Summers 1985 [labor law]). But it remains surprising how little effort has been made to explore the connection systematically, either by looking comprehensively at features of legal systems or at the full range of elements of political economy. The most important attempt to go beyond the general positing of a relation between law and politics to describe the impact of these factors on specific features of the legal system so far has been by Damaška (1986). His study attempts to take account of some of the factors comprehended by my definition of 'political economy' in a multicountry comparison of procedural systems. But his study, which makes only passing reference to literature on political economy, does not exploit the relevant social science literature as fully as I think it warrants. As a result, Damaška limits his analysis of political economy to two factors, the degree of activism of the state and the hierarchical or coordinate organization of authority within the state.

While Damaška's book has been of seminal importance in stimulating our thinking about this kind of analysis, his work has met with a critical reception. Markovits (1989) has pointed out that his first factor is too diffuse to be useful. I try to avoid this objection by taking advantage of the more nuanced structural typologies developed in the 'new institutional' literature. In addition, I argue that the approach needs to be expanded beyond civil and criminal procedure to encompass constitutional litigation, administrative process and litigation, and other more substantive aspects of the legal system (such as tort, property and contract law) as well. This chapter is thus intended as a pilot project for a more thorough-going attempt to relate the ideology and structure of legal systems to the ideology and structure of their respective political and economic systems.

The argument will be pursued in four parts. The first part defines 'abstract review', describes the form it takes in Germany and France and possible analogues in the USA, and examines the usual policy rationales advanced for and against this legal institution in these countries in order to show the puzzling differences in the way conflicting values are weighed. The second part surveys the 'new institutional' literature of political science in order to define 'political economy' and to characterize the differences in the political economies of each of the three countries involved. The third section argues the fit between each country's political economy and its position on abstract review, and also seeks to show that the conventional arguments for and against derive force from their respective political economies and cannot be fully understood without understanding that context. The concluding section argues that reference to the concept of political economy can help us understand the apparent paradox that Western European countries, like Germany and France, which so long resisted the US concept of judicial review as an inappropriate politicization of the law, have now adopted vigorous judicial review that is as politically salient as the US form (Favoreu 1990; Shapiro and Stone 1994), and moreover, have adopted it with abstract review, which seems to emphasize the tendency judicial review has to politicize the courts even more than is the case in the USA (Favoreu 1984, 52; Schwartz 1992b, 757; Stone 1992, 243, 253).

ABSTRACT REVIEW IN FRANCE, GERMANY AND THE UNITED STATES

The Institution of Abstract Review in Each Country

In the USA, the process by which courts adjudicate constitutional issues is limited primarily to what is known as 'concrete review'. In concrete review parties raise claims of constitutional rights as a defense to the actual or threatened enforcement of law against them by the state or by other private parties, or they assert a right against the state based on the violation of their constitutional rights. The party seeking review in a truly concrete case can thus show that resolution of the constitutional issue immediately affects the determination of her rights in a pending case.

France represents the opposite extreme. Constitutional review is limited to abstract review at the behest of a very limited group of public actors, namely, the President of the Republic, the Prime Minister, the President of the National Assembly, the President of the Senate, or – since 1974 – any group of 60 or more deputies or 60 or more senators. Private individuals have no right to invoke that review. Judicial review comes after the votes necessary to pass the legislation in question have been taken but before the President has signed the bill into law, so it is

usually classified as *a priori* review, and every constitutional case is necessarily 'abstract' in the sense that no specific individual rights are at
stake in a concrete controversy: although, of course, as in the case of
concrete review, many non-parties may be intensely interested in the
outcome of the case because of the effect they expect the statute to
have on them if it is found to be constitutional.

Germany has adopted a combination of concrete and abstract post-
enactment review. While abstract review accounts for a very small
proportion of the GFCC's caseload, it regularly brings politically sen-
sitive cases to the Court, such as the challenges to the abortion
statutes. Abstract review is structured roughly as in France, but with
an overlay of federalism. Abstract review can be invoked by the
federal government (the Chancellor, or Prime Minister, and the other
Ministers), by the government of any of the constituent states of the
German federation (the *Länder*), or by one-third of the members of
the lower house (the Bundestag).[3] But by far the bulk of the Court's
cases come from the type of concrete review resulting from complaints
filed by individuals directly in the Constitutional Court (so-called
Verfassungsbeschwerden, or 'constitutional complaints') (Kommers
1994, 473–75).

The private litigant seeking to raise a constitutional question in
Germany has potentially to plod a weary way by litigating his case all
the way through one of the regular court systems with jurisdiction over
his case before he is guaranteed access to the Constitutional Court,
but that path can be shortened if any of the non-constitutional courts
through which he must travel take the constitutional claim seriously
enough to refer the issue to the Constitutional Court. As Brunner
(1992, 546) has noted, court reference 'blurs the procedural line dividing concrete from abstract review' because the reference involves only
the abstract constitutional question and state actors (judges) control
whether or not the reference is made, but court references do arise
out of concrete cases.[4] In a system like Italy's where private litigants
have no right of direct access to the Constitutional Court even after
exhausting all appeals within the regular or administrative courts, the
system of reference in effect uses the judges of the regular and special
courts as a filter through which all concrete cases to be considered by
the Court must pass. However, because Germany guarantees the right
of direct access through a constitutional complaint after exhaustion of
all other judicial remedies, the reference system does not ultimately
prevent any private litigants from gaining access to the Court.
Moreover, if the lower non-constitutional courts refer the case, the

German system will conduct a constitutional challenge to the one court authorized to resolve the issue definitively (the GFCC for federal constitutional issues and the appropriate state constitutional court for state constitutional issues) much more directly than a comparable case can normally reach the US Supreme Court.

The French and German Constitutions (both drafted after the Second World War) expressly provide for abstract review,[5] but the much older US Constitution does not explicitly provide for any type of judicial review of legislation, and consequently neither authorizes nor prohibits abstract review in express terms. We know that the drafters of the US Constitution considered and rejected one form of abstract review, a Council of Revision, a body which would have been composed of members of both the executive and judicial branches and which would have had the power to accept or reject laws passed by Congress (Clinton 1984, 769–72). The Constitution itself contains only one express restraint on abstract suits, Article III's restriction of federal court power to 'cases and controversies', but that phrase has 'little necessary meaning' (Monaghan 1973, 1364).

One meaning of the phrase was settled at an early date: it prevents the federal courts from rendering 'advisory opinions' to the other branches of government on the legality of proposed executive action or legislation (Gunther 1991, 1593; Nowak and Rotunda 1995, 54–7). But while advisory opinions share some of the features of abstract review, they have one vice that is not shared: they expose the courts with the power of judicial review to the risk that they might have to sit in judgment on matters as to which they have already given their advice. While a few US states authorize their supreme courts to give advisory opinions, the practice has nowhere gained much importance (Note 1956; Bledsoe 1992; Calogero 1992), and Germany and France have rejected the practice, too (Heyde 1992, 1408–9; Rousseau 1993, 158).

The phrase also figured prominently in Chief Justice Marshall's justification of judicial review in *Marbury* v. *Madison* (1803). He characterized judicial review as a power the courts assert only reluctantly, pusuant to their obligation under Article III to decide concrete 'cases and controversies' according to law, including the Constitution as the supreme law of the land. As Bickel (1986, 115) has pointed out, Justice Marshall's argument had the effect of making justiciability requirements 'not so much limitations of the power of judicial review as necessary supports for Marshall's argument in establishing it.' While justification for judicial review is surely no longer limited to

Justice Marshall's narrow argument (Monaghan 1973, 1368), the failure of the Constitution to settle the issue of judicial review explicitly may contribute to the hesitancy of US courts to loosen justiciability requirements.

Nevertheless, the issue of abstract review surfaces in every case in which a party seeks to stretch notions of concreteness, and the US courts have permitted constitutional claims which could be viewed as partially abstract in the case of First Amendment challenges to statutes facially on grounds of overbreadth or vagueness even though a properly drawn statute could constitutionally be applied to the behavior of the party raising the claim (Nowak and Rotunda 1995, 85). But in the case of constitutional claims raised by official parties – state or federal governmental units, officers, or legislators – the US courts have insisted on rigorous requirements of concreteness. The discussion, Tribe (1988, 147) says, 'of a state's standing must begin with this inquiry: has the state made its claim in a capacity that justifies the inference of an injury in fact to the state's own interests – or is it merely acting as a conduit for the claims of its citizens?' For example, '[a] state is clearly entitled to sue to protect its sovereign interests,' such as the enforcement of its laws or recognition from other sovereigns, especially of its borders, as well as proprietary interests, such as the protection of state property and as the owner and operator of public institutions (Tribe 1988, 147–8). To the extent the state is permitted to act as a conduit for its citizens' claims, the state's standing to sue is based on concrete claims of private persons (*cf.* Tribe 1988, 147 and n.15).

The cases permitting a state to sue on behalf of its citizens under the doctrine of *parens patriae* to protect the general health, welfare, or property rights of its citizens (Tribe 1988, 148; Nowak and Rotunda 1995, 88) might seem to offer a closer analogue to European abstract review. But the importance of *parens patriae* for constitutional review has been greatly diminished by the rule that a state may not invoke this status against a federal statute because the federal government is also *parens patriae* (Tribe 1988, 149; Nowak and Rotunda 1995, 88). Consequently, states cannot generally invoke this kind of standing to challenge the constitutionality of federal legislation.[6] *A fortiori*, it has been held, the state may not use that status to challenge the constitutionality of its own legislation (*Baxley* v. *Rutland*, 1976). Moreover, the utility of *parens patriae* challenges has been circumscribed by a general tendency to require the state to demonstrate a sovereign or proprietary interest or show why the private parties whose concrete interests are at stake cannot be expected to litigate the issue (Tribe 1988, 149).

The only other official to whom US courts have accorded standing is the legislator, but never simply as a representative of his or her constituents and never simply to test the constitutionality of laws passed over his or her objection or the legality of executive enforcement of the laws (Tribe 1988, 151, 154). The Supreme Court has permitted legislators to sue to vindicate concrete, individual interests connected with official duties, such as the right not to be excluded from Congress (*Powell* v. *McCormack,* 1969), or the right not to have their votes nullified by illegal voting procedures in the legislature (*Coleman* v. *Miller,* 1939). But the Court has recently held that the change in the balance of power between the executive and legislative branches created by giving the President the line-item veto power was not a sufficiently individualized harm to each legislator's voting power to give them standing to challenge the constitutionality of the line-item veto (*Raines* v. *Byrd,* 1997).

In sum, such examples of abstract review as can be found in the USA are fundamentally different from the European versions. No public body or official has general, automatic standing to bring constitutional challenges to legislation, as in European abstract review. In general, a substantial degree of concreteness to the controversy is required for public party suit, either with respect to the public party's specific interests or, in the case of *parens patriae* suits, to the interests of the private parties represented by the state. But US law does not really reject all abstract review. Indeed, the rules of justiciability may be relaxed to permit somewhat abstract suits by private plaintiffs. What the US law firmly rejects, however, is abstract review at the behest of public bodies or officials.

Policy Arguments for and against Abstract Review

One main argument advanced for the European form of abstract review is that it permits clarification of what the law is before individuals have to act (Favoreu 1984, 53).[7] Under a system truly limited to concrete review, there can be no judicial determination of the constitutionality of a criminal statute, for example, until some private party is willing to violate the statute, run the risk of criminal penalty, and raise the constitutional claim in defense to his prosecution. This effect of concrete review is ameliorated in the USA by such devices as letting potential defendants sue for a declaratory judgment or by stretching the doctrines of ripeness, mootness and standing, but it remains the case that a citizen often cannot know whether a given law is constitutional unless he or she is willing to litigate the question or wait for another private party to do so. Private parties thus may let statutes of doubtful constitutionality abridge their rights rather than arrange their affairs to challenge the statutes, incur legal expenses to litigate, and run the risk of losing their challenge in the end. Under France's limited form of judicial review, citizens can rely on the constitutionality of statutes once promulgated because there is no possibility of subsequent judicial invalidation, and litigation started before the Constitutional Council has to be resolved within 30 days. Even under the post-enactment review system in Germany, German citizens need not shoulder the burden of constitutional litigation if an official plaintiff does it for them. So there is something to the claim, frequently made in Europe, that in contrast to concrete review, abstract review secures a beneficial certainty to the law.

Against that advantage is the argument, repeatedly mentioned in the USA, that, as Bickel (1986, 115) puts it, 'the hard, confining, and yet enlarging context of a real [i.e., concrete] controversy leads to sounder and more enduring judgments'. The US Supreme Court has claimed that requiring a personal stake in the outcome of the case 'assure[s] that concrete adverseness which sharpens the presentation of issues upon which the court so largely depends for illumination of difficult constitutional questions' (*Flast* v. *Cohen,* 1968, 99). But as Avril and Gicquel (1992, 106) point out, abstract review does not generally involve any lesser degree of adversarialness. Most cases of abstract review are brought by the political opposition in both Germany and France. The cases result from hard-fought political struggles, and there is no reason to believe that they involve any less genuine controversy than cases of concrete review, or that the lawyering by attorneys and judges will be any less zealous or skillful.

A much broader claim is the argument that abstract review weakens the courts' claim to legitimacy. As the noted comparatist with one foot on each side of the Atlantic, Cappelletti (quoted in Favoreu 1984, 52–3), said in critiquing the French Constitutional Council:

Standing reserved to several political personages and, since 1974, to a certain number of members of Parliament also, accentuates the 'political' character and obscures the 'judicial' nature of the Council; it makes of the Council a kind of hybrid organ in which the characteristics of the legislator, of a 'third legislative chamber', predominate over those of a judge, and the third chamber is obviously one without any sort of electoral base. In this manner, I think the Council immensely more vulnerable than any other system of judicial control of legislation to this recurrent objection – namely, the lack of democratic legitimacy.

Similarly, American commentators Schwartz (1992b) and Stone (1992) have viewed abstract review at the behest of members of the political branches as having the effect of thrusting the court deciding constitutional issues into the thick of partisan political battle much more directly and obviously than does concrete review. The result, it is argued, weakens the legitimacy of judicial review and leads to an undesirable expansion of judicial power.

The arguments for loss of legitimacy and unwarranted expansion of judicial power are based on both the form and speed with which a hotly contested political issue can go from the legislature to the court. Abstract review and official standing, it is argued, turn the constitutional court too obviously into a 'third chamber' of the legislature because the opposition can invoke constitutional court review on all important bills on which they lose, thus making court review an automatic part of the legislative battle. There is no need to wait for the government to apply the law to private parties and for one or more of them to resist its application. Abstract review cases reach the French and German constitutional courts literally in the heat of legislative battle; cases often do not reach any US court until years after the relevant legislative fights. Moreover, abstract review lacks the usual forms of court adjudication. There is no defendant in either Germany or France. There is no complaint. Like the legislature, in abstract review the court focuses solely on the prospective application of the law.

By contrast, cases of concrete review have the virtue of restricting courts to the function of resolving concrete disputes between clearly identified plaintiffs and defendants when they engage in judicial review. Shapiro (1980) argues that regular courts in all societies generally derive their basic legitimacy from this 'triadic conflict resolution' function. Based on Shapiro's theory, Stone (1992, 245) hypothesizes that abstract review may undermine the legitimacy of European constitutional courts more than concrete review. The US Supreme Court has adopted a very similar position, stating that 'judicial review is effective largely because it is not available simply at the behest of a partisan faction, but is exercised only to remedy a particular, concrete injury' (*Sierra Club* v. *Morton*, 1972, 740–1; *USA* v. *Richardson*, 1974, 188–92 [Powell, J., concurring, quoting *Sierra Club*]).

The Europeans by and large reject the legitimacy argument out of hand (Favoreu 1984, 53–5). Neither can it be said, despite the constant criticism to which the constitutional courts are subject, that there is any pending crisis of legitimacy for the French or German court. To the contrary, Germany and France appear to be celebrating the strong public acceptance their constitutional courts are enjoying (Favoreu 1984, 52; Kommers 1994, 486–9; Shapiro and Stone 1994, 402). The French have recently had desultory debates about adding concrete review to their system (Morton 1988, 148), but no one in Europe seriously argues in favour of abolishing abstract review. Yet in the USA, abstract review is rejected as damaging to the courts' legitimacy, and the legal certainty argument in favor of abstract review, which certainly has some force, does not appear to be accorded much weight.

How can we explain the very different weights given to these arguments on different sides of the Atlantic? Is this question not precisely the type of issue for which some basis of 'sympathetic understanding' is necessary to enable parties on both sides to take seriously the other legal system or systems?

POLITICAL ECONOMY

This chapter attempts to answer the foregoing questions by arguing that important values underlying each country's position on abstract review are identical to important values one sees in that country's 'political economy.' In order to carry out such a comparison, I first need to define what I mean by 'political economy,' and I then need to characterize the political economies of France, Germany and the USA to show how they compare. For help in those tasks, I turn to the 'new institutionalism' literature of political science.

Definition of 'Political Economy'

By the 'political economy' of a particular country, I mean to capture the characteristic combination of (1) ideology about the proper role of the state in private affairs, including economic activity, and (2) economic and political structures which influence how that ideology is implemented in that country. The utility of this approach is suggested by the literature of 'new institutionalism', which has attempted to study the connection between political and economic institutions and political and economic policy outputs.

After a long period of neglect, political science in the 1980s 'rediscovered' the state and its formal structures (Skocpol 1985; Dearlove 1989, 522–3). One seminal article was by Nettl (1968, 591–2), who suggested that 'more or less stateness is a useful variable for comparing Western societies and that the absence or presence of a well-developed concept of state relates to and identifies important empirical differences in these societies'. Subsequent work developed a typology of 'strong' and 'weak' states to express the difference between states that intervene actively in their economies and those that adopt liberal or *laissez-faire* economic policies. The strong/weak state typology proved unsatisfactory, however, because careful case studies of states usually denominated 'strong', such as France or Germany, revealed situations in which the autonomy of the supposedly strong state vanished, and classically weak states, such as the USA, turned out to have some surprisingly autonomous governmental bodies. Moreover, a state's autonomy appears to wax and wane with time (Skocpol 1985, 9–14; Hall 1986, 239; Atkinson and Coleman 1989, 47–49; Wilks and Wright 1991, 12).

One response to this variability has been to focus on structure, rather than policy outputs. In Skocpol's (1985, 28) words, we should view states 'as configurations of organization and action that influence the meanings and methods of politics for all groups and classes in society'. Here the emphasis is not so much on the actual capacity or autonomy of states as on the particular structures or institutions that govern the interaction between state and society. This type of work assumes that states 'matter because their organizational configurations, along with their overall patterns of activity, affect political culture, encourage some kinds of group formation and collective political actions (but not others), and make possible the raising of certain political issues (but not others)' (Skocpol 1985, 21). As Hall (1986, 19) explains, institutions can affect policymaking in two different ways: (1) 'the organization of policy-making affects the degree of power that any one set of actors has over the policy outcomes', and (2) 'organizational position also influences an actor's definition of his own interests, by establishing his institutional responsibilities and relationship to other actors'.

However, this mode of analysis takes us decidedly beyond the state itself to consider the organization of society, especially of the economy. The organization of interest groups into systems of 'corporatism' or 'pluralism' becomes relevant. Systems of corporate finance are relevant because they affect greatly the state's abilities to influence investment decisions (Zysman 1983, 55–80; Skocpol 1985, 17). From this point of view, '[t]he state appears as a network of institutions, deeply embedded within a constellation of ancillary institutions associated with society and the economic system' (Hall 1986, 17). The approach thus asks us to look at structure, but not just at state structure, and I join with Hall in preferring not to use a term suggesting that the relevant structure is all 'state-centric'.

Hall calls his approach simply an 'institutional' one, but I think that the term fails to say much about what I mean the term to cover. By contrast, the term 'political economy' suggests at a minimum the contrasts among *laissez-faire* capitalism, social welfarism, statism or dirigism, and the socialist command economy. The term thus foregrounds the question of how active a role the state should play in private lives, the ideological issue that I believe to be key to making sense of many of the most important differences among legal systems.

Nevertheless, I have defined 'political economy' to cover structure as well as ideology, and a number of writers use the same term to explore more nuanced questions of structure, including the contrasts between corporatist, statist and pluralist institutions, different forms of separation of powers, and different forms of business and financial organization (Yamamura and Yasuba 1987; Wilks and Wright 1991). Following Hall's (1986) approach, I assume that structures provide important evidence of dominant, enduring ideologies. As Hall (1986, 18) says, '[t]here are likely to be structural consistencies behind the persistence of distinctive national patterns of policy'. Undoubtedly such structural consistencies in the broader political and economic systems and in the legal system itself have reinforced each other over the years. Thus I take ideologies all the more seriously if there are institutions in the society that seem likely to reinforce the same values.

I also prefer the term 'political economy' over 'institutionalism' in order to indicate that my project is different from that of the 'institutionalist' literature: they seek to explain policies as the logical product of structure; I seek to compare the values implicit in the structures of the political and economic spheres to those implicit in the legal system. Institutionalists seek to demonstrate the primacy of institutions over ideas and values; I seek the ideas and values behind institutions. We are united in our belief that institutions and ideologies are likely to reinforce each other, but I agree with Ewald (1995) that a primary task of comparative law is to explain to lawyers what the cognitive world of lawyers from other systems looks like. To that extent, the comparative law project is committed to the primacy of ideas and values, and I therefore would not like to accept the 'institutionalist' label.

The Political Economies of Germany, France and the USA

The difference in goals does not reduce the utility of literature about the 'new institutionalism' for the comparative lawyer seeking to characterize the political economies of the countries under discussion in this study. Indeed, it is the literature that appears to have most carefully studied political and economic structures and their underlying ideologies. While there remains considerable debate about how to classify the political economies under discussion, there is nevertheless broad consensus on enough of the principal features to permit the sketching out of a typology of political economies for the purposes of this chapter. More nuanced descriptions of the respective political economies can be postponed to more detailed studies that consider legal features other than abstract review.

First, as a matter of intellectual history, French and German political thinkers have accorded the state a much more important and active role in society than US or British thinkers, and French and German concepts of the state have been intimately connected. As Nettl (1968, 567) points out:

> the historical experience of France since the seventeenth century was dominant in providing conscious or unconscious models for countries that underwent their national-integrative revolution in the nineteenth century, ... the real development of the historical tradition [of the state] took place in France; it is the French state, and idea of state, that provide the basic European model – even though the philosophical and intellectual tradition of ideas about the state reached the fullness of universality and precision in German hands from the beginning of the nineteenth century onward.

Most influential for Continental thinking was Hegel, who developed a positive concept of the state as the promoter of citizen welfare and the guide for civil society, thus providing the intellectual basis for the idea of the strong or interventionist state (Nettl 1968, 570–77; Caspar 1989, 318–19, 325).

In contrast to the French and German view of the 'state' as the institution embodying public power, Britain and the USA have tended to use the much narrower term 'government,' which refers most clearly to the executive branch, as the locus of public power (Nettl 1968, 570; Johnson 1978, 179–80). The word 'state' is reserved in the Anglo-American tradition primarily for the somewhat pejorative phrase, 'the welfare state' (Caspar 1989, 318–19). The intellectual traditions in the USA, reinforced by the daily struggle of the individual against nature in the settlement of the frontier, celebrate individualism and individual initiative (Bellah *et al.*, 1985, 27–51). Until the beginning of this century, the dominant American school of economics, influenced by the abundance of land, favored *laissez-faire* capitalism (Hovenkamp 1991, 183–92). Large-scale federal governmental intervention in the economy did not win majority political support until the Depression (the 1930s), and since the 1970s has once again been in full retreat (Bellah *et al.*, 1985, 250–71). While the USA has created some very interventionist governmental programs since the New Deal, there is substantial consensus among commentators that it shows a particularly high degree of ambivalence about strong governmental programs (Bellah *et al.* 1985; Skocpol 1985; Caspar 1989; Wilsford 1991). As Caspar (1989, 329) has written:

> [b]ecause regulation in the USA more often than not occurs as crisis management, it is also more readily reexamined as a crisis recedes and the usual distrust of the state and rent seeking by private interest groups reasserts itself. This ... is part of a continuum going back all the way to the late 18th century.

There is thus a sharp contrast between a continental European political philosophy that could be said to be state-centered in the significance of the role it assigns to the state, and an American political philosophy that is market-centered in the sense that it favors leaving matters to individual initiative.

We see the same overall contrast in the structures of political, economy though the situation is more complex because Germany and France have some quite different structures. France is a unitary state, a fact which makes its national government the embodiment of the French state in a way that federal states cannot match. In addition, Wilsford (1991, 38–45) sees the following structural features of the French state as constituting 'tactical advantages' for the state which make it more likely that the state actors will be able to maintain their autonomy in the face of efforts by interest groups to influence state action: (1) the powers that the government (the Prime Minister and cabinet of other ministers) has under the 1958 constitution to make law and to control the law-making process of the legislature;

(2) the fact that the legislature has been transformed by the 1958 constitution into an 'arena' legislature (one that 'cannot place its own substantive institutional imprint on legislative outcomes because it lacks the powers'); (3) the strong powers of the President of the Fifth Republic, who is separately and directly elected, to control state action; (4) the tradition of powerful ministerial cabinets, cohesive decision-making and policing units serving each cabinet minister and separate from functional units in the ministries; (5) an extensive bureaucratic elite that comes largely from two prestigious schools, which also produce most of the chief executives and scientists in French industry; (6) a judiciary of limited powers; and (7) the ideological fragmentation of private interest groups. Even though 'the policy process in France has become more pluralistic and incremental, the result of an interplay of a plurality of public and private preferences' (Safran 1995, 154), these tactical advantages of the French state mean that any group that is able to capture the main executive posts of the country (the offices of the President and the Prime Minister) has a much better chance to impose their policies on the country than would a similar group in the USA or Germany. In that sense, I think it is appropriate to refer to France as 'statist', by which is meant that it has a relatively autonomous central government that is designed to be able to impose its policies on the society it governs (cf. Safran 1995, 152).

The structures of the German political economy can also be said to be state-centered although much of the structure of the German state is quite different (a more truly parliamentary form of government instead of a presidentially dominated one; a federal state; an extensive and well trained bureaucracy, but one that does not have a comparable level of cohesion because of the far greater decentralization of German education). The German commitment to a state-centered polity is written into its Constitution, which states in Article 20 that Germany is a 'democratic and federal social-welfare state' (*demokratischer und sozialer Bundesstaat*). This provision has been interpreted to require the state to take action to protect the basic welfare of its citizens (Kommers 1991). But unlike France, which is a highly centralized unitary state despite some recent efforts at decentralization, the tactical advantages of the German state are limited by the federal structure that divides power between the federal and the *Länder* governments, and by the corporatist organization of economic interests 'in which interest groups exclusively representing given functional socioeconomic interests attain public status and the right to authoritative participation in national policy making' (Skocpol 1985,

23). Everyone who studies Germany is struck by the way in which private economic interests are brought together in umbrella organizations which are then given official roles to play in the determination of state policy (Hall 1986, 236; Katzenstein 1987, 23–30; Dyson 1992, 16; Lehmbruch 1992, 39–42). Similarly, political parties in Germany are particularly powerful and control the workings of government in a way that is not true in either France or the USA (Katzenstein 1987; Dyson 1992). France shows some elements of corporatist organization as well, but because of the ideological fragmentation of most of its interest groups, corporatism does not provide nearly as significant a check on the autonomy of state actors in France.[8]

On the one hand, German corporatism is an institution that reflects a commitment to active state participation in the economy because there would be little point in providing such a structure for private citizen input into state policy formation if the state were not intended to do very much. Indeed, the historical development of corporatism in fascist regimes shows that extreme forms of corporatism were intended precisely to enable the state to dominate society and the economy. German corporatism may be intended rather to permit society to control the state, but all forms of corporatism bespeak the same impulse to aggregate private interests in a way that permits coherent collective action. On the other hand, the far greater development of corporatist arrangements in Germany than in France creates a structure that limits the autonomy of state actors and ensures a greater role for voices from the public in formulating German state policy. Thus we should see the structure of the German political economy as representing a stronger commitment to state action than the US political economy, but a stronger commitment to individual participation than the French political economy.[9] For present purposes, it is enough to say that German corporatism and French statism are both structures that reinforce state-centered ideologies although the German version involves a more direct participation of private interests in the state.

By contrast, the USA is 'a polity in which virtually all scholars agree that there is less structural basis for [state sector] autonomy than in any other modern liberal capitalist regime' (Skocpol 1985, 12). In the USA, state power is fragmented by extensive diffusion, not only through a federal system but also through a presidential system (including congressional watchdog committees for federal agencies), that makes Congress and the President competing power centers (without tipping the balance as strongly as in France in favor of the

President). Most significant for our purposes is the system of interest group representation, in which societal groups interact with the state in a pluralist pattern of open competition among privately organized interest groups (Skocpol 1985, 12; Wilsford 1991, 54).[10] These features and 'the absence of a politically unified working class, ha[ve] encouraged and allowed U.S. capitalists to splinter along narrow interest lines and to adopt an antistate, laissez faire ideology' (Skocpol 1985, 27 [footnote omitted]). These structures have not prevented the development of some strong state institutions. (For discussion of autonomy of certain federal institutions, see Nettl 1968, 569.) The USA has even developed some corporatist structures, but not many (Salisbury 1979), and the preference in the USA is for economic and other interest groups to compete openly with opposing interest groups if they want to try to influence governmental policy decisions. Moreover, the extensive diffusion of power provides private interests with many access points to the public policy process. Skocpol (1985, 12) says that state power is 'everywhere permeated by organized societal interests'. Compromises are the likely result; 'grid-lock government' the constant danger. The state can act decisively to make significant changes only when there is a strong consensus. The pluralist structure of the political economy would thus seem to reinforce the pro-market, anti-state or weak state ideology that historically has dominated US thinking.

   In sum, Germany and France have state-centered political economies in the sense that their political economies demonstrate considerable distrust of free markets and a commitment to the idea that the state has a duty to intervene in markets to assure basic welfare; the USA has a market-centered political economy in the sense that its political economy demonstrates recurrent distrust of state action and a preference for leaving matters to private initiative and the free market. The greater degree of corporatist organization in Germany, however, combined with such features as the federal structure of its polity place the German political economy somewhat closer to that of the USA in the sense of making it more open to influence by private interests than the French political economy.

THE CONNECTION BETWEEN SYSTEMS OF JUDICIAL REVIEW AND POLITICAL ECONOMY

In none of the countries under study is the choice for or against abstract review explicitly rationalized on the grounds that it fits aspects of what I have called that country's political economy. However, there are two ways of showing the connection with political economy: (1) the superficial fit between the values underlying the country's choice and the values evident in its general political economy, and (2) the way in which those values are reflected in the policy rationales that are explicitly given in the legal literature.

The Superficial Argument of Fit

The simplest argument is that the values underlying the country's choice are the same as those underlying its general political economy. The choice of the design of this aspect of the legal system thus arguably 'fits' design choices for the broader political and economic system.

For example, the US system of concrete review leaves control over the raising of constitutional claims largely to private parties. The state, through its action or inaction, may sometimes be able to influence whether private parties feel the need to raise constitutional claims, but the state cannot relieve private parties of the need to defend their constitutional rights by bringing legal action for them. Thus control over the initiation of constitutional litigation is largely privatized. The US system of constitutional review, like its broader political economy, reflects a preference to trust in individual initiative rather than in state action. Indeed, the idea behind a system limited to concrete review is strikingly similar to Adam Smith's 'iron hand' of the market: the benefit of judicial review for the legal order will emerge from each individual's pursuit of his or her own interests in concrete suits. The US tendency to refuse to stretch standing rules in suits by public plaintiffs further demonstrates the US preference to rely on private initiative.

France represents the opposite extreme: constitutional litigation is restricted to a very small group of political elites vested with high official offices in the two political branches. Under this model, constitutional review is a product exclusively of action by state actors. Germany, with its combination of concrete and abstract post-enactment review, combines state-centered judicial review with the privatized form of concrete review. Like the corporatist organization of German political economy, Germany's system reflects the melding of state and private control. These correspondences are indicated on Table 4.1.

Table 4.1   The fit between political economy and the choice concerning abstract review

State	Political economy	Form of review
France	Highly state-centered: strong-state ideology with some corporatist structure but mainly competitive pluralist structure	Abstract review only
Germany	Moderately state-centered: strong-state ideology with highly corporatist structure	Combination of abstract and concrete review
USA	Market-centered: weak-state ideology and competitive, pluralistic structure	Concrete review only

Fit Between Policy Arguments and Political Economy

The connection to political economy goes deeper, however, than a merely superficial fit. Although the policy arguments on either side of the issue do not make express appeal to the political economy, one can appreciate the full force of the arguments only if one keeps each country's political economy in mind. Indeed, some aspects of the policy rationales are difficult to understand without that context.

For example, why do US lawyers accord so little weight to the legal certainty argument advanced in Europe as the principal justification for abstract review? The rejection makes sense in light of the US political economy. Certainty about the law is no less desirable in the USA than it is in Europe, but securing that value through abstract review brings it into conflict with the US suspicion of governmental power. In the French and German political economies, the state is conceived of as having a duty to provide basic welfare, including a constitutional legal order. Abstract review is a mechanism for the state to fulfill that function. The US political economy does not give the state such comprehensive welfare duties,[11] and as a mechanism to secure the benefits of legal certainty, abstract review seems objectionable because its reliance on state actors goes against the grain of the US political economy.

One prominent US commentator comes close to making an explicit connection to the US political economy: Brilmayer (1979) includes among the values underlying the standing requirement of concreteness the individual's interest in self-determination, by which she later explained that she means the individual's interest in being free from unwanted paternalism (Brilmayer 1980, 1732). Rejection of paternalism surely lies at the heart of both the US political economy and the US rules on justiciability. The kind of citizen required by a system limited to concrete review is a 'tough' citizen, one who is willing to run significant risks deliberately in order to vindicate his rights, not one who waits for the paternalistic arms of the state to take care of him. A few French reformers have made the same point by objecting that the French system limited to abstract review relegates French citizens to the status of 'eternal minors' (Gicquel 1993, 772 [quoting R. Badinter]; cf. Rousseau 1996, 78 [concrete, *a posteriori* review would let individuals participate in the defense of their rights]).

The connections between political economy and the legitimacy argument are more complex and ultimately more interesting. It seems apparent that the legitimacy argument gains force in a market-centered political economy but fails to have much force in a state-centered one. I argue that this correspondence makes sense because the functions a court can legitimately fulfill in a state-centered political economy, where the state has significant welfare-providing duties, are broader than in a market-centered one.

The view that legitimate court functions should be limited to the resolution of concrete disputes is clear in Justice Powell's classic statement of the legitimacy argument in the USA:

> The irreplaceable value of the power [of judicial review] lies in the protection it has afforded the constitutional rights and liberties of individual citizens and minority groups against oppressive or discriminatory government action. It is this role, not some amorphous general supervision of the operations of government, that has maintained public esteem for the federal courts and has permitted the peaceful coexistence of the countermajoritarian implications of judicial review and the democratic principles upon which our Federal Government in the final analysis rests.

(*United States* v. *Richardson.* 1974, 192 [Powell, J., concurring]; *accord Raines* v. *Byrd*, 1997, 2322.) In contrast, however, French and German jurists accept the value of a 'general supervision of the operations of government'. I argue that continental Europeans do so because their more state-centered political economies make greater demand for a mechanism for policing government action to make it consistent, effective and lawful.

The French Constitutional Council was clearly designed to serve such a policing function. General de Gaulle intended it to prevent the legislature from exceeding its limited powers under the 1958 Constitution by invading the powers of the executive (Avril and Gicquel 1992, 23–4). Stone (1992, 96–7) reports that French specialists in public law viewed the Constitutional Council as a political body, not a 'court', until the end of the 1970s, but that by the early 1980s the orthodox view had swung around 180 degrees. The earlier view was founded on a view of courts as neutral bodies which decide concrete disputes between two disputants (Stone 1992, 96). This is the function that Shapiro (1980) called 'triadic conflict resolution'. To justify the change in perception of the Constitutional Council, French jurists had to abandon that narrow definition of a court; instead, a constitutional court 'came to specify any institution charged with the power to determine, in a definitive manner, the content and applicability of constitutional law' (Stone 1992, 96). Bettermann (1982, 92) displays a similar strategy for Germany: the three functions of a court, he says in the course of arguing that the Constitutional Court exercises a judicial and not a legislative function, are (1) resolving legal disputes, (2) guaranteeing legal protection (*Rechtsschutz*), and (3) ensuring the constitutionality of law itself (*Rechtskontrolle*). In short, in order to account for the abstract review functions of their constitutional courts, French and German jurists have been forced to expand their conception of what a court does beyond that of deciding concrete disputes to include some form of general supervision of other governmental branches.

This European conception of court functions does not necessarily refute Shapiro's (1980) contention that all courts gain basic political legitimacy from triadic conflict resolution; but it does show that legitimacy is not necessarily destroyed when the court takes on other functions. Indeed, Shapiro (1980, 20–2) noted that it is common in some countries for courts to fulfill administrative duties in addition to judicial duties. The idea of courts making legal rulings outside concrete cases is attested to by a long history in England of both advisory opinions and suits by persons without injury to personal interests (Frankfurter 1930, 476–7; Berger 1969). While courts in this mode may fail to derive the full measure of legitimacy that they might get from concentrating on concrete conflict resolution, it does not follow that they necessarily lose legitimacy. Shapiro (1980, 17) recognized that courts may gain legitimacy from functions quite independent of conflict resolution, and Stone (1992, 251 [emphasis deleted]) notes that because the French and German Constitutions provide expressly for abstract review, 'Europeans desire and expect their constitutional courts to conform less to the judicial paradigm than their other courts.'

The effect of this conception on the European constitutional courts, however, is to locate them somewhat more clearly within the machinery of the state than the courts in the USA. The constitutional court serves more obviously as a sort of adviser and/or policeman to the other two branches. This type of court is more obviously part of the state machinery because it is charged with policing on behalf of important state interests. In fact, abstract review has the potential to involve the constitutional courts more deeply in the working of the government than a system limited to concrete review. For example, in Germany, there are at least two types of cases that can and do come to the Constitutional Court on abstract review but which would not be likely to come up under concrete review: international treaty cases and certain types of budget cases.[12]

The language German jurists usually use to discuss abstract review reveals that abstract review is conceived of as focusing on state interests. German jurists call abstract review 'an objective procedure' and use the term 'objective' (*objektiv*) to refer to the 'law' or 'right' (German *Recht* can signify either) which is vindicated by abstract review, in contradistinction to 'subjective law or right' (*subjektives Recht*), which is vindicated in concrete cases (Babel 1965, 11–12; Söhn 1976, 295; Stern 1982, 107; Maunz *et al.* 1993, § 76 at 3). Since objective law does not create individual rights, it probably represents state interests. Other aspects of German writing about abstract review confirm this hypothesis. For example, the GFCC has said that the purpose of abstract review is 'to serve legal peace [*Rechtsfrieden*] through clarification of the constitutional law situation' (Decision of German Constitutional Court, 30 July 1952). Other German scholars mention the 'integrity of the Constitution, legal peace, and the undamaged federal hierarchy of powers' (Isensee and Kirchhof 1987, 775) or 'protection of the legal order' (Stern 1982, 106) as the principal goals to be secured by abstract review. As Johnson (1978) has shown, Germans use terms such as 'the legal order' to talk about the state because the state is conceived of as the specific legal order set forth in the German Constitution. Thus, like their state-centered political economies, the language in which the Germans state a theoretical foundation for abstract review is state-centered.

A state which has the duty to provide basic welfare to its citizens, including the legal order and public powers which are exercised only in accordance with the legal order, naturally needs a mechanism to fulfill its duty to 'protect the legal order', and abstract review is such a mechanism.[13] Giving a court the powers of abstract review thus appears to proceed from the same impulse as that which led the French to give special arms of the executive branch, the *ministère publique* and the Council of State, supervisory powers of a sort over court cases (civil as well as criminal: Cappelletti 1975, 801–11) and over administrative action (Brickman, Jasanoff and Ilgen 1985, 101–2; Brown and Bell 1993, 276–9), respectively. Thus, 'objective rights' should be understood as state interests, the rationale for abstract review as one centered on state interests, and the courts which provide such review as special supervisory agencies of the state serving the state interest in being able to fulfill its duty to provide a constitutional legal order for its citizens. This insight makes perfectly understandable the rule in both France and Germany that once an abstract review proceeding is commenced, solely the constitutional court is in charge of the scope of the proceeding and the decision to terminate it (Söhn 1976, 309–10; Stuth 1992, 986; Rousseau 1993, 160). No individual's interest can prejudice the state's interest in vindicating its need to obtain constitutional clarity.

In the relatively stateless political economy of the USA, such a conception of the court would be foreign. To attribute interests to the state apart from those of its citizens would be to imply an activism or a penchant for action to the state inappropriate to its political economy. A court exercising 'amorphous general supervision' at the behest of other state officials would be viewed with alarm because such a mechanism could be used to coordinate and concentrate state power in the way that could facilitate activist intervention in private life. The legitimacy argument against abstract review thus strikes an especially responsive chord in the USA because it is predicated on a conception of court function that fits the market-centered political economy, but the argument has virtually no force in state-centered political economies because, in accepting a broader role for the state in private affairs, they also accept a broader role for the courts.

CONCLUSION

This chapter has sought to show how the institution of abstract review at the behest of official parties makes sense in state-centered political economies such as those of Germany or France but would not make sense in the market-centered political economy of the USA, which especially rejects automatic standing for official parties. Exploring the relationship between political economy and abstract review seems quite useful. Not only does the analysis give a basis for understanding the radically different positions taken by different legal systems on the issue of abstract review, but it also helps common law lawyers understand such puzzling terms as 'objective law or right' (*objektives Recht*). Furthermore, the analysis based on political economy helps to make sense of the differences in conception of legitimate court functions that underlie the acceptance or rejection of the legitimacy argument against abstract review.

Finally, the analysis suggests a way to understand the paradox, mentioned at the beginning of this chapter, which a number of commentators have noted about European forms of judicial review: European legal systems long resisted judicial review for fear that it would politicize the judiciary and judicialize politics, and yet abstract review, which thrusts the constitutional courts more quickly and directly into the political debate than concrete review, seems calculated to exacerbate this problem. Why have the Europeans insisted on abstract review?

This chapter has argued that abstract review fits the French and German concepts of a state and the type of judicial machinery it needs. Judicial review is accepted in Europe on the grounds that the state has to provide a constitutional legal order, yet only by including abstract review could state actors be given a way to ensure that the state fulfills its duty. So, the political economy analysis suggests, abstract review is seen in European terms as a virtually inevitable part of judicial review. Of course, I do not mean that it would be impossible to imagine a state-centered political economy that failed to adopt abstract review, but German and French adoption of abstract review does suggest that the chief values and structures of the political economy of each of these countries are so fundamental to the thinking of the participants in the culture of each country that they tend to trump other concerns.

At least they appear to have done so with respect to the design of constitutional litigation: despite the added risk of politicization, the state-based political economies of France and Germany have seemingly required a state-based procedure for constitutional litigation, although, unlike France, the less strongly state-based political economy in Germany accepts a procedure that blends private and state control over the initiation of constitutional litigation. In like manner, I believe that notions of political economy are fundamental to the explicit and implicit thinking of French, German and US lawyers about many other legal issues, and can help make sense of the persistence of a whole host of differences among these legal systems, in respect of legal structures, procedural rules and substantive law.

Notes

1. In addition to the generosity of Esco C. and Alva Obermann, who provided the funding for the seminar for which this chapter was originally prepared, I would like to acknowledge the generous support of the Iowa Law School Foundation and the Developmental Leave Program at the University of Iowa. The Obermann Center for Advanced Studies at the University of Iowa provided a welcome refuge and stimulating home for crucial stages in the development of this chapter. So many people have helped me with this project, I cannot name them all. However, I specifically want to thank: my fellow participants in the Obermann seminar; colleagues on the law faculty at Iowa, where I twice had the benefit of presenting earlier versions in faculty seminars; for written comments on earlier drafts, Professors Mark Osiel and Constantijn Kortmann, as well as Alexander Domrin and an anonymous reviewer for the University of Michigan Press; and research assistants Andrew Hawke, Alexander Klett, Karsten Kuhlmann, John Lundquist, Siegmar Pohl and Ling Zhu. Despite all that help, the chapter's shortcomings are my responsibility. Except where otherwise noted, translations are by the author.
2. Damaška (1986, 6 n.7), noting that 'Marx never attempted to link his broad models of socioeconomic structure to formal aspects of the legal process', dismisses the many subsequent attempts to do so in the Soviet Union. I am not familiar with that literature and it seems to have had no impact in the West.
3. The federal government, the governments of the *Länder*, and various other organs of government can also initiate constitutional litigation in the so-called cases of *Organstreit* and *Bund-Länder-* or *Land-Land-Streit*, German Constitution Art. 93 (1)–(4), and the communal governments can challenge laws which infringe their right to self-government, Art. 93 (4b), but these are cases of concrete review because they involve cases in which the organ of government bringing the suit is vindicating its own rights and protecting its own interests as an organ of government. See, e.g., Constitutional Court Law § 64 (requiring for *Organstreit* that the complaining state organ show that its constitutional rights are 'injured or threatened').

4. German law calls court reference *konkrete Normenkontrolle* (concrete control of norms) and does not use that term to refer to *Verfassungsbeschwerden*. The terminology should not obscure the fact that *Verfassungsbeschwerden* are the clearest examples of concrete review.

5. In fact, it is the only form of review authorized by the French Constitution, and it – together with the intermediate form of reference from regular courts – was the principal form provided by the German Constitution. The only instances of pure concrete review originally were *Organstreit* and *Bund-Länder-Streit*. Provisions for *Verfassungsbeschwerden* and communal challenges were added in 1969.

6. Unless the challenged legislation arguably invades powers the Constitution reserves to the states (Tribe 1988, 149). But in that case the state can show a concrete harm to its own sovereign interests.

7. In France, abstract review is required by the decision to limit judicial review of legislation to *a priori* review. Such review can only be abstract. But the French do not appear to limit their justifications for abstract review to that argument, and the Germans cannot in any event use that argument since their review is post-enactment.

8. There is considerable debate over the degree of corporatist organization in France (Safran 1995, 146–55; Wilson 1983, 1985; Keeler 1985). But no one would dispute that French society falls between Germany and the USA in terms of the degree of corporatism.

9. Cf. Cawson (1985, 225): 'Corporatism seems to require a state system which is strong enough to preserve its autonomy from societal interests, yet not strong enough for an independent conception of a transcendent interest to be enforced upon society in a directive mode without the participation of interest organizations.'

10. Katznelson and Prewitt (1979, 32) argue that the 'stateless' political economy of the USA is actually constituted by the Constitution: 'The Constitution does not establish a state that in turn manages the affairs of society toward some clear conception of the public welfare; rather, it establishes a political economy in which the public welfare is the aggregate of private preferences.'

11. The American state's lack of duties to provide welfare is no doubt reinforced with respect to the legal system itself by the traditions of the common law and the influence of natural law, which combine to create a sense in common law systems that the legal order is at least partially independent of the state (Johnson 1978, 190). Thus the state cannot as easily be said to have a duty to provide the legal order.

12. See, e.g., Decision of German Constitutional Court (31 July 1973) (considering merits of Bavarian state government's challenge to federal treaty with German Democratic Republic and law implementing the treaty in part on the basis that the treaty violated federal constitutional command to work toward German reunification); Decision of German Constitutional Court (18 April 1989) (considering merits of challenge by 231 members of parliament to federal budget statute authorizing Minister of Finance to borrow more money than required to cover expenses for certain investments on grounds that it violated

federal constitutional prohibition on borrowing in excess of projected expenses).

13.   Cf. Rinken (1984, 1020) noting the inclusion of the Constitutional Court in the 'tradition of "nationalization" in which the state appears as the "reality of the ethical idea" (Hegel) removed from the battle between parties and the law as an expression of the commonweal superior to and transcending the political process'.

5 A Comparative Study of the Constitutional Protection of Hate Speech in Canada and the United States: A Search for Explanations
William G. Buss

INTRODUCTION

In any constitutional system that undertakes to give legal protection to freedom of speech, questions arise about the meaning of 'speech' and the scope of the freedom. One recurrent question is whether strongly negative statements about an individual or group, based on race or ethnic identity, are protected as 'freedom of speech'. In this essay, I will treat such negative statements as 'hate speech',[1] and I will refer to the question of whether such messages are entitled to constitutional protection as the 'hate speech problem'.

Broadly speaking, the USA has said, 'Yes, hate speech is protected,' and the rest of the world has said, 'No, hate speech is not protected' (Coliver 1992; Walker 1996, 87–93). In this essay, these two opposite approaches will be considered by comparing two recent cases decided, respectively, by the Supreme Courts of Canada and the USA. I will explore considerations that might explain the different results in those cases at three levels: the first suggesting different results are fortuitous, the second suggesting that they are products of significant structural differences in the American and Canadian constitutional systems, and the third suggesting that they reflect fundamental cultural differences between the two countries.

Based on that analysis, I tentatively conclude that the American-Canadian divide represented by the divergent outcomes of the two hate speech cases considered does in fact reflect significant cultural differences concerning individualism and paternalism; assimilation and preservation of group identities; and historically-based different styles of government. I will modify this tentative conclusion, relying both on counterindications in American and Canadian constitutional law and on two examples taken from under the European constitutional law. I will, finally, conclude with an acknowledgment of an apparently irreducible Canadian-American cultural difference.

So that readers may better decide whether this essay may be of interest and what biases may be operating, three matters should be stated explicitly. First, I am a white male who does not fit any obvious 'minority' category (and not unaware of the possible influence that this fact might have on my judgment). Second, as an American lawyer, it may not surprise some readers that I find the American approach more persuasive (though not based on any assumption that hateful speech is harmless[2]), and that perspective may influence my analysis and discussion unintentionally. Finally, this essay does not itself offer a justification of the American approach (or any alternative) but only points out and attempts to explain differences between it and the approach of most of the rest of the world.

HATE SPEECH IN THE UNITED STATES AND CANADA: TWO CASES

The General Factual and Legal Setting

RAV v. *City of St. Paul, Minnesota* (1992) and *Regina* v. *Keegstra* (1990) are recent cases in which the highest courts of the USA and Canada have given extensive attention to the problem of hate speech.[3] *RAV* and *Keegstra* are both cases in which the hate speech is truly hateful: blatant (albeit symbolic) racist speech against blacks in the USA; anti-Semitic, holocaust-denying speech in Canada. In *Regina* v. *Keegstra*, the defendant, James Keegstra, was a high-school teacher whose prosecution was based on anti-Semitic comments that he had made to his students, remarkably, for ten or more years. According to the allegation, Mr Keegstra informed his students that Jews were treacherous, subversive, sadistic, money-loving, power hungry, child killers, and fabricators of the holocaust; and he required his students to demonstrate that they had learned the lesson he was teaching by their in-class and examination responses. In *RAV* v. *City of St. Paul*, the defendant was a teenager who, apparently in retaliation for a black family's moving into a 'white neighborhood', tied two legs of a chair together into the shape of a cross, and then set the home-made cross on fire inside the fenced yard of the black family.

The constitutional system in both the USA and Canada are federal systems. Each has a Supreme Court with final power to construe and enforce the national constitution.[4] Both Canada and the USA have entrenched Bills of Rights: various specific amendments in the US Constitution; a 'Charter of Fundamental Rights and Freedoms' in Canada. The American First Amendment includes a 'freedom of speech' provision; the Canadian Charter includes a 'freedom of expression' provision.

The general pattern of litigated issues arising in the two cases was similar: (1) an individual who communicated 'hate speech' was charged with criminal conduct;[5] (2) the individual set up a constitutional right of freedom of speech expression as a defense; (3) the case began in the state/provincial courts, and culminated in the highest court in the land;[6] (4) in both cases, all of the judges who spoke were strikingly united in their articulation of the value of equality (and especially racial and ethnic equality) and the value of liberty (and especially liberty of speech and expression); (5) in the highest and decisive court in each case, the judges were divided as closely as they can be: 5–4 in the US Supreme Court; 4–3 in the Canadian Supreme Court. Indeed, if one regards the issues in the two cases as truly the same issue, one cannot help noticing that the combined international vote is a dead even 8–8.

Regina v. Keegstra

Canadian Statutory and Constitutional Provisions

Keegstra was charged with and convicted of a violation of s.319(2) of Canadian criminal law, which makes the following conduct a criminal offense:

> Every one who, by communicating statements, other than in private conversation, wilfully promotes hatred against any identifiable group.[7]

Keegstra relied upon his Charter right of freedom of expression as a defense to his conviction. s.2(b) provides:

> 2. Everyone has the following fundamental freedoms: ...
> (b) freedom of thought, belief, opinion and expression, including freedom of the press and other media of communication ...

To nullify the free expression defense, the prosecutor (the 'Crown' in Canada), relied upon s.1 of the Charter which authorizes 'reasonable limits prescribed by law' that are justifiable 'in a free and democratic society'.[8]

Reasoning of the Canadian Supreme Court

In an extensive opinion for a divided Canadian Supreme Court (4–3), Chief Justice Dickson concluded that the proscribed statements were 'expression' within Charter s.2(b) but that the statutory proscription came within the permissible limits of s.1. The majority opinion discussed American constitutional law at some length. The Chief Justice said that he found the American experience 'tremendously helpful' but doubted its applicability (*Keegstra*, 741). Chief Justice Dickson's opinion discussed and rejected both the current American 'clear and present danger' rule, as articulated in *Brandenburg* v. *Ohio* (1969), and the American rule prohibiting content or viewpoint discrimination. The Chief Justice also stressed that s.1 of the Charter, and especially the phrase 'free and democratic society' brought into play 'fundamental values and aspirations of Canadian society' (*Keegstra*, 744).

The analytical framework for Dickson's opinion was provided by the test established in *Regina* v. *Oakes* (1986). Roughly parallel to the American 'compelling interest' test, *Oakes* requires that the legislation being challenged must have an objective which 'relates to concerns which are pressing and substantial in a free and democratic society' (*Keegstra*, 744) and that the means used are 'proportionate' to that objective.

The objectives of s.319(2), in preventing the harms of 'hate propaganda', were found in studies and reports of hate propaganda in Canada (particularly the Cohen Committee) (*Keegstra*, 746–7). The Court identified emotional or psychological harm to the individuals who are the targets of hate speech and harm to 'society at large' in being persuaded to believe the hateful accusations.[9]

Chief Justice Dickson conceded that s.319(2) would lack proportionality if, as argued by dissenting Justice McLachlin, it was either ineffective in preventing the harm at which it was aimed or counterproductive in the sense of aggravating rather than ameliorating the harm (*Keegstra*, 768). McLachlin argued that the statute was counterproductive since it gave hate speech publicity and raised the question in the public's mind of whether the government suppressed these ideas because there was truth in them; and she argued that the ineffectiveness of such laws was demonstrated by their failure when used in the Germany of the 1920s and 1930s.[10] In partial response, Chief Justice Dickson observed that Germany, many other countries, and the international community (through its treaties) had not been deterred by Germany's experience.

To meet the argument that s.319(2) would 'chill' protected speech because it was vague and overbroad, Chief Justice Dickson read s.319(2) narrowly, emphasizing its inapplicability to private conversation, its application only to wilful promotion of hatred (with respect to which 'promotion' was said to entail more than encouragement or advancement, and 'hatred' was said to include only the most intense and extreme emotion) (*Keegstra*, 772–3). Saying that the Charter right of freedom of expression had to be treated 'contextually' (Keegstra, 760), the Dickson opinion indicated that speech proscribed by s.319(2) contributed very little to the pursuit of truth, individual self-fulfillment and participation in the political process, and thus placed very little weight on the balancing scales of proportionality.

RAV v. City of St. Paul

American Statutory and Constitutional Provisions

In the *RAV* case, the teenager who burned a cross in a black family's enclosed yard was charged under a regulation of the city of St. Paul, Minnesota:

> Whoever places on public or private property a symbol, object, appellation, characterization or graffiti, including, but not limited to, a burning cross or Nazi swastika, which one knows or has reasonable grounds to know arouses anger, alarm or resentment in others on the basis of race, color, creed, religion or gender [is] ... guilty of a misdemeanor. (St. Paul ordinance)

At the trial level, the court granted RAV's motion to dismiss the charges on the grounds that the St. Paul ordinance violated the First Amendment of the US Constitution, which states that 'Congress shall make no law abridging the freedom of speech', and which is understood to be applicable to states of the USA and their political subdivisions through the Fourteenth Amendment. In reversing the dismissal, the Minnesota Supreme Court apparently intended to interpret the ordinance so that it would apply only to 'fighting words' (*In re Welfare of RAV* 1991). In reversing this Minnesota decision, the US Supreme Court was unanimous; but the Court was deeply divided between two technical rationales.[11]

The US Supreme Court Reasoning

Justices White and Stevens assumed that the St. Paul ordinance would have been constitutional if it had prohibited only 'fighting words'.[12] But these concurring Justices concluded that the St. Paul ordinance prohibited much speech which could not be considered fighting words and thus much protected speech. According to Justice White's opinion, 'The mere fact that expressive activity causes hurt feelings, offense, or resentment does not render the expression unprotected' (*RAV*, 414).

In his opinion for the majority, Justice Scalia relied upon another well established First Amendment doctrine: that viewpoint discrimination is one of the – if not *the* – most fundamentally unacceptable ways for government to regulate speech (Stone 1978; Stone 1983). For Scalia, the fatal flaw in the St. Paul ordinance was its prohibition of some fighting words (those based on race, religion, or gender) but not others (e.g., those based on sexual orientation, union membership, or political affiliation) (*RAV*, 391). Scalia conceded that the state had a compelling interest to protect individuals from the harm of racist speech but, he argued, that could be done without selective protection. The concurring opinions said that the government's interest could not be fully satisfied without making known its special concern, and its intention to provide special protection for the very groups in society which had been most badly treated and, consequently, in a sense, uniquely injured by fighting words (*RAV*, 407, 424–5). Scalia responded that the city of St. Paul could express its compassion for the affected racial minorities or its condemnation of the racial hate speech but it could not achieve the stated end by limiting the speech of those who disagree (*RAV*, 396).

COMPARATIVE ANALYSIS

In this part, I will compare the *Keegstra* and *RAV* cases by considering three different types of explanation, roughly corresponding to surface explanations, deeper explanations and fundamental explanations. The first level is called 'coincidental', by which I mean that the different outcomes of the two cases can be explained on the basis of nothing that generally distinguishes the two constitutional systems or the cultures of which they are a part. The second level is called 'structural', by which I mean that an explanation can be traced to the language or structure or judicial doctrines of the two constitutions. The third level is called 'cultural', by which I mean that fundamental differences between the two countries outside their legal constitutional systems tend to produce the different results that these two cases illustrate.

Coincidental Explanatory Considerations

Within any legal system two judges or two courts or the same court at different times often reach conclusions that appear to be inconsistent. Given the shared Canadian and American commitment to free speech and racial equality, the strong dissent in each case, and the cross-border division of intellectual opinion (Borovoy, and Mahoney 1988/89), a judicial appointment or two on either side of the border might change the result in either country.

Although each case was decided on the face of the statute, factual differences could conceivably have influenced the outcomes. The *Keegstra* speech involved an adult who occupied a position of trust with children and who repeatedly and systematically taught the children his hateful message.[13] The burning cross in *RAV* is a well-known symbol of lynching as well as hatred, and it conveyed a veiled threat of violent action against a specific human target. These are both very hateful, yet very different, factual grounds for not protecting the message.

Given the facial disposition of each case, different outcomes may be more likely to be attributable to the scope of the statutes. In *Keegstra*, s.319(2) prohibits speeches that 'wilfully promote hatred' against a racial group, and, as interpreted by the Canadian Supreme Court, it aims only at hate speech which involves a very high order of emotional or psychological harm and only speech that specifically intends that harm. Under the St. Paul ordinance, the harm to be prevented causes 'anger, alarm, or resentment' in 'others' (the target or a bystander) and applies to an unintending speaker who *knows or has reasonable grounds to know* that the proscribed harm will occur. Thus, as the latter prohibition seems to restrict a broader swath of speech, it might be expected that two courts with the same constitutional view would find the *RAV* but not the *Keegstra* regulation unconstitutional.

Structural Explanatory Considerations

'Structural' explanations take into account the *wording* and *relationships* of constitutional provisions; *treaty* commitments; and judicially determined *doctrinal* approaches applicable to a broader area of law than the law of hate speech.

Constitutional Language and Structure

The specific constitutional language adopted can never be ignored, but differences in the terms used by Canada ('thought, belief, opinion and expression' and 'press and other media') and the USA ('speech' and 'press') yield little of value. It is quite clear that these open-textured words can easily reach most forms of hate speech, including the examples litigated in the *Keegstra* and *RAV* cases.[14]

A more promising American-Canadian contrast stems from the approach of the Canadian Charter which combines its guarantees with express language making rights and freedoms 'subject only to such reasonable limits prescribed by law as can be demonstrably justified in a free and democratic society'. It would be grossly wrong to assume that the absence of a specifically limiting provision in the American constitution means that free speech rights in the USA are absolute. Nevertheless, the creation of a right in absolute terms may discourage judicial qualification,[15] whereas an express limitation may invite qualification.

There may be a more subtle difference, as well. The Canadian Supreme Court has interpreted s.2(b) as protecting every conceivable form of expression except expression which directly takes the form of violence (*Irwin Toy* 1989, 970). For example, verbal threats are protected under the Canadian Charter (*Keegstra*, 733) but not under the American Constitution (*Watts* v. *United States* 1969; Greenawalt 1983). In American constitutional law, many forms of speech are regarded as not covered by the First Amendment at all. In the USA, the work of determining which speech is actually protected is divided between two very different kinds of judgments: judgments about whether the speech in question is the kind of speech that functions to serve the purposes of free speech; and judgments that balance free speech values against others (Schauer 1983, 89–92). In Canada, on the other hand, because all conceivable expression is viewed as coming under s.2(b), all of the real work of determining which speech is actually protected falls on the s.1 limitation provision. Under such a broad reading, s.2(b) may seem to 'exhaust' the value implicit in freedom of expression. Consequently, when a court turns to s.1 for the balancing of expressive values against the other democratic values, the Court may tend to concentrate on the other values.

Related Constitutional Provisions

The Canadian Supreme Court's willingness to limit free expression rights in *Keegstra* was considerably enhanced, according to its opinion, by the explicit specification of other values in ss15 and 27 of the Canadian Charter. S.15(1) provides that 'every individual' is equal 'before' and 'under' the law and is given equal 'protection' and equal 'benefit' of the law without discrimination.[16] This discrete specification has been given some significance by the Canadian Supreme Court (Hogg 1992, § 52.6(a)) but, as relevant to differences in Canadian and American hate speech law, I doubt that there is any meaningful difference from the American Equal Protection Clause, which simply provides, 'No state shall ... deny any person ... the equal protection of the laws' (US Constitution, amend. XIV). Furthermore, although an *individual's* hate speech cannot *violate* the Equal Protection Clause or s.15 (because, in both cases, rights are protected only against *state* action),[17] the US Supreme Court has sometimes used the anti-discrimination value to limit First Amendment rights (*Roberts* v. *Jaycees* 1984; *Bob Jones University* v. *United States* 1983).

Nevertheless, the anti-discrimination value may have added weight in Canadian constitutional law by reason of two Charter provisions having no counterpart in the American Constitution: subsection (2) of s.15, an affirmative action provision, and s.27, a multicultural provision. From the beginning, affirmative action has been a controversial policy in the USA, and it has been a fiercely debated issue of constitutional law.[18] The argument against affirmative action (or for limiting it), has always enjoyed substantial support on the American Supreme Court.[19] Adopted at a time when the affirmative action debate in the USA had been thoroughly aired, s.15(2) in the Canadian Charter evidently reflects a very different constitutional value. In effect, it affirmatively authorizes what would otherwise be forbidden discrimination when undertaken to ameliorate the conditions of 'disadvantaged' groups. This affirmative authorization is reinforced by s.27 of the Charter, which mandates that the Charter be 'interpreted' so as to be 'consistent with the preservation and enhancement of the multicultural heritage of Canadians'.

Neither s.15(2) nor s.27 dictate any particular weight to be given to affirmative action or multicultural considerations. Neither is addressed to hate speech, as such; and neither compels the Canadian courts to uphold any or all laws regulating hate speech. Nevertheless, these provisions encourage the courts to give weight to factors that count in favor of upholding laws prohibiting or regulating hate speech. The US Constitution does not directly prevent the courts from giving weight to these same factors, and many have argued that the courts should do precisely that (Michelman 1989; Lawrence 1990). As the US Constitution has been interpreted, however, nothing has supplied the momentum created by these Charter provisions.

Freedom of Speech/Expression Jurisprudence

The established jurisprudence under the American First Amendment and the Canadian Charter (s.2(b) and 1) reveal both a significant similarity and a fundamental difference. In neither system are free speech rights entirely free from regulation, but in both systems constitutionally permissible regulations must serve a very important government interest and both require a close relationship between the government goal and a regulatory means that restricts expression. Although the specific wording of the judicially crafted Canadian and American tests is not precisely the same, each test is sufficiently general and elastic to leave considerable latitude for judicial application, and neither test would dictate a result different from the range of results possible under the other test.

The similarity, and particularly the similarly elastic nature, of these two tests provides a point of departure for emphasizing a basic difference between American and Canadian free expression jurisprudence: whereas Canada applies the *Oakes* test right across the board to all cases involving freedom of expression (indeed, to all Charter rights), in the USA the general 'compelling state interest' test is seldom applied in the resolution of free speech cases.[20] Ordinarily, the American Supreme Court adopts a categorical approach under which distinct, very demanding, tests are applied to various speech categories (e.g., obscenity, fighting words, defamation, incitement of lawless action: *Cohen* v. *California;* Ely 1975). A fundamental reason for taking this categorical approach is the fact that it cabins judicial discretion by subjecting speech to abridgement only on the basis of well defined, relatively narrow grounds and creating a strong presumption against abridgements outside these categories, and particularly against doing so on the basis of the message communicated.

Whatever the particular theory for regulating racist hate speech as such, it entails viewpoint discrimination. In any place in the world where hate speech is constitutionally prohibited, there is always a statute, such as s.319(2) in Canada, that restricts a particular message or set of messages from being communicated. Prohibiting such a message because it would lead to violence or disorder or because it was offensive to the target of the hate message would have as its ultimate objective the prevention of violence (or disorder) or offensiveness, but the prohibition would regulate that speech while permitting other speech on the basis of its message. The Canadian Supreme Court has rejected any such presumption against content or viewpoint discrimination (*Keegstra*, 740–1). The general use of the open-ended *Oakes* test rather than a categorical approach will tend to reserve to the Canadian Supreme Court a maximum discretion to protect speech when and only when it chooses to do so. That Court's receptivity to arguments based on the perceived falsity of a message means that free expression in Canada may be suppressed when the Court, in its discretion, does not approve of a particular view, and the *Keegstra* decision unambiguously illustrates this approach.

International Human Rights Treaties

In determining the objective of s.319(2) under the *Oakes* test, the *Keegstra* majority opinion placed considerable reliance on Canada's obligations under several international human rights treaties, which included both provisions guaranteeing freedom of expression and provisions requiring the prohibition of racist hate speech.[21] The Court particularly stressed the International Convention on the Elimination of All Forms of Racial Discrimination (CERD), which includes the most sweeping requirement to eliminate hate speech. Article 4 of CERD begins with a recitation that 'States Parties condemn all propaganda and all organizations which are based on ideas or theories of superiority of one race ... or which attempt to justify or promote racial hatred and discrimination. This strongly stated duty to undertake an affirmative program of speech regulation, however, is preceded and qualified by the clause, 'with due regard to the principles embodied in the Universal Declaration of Human Rights and the rights expressly set forth in Article 5 of this Convention'. Both the Universal Declaration and Article 5 include the right of freedom of expression.

Chief Justice Dickson's *Keegstra* opinion acknowledged that 'finding the correct balance between prohibiting hate propaganda and ensuring freedom of expression has been a source of debate internationally' but that Canada has a commitment under these treaties to prohibit hate propaganda and that the Canadian Supreme Court 'must have regard to that commitment in investigating the nature of the government objective behind § 319(2)' and the importance of that objective under s.1 of the Charter (*Keegstra*, 754).

Thus, while these international treaties evidently have not become part of Canada's domestic law by statutory enactment (Bayefsky 1992, 25), they do entail commitments in international law and, correspondingly, commitments to certain values shared by the international community and highly relevant to the interpretation of s.1 as applied to hate speech. The USA, in contrast to Canada, signed the CERD treaty with the reservation that any inconsistency between the treaty and the First Amendment would be resolved in favor of the First Amendment.[22] Plainly, from these different approaches international treaties play a very different role in the constitutional treatment of free speech in the two countries.

Foundational Explanatory Considerations

In his book, *Continental Divide*, Professor Seymour Martin Lipset argues that there are very different cultures in the USA and Canada, and that the differences grow rather directly out of the revolutionary and counterrevolutionary beginnings of the two countries (Lipset 1990). The American experience began in revolution against governmental authority and forever after has fostered a strong distrust of authority and a deep commitment to individualism. Canada's different early experience was one of loyalty to a monarchical (and hierarchical) government. On the southern side of the border, government was to be limited, restricted and distrusted. On the northern side, government was honored, deferred to and trusted. The American spirit was strongly anti-paternalistic; the Canadian spirit the opposite. Professor Lipset also thinks that Canada feels a significant continuity to its past and to Europe, and, by contrast that the American revolution drew a sharp line between the USA and its antecedents.

This chapter cannot independently evaluate Professor Lipset's interesting analysis. Neither can it be assumed that the Lipset thesis identifies characteristic differences that, inexorably, would bring about significant differences in American and Canadian constitutional law, either in general or in connection with the law governing freedom of speech. Lipset himself gives reason to be cautious about extrapolations from his thesis. He mentions the greater protection of free speech and press in the USA as a defining difference, but he also says that, 'By enacting the Charter [with its entrenched Bill of Rights], Canada has gone far toward joining the United States culturally' (Lipset 1990, 226–7). Certainly, however valid the generalizable between-country differences, one would not assume that they would be reflected in the outcomes of two arbitrarily chosen cases dealing with hate speech. Nevertheless, without assuming a straight-line determinism, one can evaluate the results and the reasoning of the courts in the *Keegstra* and *RAV* cases against the large cultural themes advanced by Professor Lipset. One can ask whether there is coherence between the judicial opinions and the characteristic between-country differences manifested in certain themes falling along a continental divide (Kress 1996).

Beginning with the structural differences already discussed, it is possible to argue that many of these differences between Canadian and American constitutional law may be explained in terms of these deeper cultural themes. The different approaches of the two constitutional systems to viewpoint discrimination and to affirmative action appear to reflect different cultural attitudes toward paternalism and individualism. Canada's constitutional protection of affirmative action and cultural diversity may reflect a deeper commitment to a multicultural society. Canada's commitments under international human rights treaties were also a contributing factor to the *Keegstra* results for which there is no American parallel, and that difference may reflect the different relationships of Canada and the USA with Europe. So, too, in contrast to the American tradition of popular sovereignty, the Canadian tradition of parliamentary sovereignty (partially encompassed in Charter s.1 and 33) may reflect both a more tentative commitment to individualism and a closer continuity to European constitutionalism.

Paternalism/Anti-paternalism

In the earlier discussion, I argued that the affirmative action provision of the Canadian Charter, s.15(2), for which there is no American equivalent, revealed a significantly different view of equality. The American hostility to affirmative action has been partially based on the individualistically oriented ideal of color-blindness and the related distrust of government to make wise and competent distinctions favoring some groups over others on the basis of racial or ethnic identity (*Bakke*, 295–7 (Powell, J.); *Croson*, 493; *Fullilove*, 532 (Stevens, J. dissenting)). The contrasting Canadian ideal would expect government protection of disadvantaged groups and would trust the government to make fair and accurate determinations of which groups were entitled to protection. Protection from hate speech would be one realization of this ideal.

Furthermore, I observed that, under the free expression jurisprudence developed in the USA (but not in Canada), a strong rule against permitting government to regulate speech on the basis of the viewpoint of the speaker's message had emerged. This rule, too, is substantially based on the American distrust of government actors to make wise and fair distinctions. The *RAV* majority opinion was based on the fundamental position of American constitutional law's rejection of viewpoint discrimination. By sharp contrast, the Canadian Supreme Court unapologetically relied upon the government's fear that a hated message might be persuasive to the audience which hears it. (*Keegstra*, 747–78).

If one were predicting results and rationales on the basis of cultural differences attributed to the USA and Canada by Professor Lipset, these *RAV* and *Keegstra* results and rationales are precisely those that one would predict. The prediction would begin with Professor Lipset's conclusion that the USA has cultural traditions that veer in the direction of individualism and that Canada's veer in the direction of accepting a significant paternalistic role of government. In its strongest form, Canada's characteristic paternalism would lead to the conclusion that Canada would approve the government's limitation of speech to protect its citizens from receiving messages that they should not hear because, to the detriment of themselves and others, they might find those messages persuasive; and the characteristic American individualism would lead to the prediction that citizens would be left to decide for themselves what to believe in the USA. In a less strong (and more plausible) form, this cultural distinction would lead to the prediction that, *if* the USA and Canada reached different results (as to whether such messages should be limited), it would be the USA which would say no (the message should not be limited: the individual hearer should be left to decide for him/herself) and Canada which would say yes (limit the message: the government should protect the individual hearer from reaching erroneous conclusions).

Melting Pot/Mosaic

Professor Lipset also distinguishes the cultures of the USA and Canada in terms of their different tendencies to accept the continued presence within the society of racially, ethnically or culturally distinct groups:

> American universalism – the desire to incorporate diverse groups into a culturally unified whole – is inherent in the country's founding ideology. Canadian particularism – the preservation of sub-national group loyalties, as well as the strength of the provinces vis-a-vis the federal government – is rooted in the decision of the Francophone clerical elite to remain loyal to the British monarchy as a protection against Puritanism and democratic populism across the border. (Lipset, 172)

The distinction, according to Lipset, even extends to the marginally better treatment of Indians in Canada than in the USA. Assuming the accuracy of this distinction, it can plainly be seen to be manifested in the different approach to hate speech. That is true whether one emphasizes the inclusion of s.27 in the Charter or the attitude of the Canadian Supreme Court in interpreting s.2(b) and s.1 in the light of that section. S.27 is an unambiguous endorsement of a multicultural value, and it contains an express requirement that all Charter provisions be interpreted in a way that gives recognition to this endorsement. Using the latitude available in interpreting in a manner which is 'consistent with' the preservation and enhancement of the multicultural heritage, the Canadian Supreme Court in *Keegstra* stressed the damage to minority cultures if legislation restricting hate speech aimed at such groups were held to violate the right of freedom of expression (Lipset 1990, 757–8).

This cultural distinction can also be used to explain the American predisposition toward protecting hate speech. If the metaphor for Canada is the mosaic pattern of discrete entities, the American metaphor is the melting pot which attempts to assimilate the distinct parts. So, under this analysis, it might be expected that the American emphasis is put on the common participation of all groups in the democratic process. Political speech is the ultimate speech value, and the use of speech to exchange ideas in order to make political decisions is the ultimate theoretical justification for protecting freedom of speech. Thus, under the cultural bias of the USA, the views of all – bad or good, wise or stupid – must be freely available, and the protection against hate speech is the protection of answering false speech with true speech in the universalist market place of ideas.

Treaty Approval

A somewhat similar analysis can be developed on the basis of Canada's unqualified ratification of the international human rights treaties to which the *Keegstra* court gave weight in upholding the constitutionality of s.319(2) against a free expression challenge (*Keegstra,* 757–8) in contrast to the American ratification of those treaties with a reservation based on the First Amendment, thus avoiding any direct influence on the hate speech issue.[23] These different Canadian and American approaches to the human rights treaties can once again be explained in terms of the culturally different approaches to individualism and paternalism. As pointed out earlier, these treaties include both obligations to protect freedom of speech and obligations to prohibit hate speech, and thus require a reconciliation of these potentially conflicting obligations. Yet, however that reconciliation is achieved, these treaties display a strong facial indication that some qualifications of expressive freedom will be required to protect certain harmful forms of expression. Adopting the international treaties without reservation meant a commitment by the Canadian government to take some kind of *appropriate* measures to limit an individual's right to express racist hate speech in order to protect others (from the harm of speech-caused violence, of targeted offensiveness, and of being persuaded of false and dangerous views). The American reservation evidently reflected a very different primary commitment. Embedded in the American conception of freedom of speech, individuals are given broad expressive freedom and must protect themselves from being offended or coming to have false beliefs (and from the harm of speech-induced violence which the speech might cause).

Alternatively, Professor Lipset suggests the revolutionary and counterrevolutionary histories of the American and Canadian people resulted in a turning-away from its European past by the USA, and Canada's continuing to retain close ties and an identification with Europe. 'Canada's closer links to its European origins have helped perpetuate elements of an older set of beliefs and more conservative behavior' (Lipset 1990, 4). If one places this latter explanatory construction on the differing Canadian and American treaty commitments, other considerations than the paternalism-individualism division deserve emphasis. These treaties were a response to the experience of the Second World War, and especially Nazism, anti-Semitism, the holocaust. In large measure, these treaties had their source in the same historical events that led European countries to develop systems of judicial enforcement of individual constitutional rights and, collectively, to create an internationally enforceable judicial system of individual rights through the European Convention on Human Rights. The USA Constitution was an obvious and significant model for this legal shift to systems in which legislative action was subjected to a judicially enforceable limitation. But, of course, the American model was not adopted without significant modification to suit the needs and the institutions of the European nations.[24]

One significant substantive difference between the American model and the newly created individual rights systems concerned the accommodation of freedom of expression and the harms of expression. In conclusory terms, from the vantage point of 1998, one can say that the USA has developed a body of constitutional law which weighs the interest in freedom of expression more heavily; 'Europe' has developed constitutional systems which weigh the interest in being protected from the harms of hate speech more heavily. For example, in Germany the Basic Law made human dignity the most fundamental value (Basic Law, Article 1) and not subject to amendment (Basic Law, Article 79(3)).

One explanation for the different constitutional choices that the USA and European nations have made is the different historical experiences they have had. The USA did not experience the horror of the Second World War in the way Europe did. It did not have the direct experience of Nazism and the holocaust. It did not have the destruction of property and societies. It did not have death tolls of the same magnitude. But what of Canada on the same side of the Atlantic as the USA? Of course, one might say that choosing the European perspective simply doubles back to the individualism–paternalism dichotomy. Alternatively, it is possible that, independent of any predisposition about individual freedom versus government protection, an *a priori* inclination to identify with Europe would make Canada more willing to accept and adopt the lessons of the European experience for itself or, at any rate, to adopt the conclusion drawn by the European community.

Sovereignty

In contrast to the American revolution and popular sovereignty, Canadian constitutionalism has experienced counterrevolution and parliamentary sovereignty. At least until the adoption of the Charter in 1982, parliamentary sovereignty had been the prevailing philosophy in Canada. This fact exemplifies a Canadian-European continuity in two senses. Canada's commitment to parliamentary sovereignty resulted directly from its constitutional tie to the UK that continued in substance well into the twentieth century. More generally, Canada's experience shared the commitment of European democracies where parliamentary sovereignty has been the dominant position up to the present time. Indeed, even when they adopted enforceable individual rights constitutions, most European countries created a distinct constitutional court because the lack of power of ordinary courts to determine the validity of legislation was so deeply established (Merryman 1985, 107). Parliamentary sovereignty continued to prevail in Canada when it adopted a Bill of Rights in 1960 since the rights created were not applicable to provincial legislation and were subject to Parliamentary override which satisfied certain formalities.[25] Even with the adoption in 1982 of the Canada Act and the Charter of Rights and Freedoms, parliamentary sovereignty survives, albeit in a qualified or weakened form, through ss1 and 33.

As applied to Charter §§ 2 and 7–15, s.33 gives both the Canadian Parliament and provincial legislatures the power, if specified procedures are satisfied, to limit or eliminate the rights otherwise guaranteed by the Charter for up to five years at a time. S.1 itself authorizes legislative limitations on Charter rights that are 'reasonable', 'prescribed by law', and 'justified in a ... democratic society', and thus seems to invite a recognition of limitations that represent the democratic will of Canada as manifested through laws duly enacted through the legislative process. In a system accustomed to equate what the legislative process produces with what is justifiable in a democratic society, this invitation to defer is likely to influence the Court's application of section 1. Moreover, this potential to carry forward parliamentary supremacy is reinforced by section 33 of the Charter. It must occur to the courts that, given the power of the legislative branch to have its way by a direct override of a Charter right, the judicial branch should be slow to challenge the legislative conception of what is 'justified' in a 'democratic society'. Thus, section 33 is not only a direct constitutional endorsement of a qualified parliamentary sovereignty but an indirect means of encouraging the courts to continue to follow their traditional allegiance to parliamentary sovereignty in their interpretation of section 1.

Apart from its general residual dimension of parliamentary sovereignty, which stands in contrast to American constitutional law, the Canadian-American contrast has special cultural significance for freedom of speech. During the early days of the American Republic, political thinkers derived a very powerful significance from the then *new* American concept of popular sovereignty (Levy 1985; Rabban 1985). Particularly in connection with the debates over the Alien and Sedition Acts passed during the Adams administration, the argument was made that the US Constitution required a much broader conception of freedom of speech than that which prevailed at common law according to Blackstone. Since sovereignty in the USA was ultimately held by the people, it was argued, the people had to be free to criticize government officials, their agents, and to exchange views among themselves, the ultimate governors (Levy 1985, 220–81; Rabban 1985, 828–34, 849–54). This line of argument has continued to be an important, and probably the most important, theoretical justification for a very far-reaching, robust freedom of speech down to the present time (Meiklejohn 1948; Schauer 1991).

POSTSCRIPT: QUALIFICATIONS AND MODIFICATIONS

In the analysis just completed, a number of differences in Canadian and American constitutional law have been identified, and a number of possible cultural explanations for these differences have been explored. These explanations do not purport to prove that certain cultural characteristics dictated the particular result of the *Keegstra* and *RAV* hate speech decisions. The explanations, rather, are proposed in the form of important considerations that make Canadian and American societies different and make the different directions of the constitutional law and the particular decisions in the two countries seem comprehensible. In this part, I do not undertake to destroy the plausibility of their explanatory analysis, fragile as it may be; but I want to soften somewhat the suggestion that a bright line and a sharp contrast separates the American law dealing with hate speech from that of Canada and the rest of the world.

Conceiving this section as an adjustment of focus to bring the bigger picture into proper perspective, I will proceed in two simple steps. First, I will point out certain respects in which a picture of Canadian-American contrast might be qualified. Second, drawing upon two examples from European constitutional systems, I will point out that the apparent dichotomy between the American way (always protecting hate speech) and the alternative, Canadian/rest of the world, way (never protecting hate speech) must be modified.

Qualifying the American-Canadian Contrast

As noted previously, any broad generalizations about the Canadian and American law of hate speech based on *Keegstra* and *RAV* must be qualified in light of the dissimilarities of the hateful expression involved and the regulations under which the hate speaker was charged and, especially, in light of the divided votes of the two highest courts and a division of intellectual criticism in the two countries. Although political opinion, too, is divided, much legislation in each country has attempted to regulate hate speech.[26] To these qualifications of any easy conclusions concerning *Keegstra* and *RAV*, one can tease out other considerations from the two opinions. For example, a broader ordinance regulating hate speech as fighting words evidently would have satisfied Justice Scalia and a narrower ordinance clearly would have satisfied the *RAV* concurrers. The concurring opinion of Justice Stevens seemed to indicate that a regulation of *threatening* hate speech would be constitutional. Threatening speech is generally treated as unprotected speech (*Watts* v. *United States*; Greenawalt 1995) and a burning cross could certainly communicate a threat to the black family who owned the property where the cross was burned.[27]

For Canada's part, the *Keegstra* opinion emphasized that private conversations were not covered, and it deliberately construed the statute to limit severely the scope of the words 'promotion' and 'hatred.' In construing the defenses provided under section 319(3), the Court acknowledged the potential vagueness and broad reach of terms such as 'reasonable' and 'good faith', but coupled that concession with the assurance that inappropriately broad applications would be prevented by the courts (*Keegstra*, 772–3, 776–8). In a subsequent case (*Zundel* v. *Regina,* 1992) the Canadian Supreme Court, applying the *Oakes* test, found neither a sufficiently important state objective nor a sufficiently narrowly tailored means to uphold a statute regulating hate speech in the form of holocaust denial.

Modifying the Either-Or Paradigm

Added to the preceding suggestive bits from the law of Canada and the USA, the following two 'European cases' should give one pause in concluding that the constitutional systems of the world can be neatly divided between those that do and those that do not protect hate speech as part of the right of freedom of expression.

*The European Convention on Human Rights:*Jersild v. Denmark *(1994)*

A Danish television journalist (hereinafter the 'producer') arranged, edited and broadcast an interview with several members of a group of young people known as the 'Green Jackets'. In the program televising this interview, the Green Jacket members made a number of extremely racist comments about 'blacks' and 'immigrants'. The Green Jacket members were charged with violating a Danish criminal statute which makes it unlawful for any person to publicly make a 'statement ... threatening, insulting or degrading a group of persons on account of their race, colour, national or ethnic origin'; and the producer was charged with aiding and abetting the Green Jackets' violation. The producer's conviction was confirmed by the Supreme Court of Denmark even though Danish law had been amended (during the litigation) in a way that might have precluded treating the producer's acts as criminal violations. The producer applied to the European Court of Human Rights (ECHR) on the ground that his conviction under Danish law violated Article 10 of the European Convention on Human Rights. The Danish Government conceded that Denmark's criminal law interfered with the producer's right to freedom of expression under paragraph 1 of Article 10, and the producer conceded that the aim of the Danish criminal statute to protect 'the reputation or rights of others', was a legitimate aim under paragraph 2 of Article 10. The European Court held that the statute was not 'necessary in a democratic society', and thus did not satisfy the conditions of paragraph 2 for limiting the free expression rights of paragraph 1. In other words, the Danish statute had a permissible end but did not use a permissible means.

Denmark argued that its statute was enacted to satisfy the mandate of Article 4 of the 1965 CERD, which (as we have seen) required Denmark to make 'all dissemination of ideas based on racial superiority or hatred' a criminal offence. The producer argued that this obligation was qualified by the 'due regard' clause under which the Denmark's treaty commitment was to be carried out: 'with due regard to the principles embodied in the Universal Declaration of Human Rights and the rights set forth in Article 5 of this Convention – which included the "right to freedom of opinion and expression"'. The ECHR noted that there was continuing disagreement about how the obligation under Article 4 of CERD should be balanced, through the due regard clause, against CERD's Article 5 rights; that it was 'not for the [European] Court to interpret the "due regard" clause in

Article 4'; but that the European Court's 'interpretation of Article 10 of the European Convention in the present case is compatible with Denmark's obligations under the UN Convention'. Thus, without offering any elaborate explanation, the ECHR denied that it was interpreting the 'due regard' clause, yet it necessarily interpreted that clause in asserting that the Court's interpretation of the European Convention was consistent with a proper understanding of the UN Convention.

At first blush, this judgment based on international treaty law seems modest enough. After all, the hateful words were not those of the producer; the motive of the producer was not to advance the cause of the hate speech message; and the publication of the Green Jacket views may have contributed to public awareness of the threat posed by the Green Jackets. On the other hand, this was clearly a case where a 'European' court did find that the interest in free expression outweighed the interest in suppressing hate speech; yet, as the conviction of the producer by the Danish courts shows, there was a substantial basis for rejecting the free expression claim. The ECHR struck the balance in favor of free expression even though it would ordinarily give a deferential 'margin of appreciation' to the Danish decision interpreting Denmark's democratic needs; and it did so even though Denmark's decision suppressing hate speech was supported by the UN (CERD) Convention. Finally, the producer's good motives might have been thought by Denmark to be undermined by his self-interest in exploiting the hateful views which were publicized. Indeed, it seems clear that the producer provided the Green Jackets with a much larger audience than they could have earned by themselves; and, if the effect of the broadcast was a net benefit to benign racial views, that was a result of the repellent nature of the Green Jackets' position as well as the fact that those views were broadcast. In short, if the broadcast produced a net good, that was a direct result of the exposure of the Green Jackets' vile views in the market place of ideas.

The Federal Republic of Germany: The Case of the 'Auschwitz Lie'

Laws prohibiting hate speech in Europe (and Canada) are at least partly a response to the phenomena of National Socialism and the holocaust. Nowhere is the rightness of such laws felt more strongly than in Germany, and no laws more directly evoke a sense of righteousness than those aimed at punishing the denial of the holocaust, the so-called 'Auschwitz lie' (one of Mr Keegstra's hateful utterances). An article by Professor Eric Stein discusses the history and controversy of such laws in Germany (Stein 1986).

Several points made in the article are relevant to my present purpose: (1) attempts were made to challenge the constitutionality of the laws prohibiting the communication of the Auschwitz lie under the freedom of expression provisions of German Basic Law, but these cases never reached the Federal Constitutional Court because either the ordinary courts or a screening committee of the Constitutional Court (Stein 1986, 287–8) determined there was not a substantial constitutional claim.[28] (2) In a number of instances, lower courts applied the relevant German laws in a manner that weakened the prohibitions against dissemination of the Auschwitz lie (Stein 1986, 291–304, 315). (3) The perception that the existing law was ineffective in suppressing the repetition of the Auschwitz lie led to proposals for statutory change (Stein 1986, 280, 298, 304, 305, 315). (4) Both the political process involved in the revision and the ultimate modification of the law were controversial (Stein 1986, 305–22). (5) As ultimately adopted, the revision of the criminal law prohibited not only the Auschwitz lie concerning Jewish victims of the holocaust but also lies about other 'comparable' forms of 'genocide' such as that committed against Germans in Silesia after the Second World War.[29]

According to Professor Stein, the political debate that culminated in this law included several relevant German perspectives: (1) laws such as this were ineffective as they do not change the mind of those who believe the holocaust was a lie and do give a propaganda platform for such people (Stein 1986, 314–15). Recall that essentially the same argument was advanced by the *Keegstra* dissent but rejected by the *Keegstra* majority. (2) The inclusion of the 'Silesian parallel' dilutes the unique aspect of the holocaust and thus reduces the effectiveness of laws prohibiting insulting lies (Stein 1986, 315–6). This argument is very similar to the one which the concurring opinions in the *RAV* case found persuasive as a justification for permitting the City of St. Paul to single out the worst form of fighting words based on their hate message. (3) The courts were an ineffective and inappropriate forum for dealing with neo-Nazi propaganda, a function which can only be performed by family, school, and political discourse (Stein 1986, 315). This, of course, is the conventional argument of American free speech theory (and implicitly relied upon by the majority in *RAV*): speech is not to be suppressed when education and answering speech is available.

As one reads between the lines of Professor Stein's article, one might make the following observation:[30] in the on-going tension between free speech and hate speech in Germany, the criminalization of one particularly destructive form of denying past events led to the extension of the criminal prohibition to other somewhat comparably harmful denials. But, however violent and wrong the forced removal of Germans from Silesia, the legislative equation of that wrong to the holocaust against Jews 'jettisoned' 'the idea that the administered genocide was a unique, an unparalleled crime' (Stein 1986, 321). Reinforcing this legislative dilution is the inexorable dilution from the passing of time as, for more and more Germans, the events of 1933–45 more and more become history and less and less the felt experience of those who lived through it or learned from those who did (Stein 1986, 299).[31] This combination of political equating and historical distancing is likely to produce a gradual shift toward protecting freedom of speech more because the fierce consensus that certain words must not be spoken will diminish, as Professor Stein speculates has already begun to occur in various subtle ways (such as decisions by younger trial judges who are 'without oppressive memories' and 'without a sense of personal guilt': Stein 1986, 299).

Summary

An isolated case decided by the ECHR and a somewhat hazy prediction drawn out of a particular legislative-political development in Germany hardly add up to a radical change from denying to protecting hate speech. Nevertheless, they do raise a caution about a too-ready acceptance of a polarized constitutional universe in which all constitutional systems, except the American, disdain protection of hate speech and the USA unwaveringly protects all hate speech. Added to the American and Canadian evidence blurring the line that divides them in their treatment of hate speech, these European signs of complexity and ambiguity point to overlapping fields and not polar stations north and south of the border.

CONCLUSION

In the third part of this chapter, three levels of possible explanations of the different treatment of hate speech in the Canadian *Keegstra* and American *RAV* cases were explored. Differences in the facts and the statutes involved in the two cases and the divided court in each case all suggest that the constitutional protection of hate speech in *RAV* and the denial of protection in *Keegstra* may be more coincidental than reflective of any significant Canadian-American difference. On the other hand, differences in the language and structure of the American Constitution and the Canadian Charter of Rights and Freedoms; general differences in the free speech jurisprudence under the two constitutional systems; and the different constitutional roles given to international human rights treaties all suggest that the outcomes of *RAV* and *Keegstra* may reflect pervasive and durable differences between Canadian and American constitutional law. Of potentially much greater significance, several basic cultural distinctions that have been attributed, respectively, to the USA and Canada seem capable of explaining the different *RAV* and *Keegstra* results. The deep strain of anti-paternalism, the ideal of assimilating all groups into a 'melting pot', and the relative lack of identification with European modes of governance all tend to characterize the USA and separate it from Canada, which has tended to trust paternalistic approaches, has been committed to a 'mosaic' ideal of preserving the identity of separate groups, and has adopted European patterns of governance (historically in the form of parliamentary sovereignty and currently in unqualified adherence to human rights treaties). All of these distinctions would predict that the fundamental constitutional law of the USA would be weighted in favor of the individualism of the market place of ideas and against the paternalistic protection from harm of groups threatened by the communication of despicable words. These same distinctions would predict that the fundamental constitutional law of Canada would be weighted in precisely the opposite way.

The coherence of these predictions with the different hate speech results in the USA and Canada should not be converted into a determinism that these different results must and always will follow. As the discussion in the fourth part demonstrates, in any system that values both free speech and equality, it is unlikely that a clash of those values will always be resolved in the same way. That is apparent from the indications in both the USA and Canada that some hate speech problems will be resolved in the opposite direction of the results in *RAV* and *Keegstra*. That is also strongly suggested by the decision in the *Jersild* case by the ECHR and by the implications of the 'Auschwitz lie' controversy under the German constitutional system.

There is also much evidence that, in at least one fundamental respect, there is a deep and pervasive difference between the constitutional law of free speech of the USA, on the one hand, and the constitutional law of free speech that prevails in Canada and, it would seem, throughout most of the world. This difference may be highlighted by recalling two parallel and opposing statements, one from *RAV* and one from *Keegstra*. In his concurring opinion in *RAV,* Justice Stevens said:

> Petitioner is free to burn a cross to announce a rally or to express his views about racial supremacy, he may do so on private property or public land, at day or at night, so long as the burning is not so threatening and so directed at an individual as to [come within the fighting words doctrine]. (*RAV*, 436)[32]

By contrast, the Chief Justice Dickson, in *Keegstra*, said that one of the harms to be avoided by suppressing hate speech is 'its influence upon society at large. The Cohen Committee noted that individuals can be persuaded to believe "almost anything"' (*Keegstra*, 747). In a similar fashion, there was no doubt by any Danish court or by the ECHR that the racist statements of the Green Jackets (even if not the broadcast journalist who arranged for the television dissemination of their statements) could be criminally punished. Similar, also, was the ease with which the German courts generally assumed that the 'Auschlitz lie' statements lacked constitutional protection (however politically controversial it might be to decide how the law prohibiting such statements might be expanded and enforced).

At this point of irreducible difference, it seems, the American system prefers to trust the individual audience, and not democratic governments, to make correct judgments about what to believe, whereas Canada and other constitutional systems place their trust in democratically elected government bodies to exercise judgment about which views are too abhorrent to leave to individual evaluation. If, indeed, the experience of Germany in the middle of the twentieth century is influencing these choices, that experience may be thought, paradoxically, to support both predispositions: the German experience teaches that individuals are capable of believing truly vicious racist communications at immeasurable cost, *and* it teaches that a government may have truly destructive power if it controls which views may be expressed and which suppressed.

Notes

1. The target groups of hateful speech can be defined in many ways. For example, the University of Michigan speech code included 'race, ethnicity, religion, sex, sexual orientation, creed, national origin, ancestry, age, mental status, handicap or Vietnam-era veteran status': *Doe* v. *University of Michigan* (1989). In this essay, I use the term narrowly so that the target groups – particularly blacks and Jews – are those whose suffering from discrimination is the least debatable and whose claim for protection is correspondingly strong.

2. Despite serious harms to targeted individuals and to society, the American approach seems more persuasive to me because of the importance of free speech and the absence of a comprehensive argument for a meaningful reduction of hate speech at an acceptable cost in enforcement and in avoiding an excessive level of thought control. For a sampling of the voluminous literature, see Alexander (1996); Gates (1994); Lederer and Delgado (1995); Matsuda *et al.* (1993); and Post (1993).

3. Although *Keegstra* was decided before *RAV*, the Canadian, but not the American, Supreme Court treated the constitutional law of the other country as possibly relevant. See generally Glendon (1991).

4. Unlike the US Supreme Court, the Canadian Supreme Court also has final power to decide questions of provincial law. See Hogg (1992), § 8.5(a).

5. Criminal law is a function of state government in the USA and of the national government in Canada. Compare *United States* v. *Lopez* (1995), with Hogg (1992), § 18.1.

6. The two cases followed equal and opposite serpentine paths: in the USA, the individual defendant won in the trial court, lost before the state highest court, then won before the national highest court; in Canada, it is the prosecution which won, lost, then finally won.

7. An identifiable group is defined as 'Any section of the public distinguished by colour, race, religion or ethic origin': Criminal Code, RSC, 1985 c. C-46 § 319(2).

8. The requirement that the limiting law be 'prescribed by law' encompasses a void-for-vagueness concept. See Hogg (1992), §§ 335.7(a) and (c). Identical language in the European Convention on Human Rights and the New Zealand Bill of Rights Act 1990, respectively, have been interpreted to contain an identical limit: *Sunday Times* v. *United Kingdom* 1979; *Ministry of Transport* v. *Noort* 1992.

9. Quoting from the Cohen Committee, the Court said, 'Individuals can be persuaded to believe "almost anything",' and, paraphrasing the American legal scholar, Mari Matsuda, said that even when the hate message is 'outwardly rejected', it may persist as an idea that holds some truth to that audience.

10. McLachlin cited Neier (1979), 160–8, who argued that the failure of the Weimar Republic was not in its excessive permissiveness concerning anti-Semitic speech, but its failure to enforce its laws prohibiting violent conduct by Nazis.

11. The bitterness of the split is revealed in this statement by Justice White: '[The majority's] decision is an arid, doctrinaire interpretation, driven by the frequently irresistible impulse of judges to tinker with the First Amendment. The decision is mischievous at best and will surely confuse the lower courts. I join the judgment, but not the folly of the opinion': *RAV*, 505 US at 415 (concurring).

12. Despite the conventional wisdom that 'fighting words' are not within the protection of 'the freedom of speech,' *Chaplinsky* v. *New Hampshire* (1942), 315 US 568; *Cohen* v. *California*. 1971, 403 US 15, 20, there has been some disagreement about the existence and extent of the fighting words exception. See Gard (1980) 531, 534–5; Greenawalt (1995).

13. In the USA, a public school teacher would have no constitutional right to teach any message disapproved of by a public school employer, let alone such a despicable message. See *Board of Education, Island Trees Union Free School District v. Pico* (1982), 457 US 853, 862, 869, 871 (plurality); *Cary* v. *Board of Education* (1979), 598 F.2d 535 (10th Cir.); Buss (1989). Nothing in the Canadian Supreme Court opinion indicates that the public school dimension played a role in its decision. But, on remand, the Alberta Court of Appeals overturned Keegstra's conviction because of a voir dire error which grew out of a suggestion that Keegstra's community had approved of his views. See *Regina.* v. *Keegstra*, 1991, 63 CCC (3d) 110, 16–17.

14. The European Convention of Human Rights, Article 10, includes, as part of the right of freedom of expression, the right to *receive* and *impart* 'information and ideas', but only the right to *hold* 'opinions', but it is hard to believe that receiving information but not opinions would be protected. The USA and Canada, each without an express right to receive, have judicially found such a right: *Lamont* v. *Postmaster General* (1965), 381 US 301; *Irwin Toy* v. *Quebec* (1989), 1 SCR 927, 968–71.

   There is no scarcity of examples to illustrate the judicial ingenuity in finding sound policy within the available constitutional language. The German Constitutional Court has minimized the consequence of the fact that some forms of constitutional speech but not others are limited by the 'general laws'. See *Mephisto* (1971), 30 BverfGE 173; *Luth.*, (1958), 7 BVerfGE 198; Kommers (1989), 370–4, 430; Quint (1989), 283–4, 290–302. Without any freedom of speech provision in its Constitution whatsoever – an omission that was intentional: see Goldsworthy (1992), 151 – the High Court of Australia has held that the character of the Australian constitutional system, as a representative democracy, mandates the existence of a constitutional right of communication which is enforceable by the courts in the face of inconsistent legislation: *Australian Capital Television Pty Ltd.* v. *Commonwealth of Australia* (1992), 108.

15. As stated by Professor MacKinnon (1985, 1 and 5), 'Although absolutism has never been the law of the First Amendment, it has left its impression upon it.'

16. S.15(1) goes on to elaborate: 'in particular, without discrimination based on race, national or ethnic origin, colour religion, sex, age or mental or physical disability'.

17. Some American scholars (Michelman, 1989; Lawrence,1990) have argued that state action limitation has been understood too restrictively.

18. For the primary Supreme Court cases see *Adarand Constructors, Inc.* v. *Pena* (1995), 518 US, 115 S.Ct. 2097; *Metro Broadcasting, Inc.* v. *FCC* (1990), 497 US 547; *Richmond* v. *J.A. Croson Co,* (1989), 488 US 469; *Wygant* v. *Jackson Board of Education* (1986), 476 US 267; *Fullilove* v. *Klutznick* (1980), 448 US 448; *Regents of Univ. of California* v. *Bakke* (1978), 438 US 265. See also Karst and Horowitz (1979).

19. Of course, there have always also been counterarguments, and I make no attempt here to discuss the persuasiveness or even the genuineness of either the arguments or counterarguments.

20. In *Simon & Schuster, Inc.* v. *New York State Crime Victims Board* (1991), 502 US 105, 124, Justice Kennedy, in a concurring opinion, argued that it was never appropriate to use the 'ad hoc balancing' of the compelling interest test to determine whether a regulation of speech is permitted.

21. The treaties relied upon were: Universal Declaration of Human Rights; International Covenant on Civil and Political Rights; International Convention on the Elimination of All Forms of Racial Discrimination; these are all reproduced in Brownlie (1981).

22. 'The Constitution of the United States contains provisions for the protection of individual rights, such as the right of free speech, and nothing in the Convention shall be deemed to require or to authorize legislation or other action by the United States of America incompatible with the provisions of the Constitution of the United States of America:' *Human Rights: Status of International Instruments* (1987) 117.

23. Of course, nothing would prevent the Supreme Court from regarding the international treaties as encompassing universal values relevant to the interpretation of the First Amendment. *But see Stanford* v. *Kentucky* (1989), 492 US 361, 369 n. 1 (international values irrelevant to interpretation of Eighth Amendment cruel and unusual punishment provision). Moreover, the effect of a treaty commitment on state (or local) legislation in the USA is not clear. An unqualified commitment of the USA to a treaty's affirmative obligation to eliminate racist speech would apply to the federal government, and the states might be affected by federal supremacy or simply influenced by the national policy.

24. One important distinction has been the creation of special 'Constitutional' courts which are unlike the American Supreme Court because, on the one hand, the constitutional courts have no general jurisdiction to decide legal issues and, on the other hand, these special courts have exclusive jurisdiction to decide constitutional issues in various procedural frameworks other than as an incidental aspect of deciding 'cases or controversies': see Merryman (1985) 37–8.

25. S.1 of the 1960 Canadian Bill of Rights recites certain rights that are 'recognized' but s.2 states that 'every law of Canada' shall be construed so as not to abrogate any of the recognized rights 'unless it is expressly declared by an Act of the Parliament of Canada that it shall operate notwithstanding the Canadian Bill of Rights'.

26. At least in the USA, moreover, there would be more such regulation but for the likelihood of its invalidity under the First Amendment. For

example, the drive to adopt speech codes to prevent hate speech on college campuses has been chilled by adverse decisions by the courts. See *Post* v. *Board of Regents of the University of Wisconsin* (1991), 774 F. Supp. 1163; *Doe* v. *University of Michigan* (1989), 721 F. Supp. 852; Weinstein (1991). Indeed, judicial actions represent a weaker indication of *current* national values than do the legislative actions being challenged. We can respond truly that, in the American and Canadian constitutional system, the courts are the ultimate guardians of constitutional values. But that, in turn, serves to remind us of the built-in tensions of a democratic system with judicial review, and of the elusiveness of relating a nation's cultural heritage to particular constitutional doctrines or judicial decisions.

27. It would seem that a court should construe the imprecise symbol as intended and reasonably perceived as a threat. Cf. *NLRB* v. *Gissell Packing Co.* (1969), 395 US 575 (employer's message construed by employees as a threat). Justice Scalia noted that RAV had not been charged with a statute prohibiting 'terroristic threats': 550 US at 380 n. 1.

28. Under s.5, subsection (2) of the Basic Law, the constitutional right of freedom of opinion is limited by 'the general laws ... and the right to inviolability of personal honour' and, in the case of the Auschwitz lie or other forms of hate speech, this intrinsic limitation is strongly underlined by the independent constitutional rights to dignity and individual personality.

29. The revised statute prohibited a public statement or publicly accessible writing of an insult 'if the insulted person was persecuted as a member of a group under the National Socialist or another violent and arbitrary dominance'.

30. As Professor Stein does not himself say this in so many words, I do not attribute these inferences to him. Yet I believe my own conclusions are at least suggested by him, and I would readily credit them to him.

31. Based on interviews with German people, the *New York Times Magazine* (3 December 1995) described the complex responses to the Nazi holocaust period by successive generations of Germans.

32. This view is deeply embedded in American constitutional law. Dworkin (1991, 14) has written, 'It would plainly be unconstitutional to ban speech directly *advocating* that women occupy inferior roles, or none at all, in commerce and the professions even if that speech fell on willing male ears and achieved its goals.' Scanlon (1972, 204, 213) has explained, as the 'Millian Principle', harms that cannot contribute to the justification for restricting speech: 'harmful consequences of acts performed as a result of those acts of expression, where the connection between the acts of expression and the subsequent harmful acts consists merely in the fact that the act of expression led the agents to believe ... these acts to be worth performing'.

6 Intercultural Citizenship: Statutory Interpretation and Belonging in Britain[1]
Susan Sterett

INTRODUCTION: CULTURAL BELONGING AND CONSTITUTIONALISM

Political disputes over those who have settled in Europe after the Second World War and in what sense they can actually belong in European states are constitutional disputes in a most fundamental sense: who constitutes a polity and how are we to decide? Since Western Europe has halted most immigration since the 1970s, people settle through family connections. Belonging provides a crucial question of contemporary constitutionalism; as Tully (1995, 202–7) has put it, many of the disputes within national states concerning belonging are intercultural, and many groups of people are themselves intercultural. To bring a husband, a child or, a parent to settle in the country in which one lives makes plain the connections between here and there, between Europe and the countries from which people have emigrated. Individual national states include people with a variety of histories and complex mixtures of cultural practices, yet the ethic of modern constitutionalism is one of uniformity (Tully 1995, 67–8).

Anthropologists have argued against pretending to a uniformity and closure in cultures that erases tensions and disagreements (Abu-Lughod 1994); legal cases provide an excellent site to explore exactly that complexity, the particular stories people tell and how national states accommodate those stories or impose expectations of uniformity. Legal cases illuminate and ground the disputes in Europe over what it means to belong. This chapter will address cases concerning the legitimacy of marriage in Britain when citizens try to bring in spouses from other national states, primarily from the Indian subcontinent. In doing so, I will illustrate just how complex and blurred the boundaries are between the cultural practices of one place and another.

Comparative law sometimes addresses how law treats a particular question in a national state other than the USA. Another possible topic for comparative law is to address how multiple legal/political systems treat a problem – hate speech, for example, or constitutional review, to name examples addressed in this collection – and interpret the different meanings of these issues in the different national states, or explain why the different states treat questions differently. But differences in cultures across national states are now partly internal to national states, with mass migration and the beginnings of recognition of the different peoples within states. A matter for comparative law can be addressing how cultural difference is understood within legal systems. A cautious approach to cultural difference can entail a contrast between custom and state law or, as James Tully has put it in his analysis of constitutionalism in a world of diversity, a contrast between the ancient constitution, which recognizes custom, and the modern constitution, which imposes order and uniformity (Tully 1995, ch.3). When states try to recognize custom, they can ignore its dynamic nature, taking it as frozen in place and not subject to remaking by participants.

How to handle cultural difference becomes especially complex if we recognize that cultural difference is incorporated within national states, that cultures are not smooth 'billiard balls', as Tully puts it, but rather:

> [Cultures] are continuously contested, imagined and reimagined, transformed and negotiated, both by their members and through their interaction with others .... Cultural diversity is a tangled labyrinth of intertwining cultural differences *and* similarities, not a panopticon of fixed, independent and incommensurable worldviews in which we are either prisoners or cosmopolitan spectators in the central tower. (Tully 1995, 11)

Customs are not unthought and unchanging.

The marriage cases in British immigration provide an opportunity to rethink the problem of cultural diversity. A first attempt to understand the marriage cases would be to say that these cases, which often involve marriages partly arranged by families between a British citizen and someone from the Indian subcontinent, address whether the British state in imposing uniformity will recognize diversity of marriage practices among its citizenry. That approach treats arranged marriage as something wholly alien to British culture and addresses whether the state can incorporate something so different. As we shall see, the case law itself confounds that approach completely. Men and women marrying make choices, agreeing to marry a partner chosen through family but insisting on some autonomy, mixing practices in a way that seems suspicious to immigration officials. If Asian marriages do not conform to a stereotype that would make them seem wholly alien to Britain, English marriages can in turn not wholly conform to the romantic individual choice based on love that has become the cultural expectation in recent centuries. British judges when criticizing immigration officials will sometimes note how motives for marriage can be complex, drawing on examples from European and North American history and explaining how a long-standing marriage can transcend whatever the motives for a marriage might have been. If the first approach to understanding arranged marriage and how marriages are handled in law would counterpoise custom with positive law, a more subtle approach would recognize that the very problem in adjudication is trying to draw those lines.

JUDICIAL REVIEW AND IMMIGRATION

Under British constitutional doctrine, administrators are accountable to ministers who in turn are accountable to Parliament, not to courts (Atiyah and Summers 1987).[2] However, decisions under statutes sometimes seem to be quasi-constitutional, interpreting statutes through expectations of fairness despite what those who drafted legislation might have meant (Craig 1990; Loughlin 1992). Courts judge immigration cases in two ways. The first, and most important, is under the remedy of judicial review. Judicial review allows courts to judge whether an administrator has made a decision that is procedurally improper or substantively outside the boundaries of a statute. The grounds for review were synthesized in 1985 as procedural impropriety, illegality and irrationality (*Council of Civil Service Unions v. Minister for the Civil Service*, 1984, 950–1). Judges are not to substitute their judgement for that of administrators who better understand the particular policies under scrutiny. They are only to overturn decisions no reasonable administrator could make.

Judicial review has two stages. An applicant files for leave to apply for judicial review. If a judge grants leave, the case can go to a substantive hearing. Second, judges sometimes hear cases on appeal, and administrative officials also hear internal administrative appeals. Under appeal, a judge or appellate official has to decide whether the administrative officials decided correctly. Judges only decide appeals if they have specific statutory authority to do so; those harmed by administrative decisions within the meaning of a statute can always apply for judicial review. Judicial review does not depend on specific administrative authority. The British state instituted judicial review as a specific remedy in 1978, then enacted it in a consolidating statute in 1981. Since then it has been a remedy for administrative decisions that has addressed some of the more pressing issues of the 1980s and 1990s, including the supervision of local government by central government (Sterett 1997, ch.4).

Immigration decisions comprise a significant part of the judicial review case load (Bridges, Meszaros and Sunkin 1996). Cases have also appeared before the ECJ and the ECHR. A relatively small and cohesive group of lawyers takes these cases (Dhavan 1989; Sunkin, Bridges and Meszaros 1993; Sterett 1994); they also sometimes win for clients.[3] Analysis of judicial review in Britain seldom includes immigration decisions; elite lawyers interested in judicial review are interested in constitutionalist accountability, not the intricate fact-based cases that comprise the immigration case load (see, e.g., Woolf 1990).

Courts do influence who may stay and who may not, most directly through overturning administrators. Officials also believe they might lose in court, sometimes leading them to concede cases. Yet scholarship on immigration usually does not discuss what the courts do in routine cases, even if scholars (Ireland 1995; Joppke 1997, 1998) might note rather broadly that constitutional standards make it difficult to restrict asylum-seeking or unwanted immigration. Indeed, Freeman (1994) in a recent commentary on immigration policy in Britain has dismissed the courts as 'not interventionist' and therefore not contributing to policy. Missing the court decisions allows a general wave toward the significance of the expansion of human rights without ever engaging the hesitancy even in ECHR decisions. Conversely, noting generally the importance of constitutions and the fact that Britain does not have one misses the importance of statutory interpretation in shaping the rights that people do have. Those rights are often much less absolute than analysts of immigration imply.

I will focus on decisions regarding the 'primary purpose' of marriage rules. Marriage cases are a substantial part of family settlement claims. Acceptances based on marriage were 55 per cent of the total immigration for 1994 (Home Office, 1995, 4). The significance of marriage as part of the immigration caseload increases when children are included. Of the 15 510 applications from the Indian subcontinent for entry to settle in 1994, 16 per cent were children, 43 per cent were wives and 30 per cent were husbands (Home Office 1995, 8). The primary purpose rules are an important focus of activism around immigration in part because immigration of a husband, wife or fiancé(e) is such a substantial part of immigration to Britain. To understand the bitter debates over the marriage cases, I will first outline the context for immigration in Britain.

IMMIGRATION IN BRITAIN

Citizenship questions in Britain have historically overlapped with immigration from the Commonwealth. Most 'black' people in Britain today were born in Britain (Anwar 1991). The families of most black citizens were at one time from one of the 'New Commonwealth' countries, to use state parlance. Yet a popular political perception is often that all black people living in Britain do not belong and are immigrants (Goulbourne 1991). Before 1962, all citizens of the Commonwealth countries had British subject status and all could freely settle in Britain. New Commonwealth citizens were encouraged by employers to move to Britain in the 1950s, though the British government never had a guestworker programme (Layton-Henry 1992, ch.1; Byron 1994). Most people who emigrated to Britain were from the Commonwealth countries, so when Britain began to restrict immigration in 1962 they were restricting rights of those who were subjects. As Rogers Brubaker has put it, in Britain the question in immigration has been which 'citizens' could settle, while the question in most states is which settlers could become citizens (Brubaker 1989). The 1971 Immigration Act distinguished between 'patrials' and 'nonpatrials'. The former were those with a parent or grandparent from Britain; they had greater settlement rights than the latter. Since Britain was a white country, patrials were white and the patrial/nonpatrial distinction allowed greater settlement rights to white subjects in the Commonwealth than to Asian or Afro-Caribbean. In 1981 the Conservative Government enacted the British Nationality Act creating different categories of citizenship to accord with settlement rights; the statute deprived Commonwealth citizens of their entitlement to citizenship (Layton-Henry 1992, 191–4). No government has tried to hide the racial distinctions in these rules; instead, governments repeatedly argue that good race relations requires restricting immigration (Messina 1989; Layton-Henry 1992, chs 4, 7, 8). Formal legal citizenship status is therefore not very helpful in analyzing membership; instead the particularities of how one is treated by the state and by one's community is a more amorphous but more accurate way of evaluating whether one belongs, or, as Harry Goulbourne puts it, whether one is legitimately part of society (Goulbourne 1991, 17). Since marriage is still a central institution of civil society, how a state treats marriage is one measure of legitimate belonging.

PRIMARY PURPOSE OF MARRIAGE

British immigration rules allow the spouse of a person settled in Britain to settle there also. The spouse may settle only if the 'primary purpose' of the marriage was not immigration. The rules state that applicants must prove that they did not marry in order to gain entry into the UK, that each intends to live permanently with the other, and that they have met (HC 169 1983, paragraph 54). In addition, applicants must demonstrate that they have adequate accommodation and income without recourse to public funds (HC 169 1983). When a marriage is genuine, a legally settled British person can sponsor a spouse from abroad to settle in Britain. The suspicion on the part of the immigration officials is that marriages involving a spouse who is legally settled in Britain and one who is not, particularly arranged marriages, are not genuine. Cases from the Indian subcontinent comprise the largest single grouping of applications to settle, as well as acceptances based on marriage (Home Office 1995, Tables 1.4, 3.1). In 1994, of 12 080 husbands accepted for settlement, 4810 were from the Indian subcontinent (Home Office 1995, Table 1.4). In that same year, the state received 4700 new applications from husbands from the Indian subcontinent (Home Office 1995, Table 2.1). It is in those cases that the question of an arranged marriage is most likely to arise. Advocates see the primary purpose rules as impossible for applicants should immigration officials choose to make them impossible. The rules require, as one advocate put it, an applicant to 'prove a negative', that one's purpose in emigrating was *not* immigration. Even some of the judges have found the rules exasperating. In explaining frustration, judges have sometimes drawn on Western analogies to diminish the sense of cultural difference. In doing so, they note that the negative to be proved, what the purpose of the marriage was *not*, is often not what is most important about a marriage. As Justice Schiemann explained in a 1993 case:

To draw an analogy with English society at the turn of the century, the fact that an American heiress was so keen to be a duchess that she was prepared to marry an Englishman whom she did not love would not lead one to suppose that the primary purpose of the marriage was for her to secure admission to the United Kingdom. She may have been after his title and he after her money.

Marie Antoinette married Louis XVI for dynastic reasons rather than as a love match but no one would regard that fact as indicating that the primary purpose of the marriage was to secure admission for Marie Antoinette into France. (*R.* v. *Immigration Appeal Tribunal ex p. Iqbal* 1993)[4]

The judge's discussion of the problems of the primary purpose rules, not in the context of Muslim society but in Anglo-American and French, questions the tenaciously held assumptions among officials that Western marriages are what the officials call 'love matches' and Muslim marriages concern immigration. Justice Schiemann reminds immigration officials that a family is not only a romantic thing and has not been within recent Western memory, leaving aside that romantic imagery may not capture all Western marriages today either. But in the interpretations of primary purpose, romantic imagery as appropriate to marriage, a stereotyped understanding of what an arranged marriage is, and submission of the wife to the husband characterize judgement. The cultural stereotypes are noted repeatedly in anecdotes lawyers tell. A solicitor speaking of one of his clients made an almost identical point concerning what the officials ignore and what they notice in cultures. He was making representations to the local Member of Parliament (MP) on behalf of a woman legally settled in Britain who was divorced and older than her husband. The immigration officials had denied entry clearance to her husband on the basis that men in the Indian subcontinent did not marry women older than themselves and a divorcee was not desirable within that culture. The primary purpose of the marriage was therefore most likely to be immigration, as the officials saw it. The divorced MP had married an American woman much younger than himself; she had no trouble legally settling. The irony, the solicitor believed, was evident to both himself and the MP.

Beliefs about what it means to be a family have influenced legal interpretations in the tribunals and in the courts of the primary purpose rules for settlement in Britain. Administrative officials evaluate whether a marriage is genuine and in doing so judge how a woman from Anglo-Indian or Anglo-Pakistani[5] culture living in England is likely to act. Judges decide whether administrative officials could have reached the conclusions they did. This standard requires deference to administrative officials and a reluctance to judge the facts, but inevitably the judges in part evaluate facts in determining whether an administrator could have decided what he or she did.

FOR LOVE AND FOR FAMILY

The European Court of Human Rights

Both domestic and supranational courts have shaped the primary purpose rules. An ECHR decision in 1985 struck down the existing primary purpose rules. Those rules allowed settled husbands to bring in wives freely, but required that wives prove that the settlement of their immigrant husbands satisfied the primary purpose rules. The justification that Britain offered was that it faced very high unemployment and that women participated in the labor force at a lesser rate than did men. Britain also recognized the racially discriminatory impact of the rules; it argued, as the government does repeatedly, that restrictive immigration rules were necessary to good race relations.

Lawyers challenged these rules on several grounds, first to the European Commission of Human Rights then the ECHR (*Abdulaziz, Cabales and Balkandali* v. *United Kingdom*, 1985). First, lawyers argued that the rules violated Article 8, which guarantees a right to family life. Second, they argued that they violated the Article 14 prohibition against sex discrimination. Next, they claimed they violated the prohibition against race discrimination. Lawyers also claimed that there was no internal adequate relief for these violations, which contravenes Article 13.

The Commission decided in favor of the claimants on all grounds (*Abdulaziz*, 1985, 29). The Commission then referred the case to the European Court. The Court first addressed what counted as a family for the purpose of a right to family life. It required that the applicants be married. Even with that restrictive interpretation of what it meant to be a family, the Court held that the rules did not violate a right to family life. The Court agreed with the British government, that if family life were the most important thing to the people involved they could choose to live in the husband's country of origin. More than that, the Court held that the claimants had got themselves into the situation. They knew the rules before they were married (*Abdulaziz*, 1985, 33–4). To say that people knew of the deprivation of what they claimed as a right, however, does not actually decide whether that deprivation is wrong.

The Court unanimously agreed that the rules violated the prohibition against sex discrimination. The Court approached it from the point of view of 'equal treatment' as meaning same treatment. The Court found that women's and men's labor force participation were not that different. In any case the numbers of people settling on the basis of marriage were very small, therefore having little effect on unemployment even if the government could show that immigrants directly gained jobs at the expense of people already settled in Britain (*Abdulaziz*, 1985, 36–9). Finally, the Court dismissed the British government's argument that strict immigration regulation was necessary to good race relations in Britain. The Court held that that approach wrongly put the burden of addressing racism on those who were new to the country. Yet the Court held that, despite the policy's disparate impact on people from the Indian subcontinent, it did not constitute race discrimination.

The interpretation by the Court of what it means to discriminate by race avoided principles of equal treatment as much as possible. In the Court's words, 'to give preferential treatment to [a Contracting State's] nationals or to persons from countries with which it had the closest links did not constitute "racial discrimination"' (*Abdulaziz*, 1985, 39). The ancestry rules were 'for the benefit of persons having close links with the United Kingdom' (*Abdulaziz*, 1985, 40). The Court acknowledged that the point of the immigration rules had been to prevent immigration from the New Commonwealth and Pakistan. But it then defined the benefits to those who had family from Britain as the grounds for comparison, focusing only on comparisons between 'non-patrials': that is, everyone not from the Old Commonwealth countries that were the beneficiaries of the patrial/non-patrial distinction. The Court held that state policy treated all non-patrials the same and it was only an accident in who wanted to immigrate to Britain that the rules affected darker-skinned people more than lighter-skinned. The British Nationality Act, the immigration rules, and finally even the ECHR in approving the Act and rules, affirmed a biological understanding of what it meant to belong.

The British government's response to the ECHR was to level down. Anticipating the ECHR's decision, in 1983 the government changed the rules so that both men and women trying to bring a spouse into the country had to prove the primary purpose of the marriage was not immigration.[6] After the 1983 rules imposing the primary purpose requirements went into effect, lawyers and activists within the community decided to work on gaining at least a moderately favorable interpretation of the law before immigration tribunals and then the courts. I will note cases that set the standards for evaluating the validity of marriage within the rules, then cases that illustrate the assumptions about the uniformity of cultural difference so important to adjudicators.

Making a Marriage: The Domestic Courts

The Kumars applied for entrance for Mr Kumar, a citizen of India. They were denied, and their case became a test case. The couple had a child; Mrs Kumar had become pregnant while the couple lived together in India. The immigration adjudicator had not seen the pregnancy as relevant; the Kumars and their lawyers challenged the decision excluding Mr Kumar from the country. They argued that the child should demonstrate that the marriage was genuine. In response, in 1986 the Court of Appeal held that if a couple could show evidence of 'intervening devotion' between the time of marriage and the time of decision regarding the application for entry, that evidence would cast a 'flood of light' on whether the primary purpose of the marriage had been immigration (*R. v. Immigration Appeal Tribunal, ex p. Kumar*, 1986).

In *Kumar* the Master of the Rolls (the chief judge in the Court of Appeal) pointed out how difficult the primary purpose rules were to satisfy for applicants; they could require one to choose between one's country of settlement and one's marriage. He noted that a woman settled in the UK would be quite likely to want to live there, making it unlikely she would marry someone unwilling to move there. Yet should the spouse admit to wanting to move there it would count against the couple with the immigration officials when they tried to settle as a family in the UK (1986, 447). As Justice Schiemann explained in his reflection on American heiresses and Marie Antoinette, one could want to settle in a country without settlement being the primary purpose of the marriage. Settlement then becomes only an additional benefit of marriage: neither irrelevant nor the sole basis of the marriage.

Two years after *Kumar*, the High Court consolidated instructions for immigration officials in primary purpose cases, including the importance of intervening devotion, in *Hoque and Singh* (1998). Double binds had not disappeared and judges noticed them. Lord Justice Slade rebuked the administrators of the law by pointing out 'the very fact that an applicant is applying for entry ... presupposes that he intends to settle *in the United Kingdom* with his wife' (at 235). The application presupposed settlement, yet the primary purpose rules used to evaluate the application presupposed that settlement is illegitimate.

Instructions from the courts to attend to intervening devotion still allowed substantial practical discretion to immigration officials. One of the applicants in *Hoque and Singh*, Matwinder Singh, still lost when the case was remitted to the Immigration Appeal Tribunal. The Singhs had a child but that was not enough (*R. v. Immigration Appeal Tribunal ex p. Singh*, 1990). The tribunal held in its interpretation of arranged marriage that:

> From its experience of 'the normal course of events' in Sikh society, of marriages being arranged by parents 'commonly between cousins or those more distantly related', it concluded that marriage between persons who were previously unaware of one another's existence [then met, fell in love and decided to marry] is at the very least unusual, but that is the scenario presented to us here (quoted in Scannell 1990, 18).

In other words, the Singhs' marriage was not an arranged marriage; the Singhs claimed they had fallen in love. It is in what the officials call 'love matches' that lawyers argue they have found the most problems for those from the Indian subcontinent. The tribunal suspected that such marriages could not exist within Sikh culture. The Singhs won in their second round before the Divisional Court on judicial review in 1990, almost seven years after they married. The judge noted that 'even with a Sikh background a young couple may meet and fall in love in the way acknowledged and understood in the western community' (quoted in Scannell 1990 19).

Interpretation did not end with the courts deciding that intervening devotion would contribute to a determination of the purpose of a marriage. Determining the purpose of a marriage requires, at least as immigration officials see it, the likelihood of a particular couple getting married and making the choices they make if they intend their marriage to be genuine. Is it likely that two people in a marriage would want to live in the woman's country of settlement rather than the man's? Is it likely that a couple in a genuine marriage would marry after only knowing each other a short time? Answering these questions invites generalizations about cultures that might have little to do with how people make choices.

In 1991 the Court of Appeal decided the case of *Sumeina Masood*. The question that was central was whether the couple intended to live together. In *Hoque and Singh*, the Court had held that it was wrong to conclude that the primary purpose of a marriage was immigration just because an applicant intended to live with his wife in England. In *Masood*, Lord Justice Glidewell held that:

> not to put too fine a point on it, the wife had the whip hand. She was the person who was saying quite firmly, 'I am established in the United Kingdom, I am a British citizen, I have a job, and I have a home. I very much hope that you can come and join me, but I am not going to live with you permanently unless you can.' That is the effect of it, and the ECO [entry clearance officer] was quite entitled to take the view at that point that the husband's intention to live with her, which was no doubt based upon a sincere wish to do so, was itself contingent upon him obtaining an entry clearance certificate … [I]t followed that it was but a short step to the conclusion that the marriage was entered into primarily to obtain admission to the United Kingdom (as quoted in Scannell 1992, 19).

The judge did not portray the case of the two wanting to live together in Britain, where the wife was more established. Instead, the woman was in control and if she was in control an intention to live together could not be any real intention; it was too dependent on her wishes. Not explicitly stated in this case, but clear in the next one and implicit in this one, is a belief that if a woman is in control, the marriage could not be genuine. In Scotland, a judge had settled a similar case in the favor of the applicant, seeing it as no hindrance that a couple needed to decide to live somewhere and they could choose to live in the country in which she was settled (*Mohammed Safter* v. *Secretary of State for the Home Department*, 1991).

Abid Hussein, a citizen of Pakistan, married Mehmuda Shaheen on 26 April 1987. They applied for entry clearance into Britain soon afterwards. The immigration officials denied the application on 14 June 1988 on the basis that the officer was not satisfied that the marriage had not been entered into with the primary purpose of immigration. The Immigration Appeals Tribunal considered the case in July of 1990. The couple had lived together in total for about one year. They had two children together. The Immigration Appeals Tribunal held that the primary purpose of the marriage had been immigration and Mr Hussein could therefore not settle in Britain. As the High Court decided in its review of the case, 'Some might think that [the two children] showed considerable devotion, but the tribunal were entitled to make the finding that they did in all the circumstances.' Since the tribunal's consideration of the case, and before the High Court got the case, the couple had lived together for ten more months in Pakistan and had a third child. Justice MacPherson decided that the tribunal had not erred in law and advised the couple to reapply for entry clearance. The High Court recommended that they ought to reapply, suggesting that immigration officials would see the case differently now that the couple had lived together longer and had had a third child. The waiting time to first interview for reapplicants in the Indian subcontinent was between five and ten months in 1994 (Home Office 1995, Table 2.5). Such decisions illuminate why immigration lawyers talk of the primary purpose rules as creating 'an endless stream of human misery'.

That a man would settle in the country of his wife is suspect to some adjudicators and judges. The judge's comment about a woman who has the 'whip hand' suggests a suspiciousness when people are doing something in a marriage other than what a judge or adjudicator thinks is appropriate. As we have seen, not all judges share that suspicion. But it reaches beyond the question of in which country a couple will settle to scrutiny of home arrangements.

Beliefs about gender and family appear as well in *R. v. Immigration Appeal Tribunal ex p. Amin*. In June 1987 Mr Amin, a citizen of Pakistan, married a woman permanently settled in Britain. She returned to Britain in February 1988 and had a child in June 1988. Justice Schiemann quoted extensively from the immigration adjudicator who decided the case. The adjudicator stated that the wife (never named in the court decision) had made it clear that she liked living in Britain better than she liked living in Pakistan:

> She said that after the marriage the appellant [Amin] wanted her to stay in Pakistan but she told him she did not like it there and he agreed she should go. She had told him of the comparative freedom she enjoyed in England which enabled her to go to work.

Mr Amin told the adjudicator that the couple intended that the woman would work for wages and he would care for the children while living in Britain.[7]

The immigration adjudicator then interpreted this story:

> For an appellant with his background, living in a village, trained as
> Imam, not permitted any contact with the sponsor other than a
> viewing before marriage, to so readily accede to the wishes of a wife
> whose traditional role is submissive, to join her household and not
> only that, to denigrate his position by allowing her to keep him, as I
> have been told, is totally unacceptable and runs completely contrary
> to his upbringing.

The adjudicator concluded that the primary purpose of the marriage had been immigration. The adjudicator based her decision on a
stereotyped and unchanging version of what Pakistani culture must
be. The price of claiming that a marriage within Muslim practices was
legitimate was that the woman could not assert any economic independence and neither could her preferences matter within the marriage.[8] The adjudicator completely avoided any discussion of what the
wife's culture might be, given that she had grown up in England within
an (Anglo-) Pakistani family.

The judge reviewing the adjudicator's decision, Justice Schiemann,
held that he could not overturn the adjudicator's decision because a
reasonable adjudicator could reach the decision she did. However, he
did hold that the adjudicator had not been clear enough in her
reasons for her decision. He therefore referred the case back to the
administrator. Along the way, he rebuked the adjudicator:

> But it is not clear to me on reading the adjudicator's decision what
> precisely it is that she is describing as an 'incredible arrangement.'
> On the face of it, it appears to be an arrangement that if the
> husband comes over here the wife will be prepared to support him
> whilst he remains at home looking after the child (at 374).

Of course, the judge has just stated what the 'incredible arrangement'
was: the adjudicator could not believe that the couple would reverse
what the adjudicator expected men and women to do in a marriage.

In her analysis of Western social contract theory, Carole Pateman
has argued that the sexual contract has preceded the social contract.
Political theory often assumes the reproduction of humanity. Those
who participate in a social contract are taken to be unencumbered
heads of households. Such independence of all ties is usually associated with men (Pateman 1988, chs 1 and 5). Pateman argues, therefore, that social contract theory depends on a sexual contract
precedent to citizenship. Under that sexual contract women are subor-

dinate to men. Consequently, she argues, the basis of women's citizenship has been child-bearing and child-rearing.

Pateman's analysis is suggestive for understanding the incorporation of men as new members of the polity. By pointing to different bases of incorporation by gender Pateman's analysis provides the beginning of a framework for analyzing the caution with which adjudicators approach the primary purpose cases. As noted above, husbands are turned down for entry more than wives, and many of the challenged cases involve women legally settled in Britain trying to bring in their husbands. Children have often been the marker of the 'intervening devotion' required in a genuine marriage, so that men are claiming entry in part on the basis of relationship to children. To use Pateman's analysis, this places men in a feminized position. To claim membership on the basis of children associates men with dependency rather than independence, a position more appropriate to women than to men (Fraser and Gordon 1994). Furthermore, applicants must show that they will not have recourse to public funds. That usually means that spouses must show that they can maintain the applicant. For men, this is a feminized position.[9]

The Home Office has turned down applications for entry for people with children who are in what could seem to be quite a conventional marriage understood in Anglo terms. Indeed, as the Master of the Rolls explained in some frustration in *Kumar* (1986), a marriage where parties had not met, or 'so far removed from the English context', would not ever be in court because the spouse could not, under the rules, apply for entry clearance (at 454). Both courts and immigration officials have an obligation to interpret the rules in such a way to allow for arranged marriages, allowing for a rough cultural pluralism to accommodate those who are settled in Britain and often British citizens. Despite the citizenship of many of South Asian ethnicity, cultural acceptance in Britain is limited (Layton-Henry 1992). The price of the legal acceptance of cultural pluralism is that cultures remain frozen in place. To have an arranged marriage that immigration adjudicators believe is genuine under *Amin* would require an enactment of a stereotype of a wholly submissive woman held to the adjudicator's understanding of what culture within the Indian subcontinent is. To the adjudicator, a woman who would participate in an arranged marriage is one who would settle in her husband's country and not raise the possibility of living elsewhere. This representation is something close to self-defeating in terms of the assimilation to dominant culture British political elites claim to want from people of color

(Messina 1989). If a woman has been living her whole life in Britain, it would make sense that she might feel more at home in Britain than elsewhere. Furthermore, given that women participating in such marriages are legally settled in Britain, it is not clear why marrying someone from the Indian subcontinent is not part of British culture if someone British is doing it.[10] Yet when a woman chooses to get married, the British immigration adjudicators often see choices as either/or: either she does not participate in a marriage to a man from Pakistan and retains her ability to make a family life in the UK, or she participates in a marriage with a man from Pakistan and must thereby renounce her connection to the UK.

This dichotomy does not accurately capture what James Clifford has called the 'predicament of culture' (Clifford 1988), and neither does it accord with the contested nature of culture that James Tully has argued constitutes intercultural engagements within national states today. The immigration service sees cultures as wholly isolated from each other and unchanging. They are not (Clifford 1988). In particular in Britain Asian women have contested representations of themselves as wholly passive. Women's movements have also criticized arranged marriages. The critique is not based on genuineness of a marriage, but instead on parental control of young women.[11] Women who have organized around the issue of arranged marriages have insisted that challenging parental control is not a matter for the state; to exclude someone after a marriage and perhaps after the couple has had children does nothing to help and indeed can make young women who have settled in Britain more vulnerable to their families (Kulli 1990; Southall Black Sisters 1990). The rules can provide leverage to abusive husbands who can threaten their wives with deportation should the marriage break up, a threat the Southall Black Sisters noted (*The Observer,* 18 October 1992, p. 3). Parental control of marriage is neither wholly accepted nor wholly rejected (Modood, Beison and Virdee 1994 1994; Puar 1995). Partial acceptance does not imply complete submission.

Writing of cultures as though they were uniform so thoroughly misrepresents how people live and explain their lives that Lila Abu-Lughod has argued that anthropology needs to tell particular stories of how people make their lives in any cultural context (Abu-Lughod 1994). Cultures are not isolated from each other; people who live in Britain grow up with British music, pubs, schools, theater, and interpretations of accents. Those with families from the Indian subcontinent also grow up with family connections to India or Pakistan and struggles over family, marriage, schooling, and religion that might sometimes differ from those in the dominant culture. Paul Gilroy has argued that the rich mixture of cultures requires a recognition of a black British culture (Gilroy 1994). To recognize ambiguity and improvisation might make the primary purpose rules extremely difficult to administer to the extent the rules must depend on assumptions about what are likely practices within cultures. To keep the rules is to keep something administratively convenient that restricts immigration, not something that allows a recognition of real cultural differences – and similarities. Legal cases are particular stories, highly stylized and told to fit into interpretations of the rules, both by the government and by the applicants' representatives.

Legal stories are one form of storytelling, but they do not provide the main understanding of Asian ethnicity culture in Britain. Arranged marriages attract attention of the mainstream British popular press (see e.g., Simmons 1995); for some Asian activists the attention amounts to voyeurism. Primary purpose rules provide occasion for discussion of 'bogus marriages' and 'marriage scams' (see, e.g., Dyer and Carvel 1992; Hooley 1992; Millward 1995; Simmons 1995; Walters 1995). In the local press in areas with substantial Afro-Caribbean and South Asian population, the coverage is more sympathetic and indeed does focus on particular stories of people unable to live together by virtue of having run into the suspicions of the Home Office (*Birmingham Post* 1993; *Wolverhampton Express and Star* 1992, 1993, 1994a, 1994b).

The stories in the local press always focus on love, on the romantic longing of a separated couple. The portrayal links with another assumption within the primary purpose rules, an assumption that also exists in Anglo-American common law regarding family life. Marriage is the primary unit of what constitutes a family (Fineman 1995). As Martha Fineman has argued, that does not have to be true (Fineman 1995). Fineman argues that a child and caretaker could instead be the most basic dyad of family life. She stresses that such a dyad would not be the only unit of family life, just the most basic. To assume a dyad as the *only* family life would cut out an immigrating parent more thoroughly than the past interpretations of the primary purpose rules have. But Fineman's insight is useful in illuminating problems with the primary purpose rules. If the focus becomes the children, the purpose of the entry into the marriage seems almost puzzlingly irrelevant. However, focus on the children ignores the needs of the adults. The interpretation of intervening devotion as meaning children also encourages those married for a very short time to have children when it might have been better to wait (interviews 1995–6).

Were the assumption about which relationship mattered different, the questions for immigration officials would not regard the evidence of intervening devotion within what Fineman calls the sexual dyad. Instead, the relevant question would be what kind of relationship the person who wishes to settle in Britain has with the now-existing children. Such questions would still enact cultural assumptions about what it means to be a family and what it means to care.[12] Those assumptions would center not on what Fineman has pointed out is a very fragile bond (that is, the bond between adults), but instead on a bond based on what children need. Whatever the nature or purpose of the marriage, children need care. It is of course not clear that any particular parent would provide that care. In addition, that approach would not address marriages without children and invites a focus on reproduction perhaps as intrusive as the focus on devotion is.[13] Centering on a different relationship, however, would transform the way that families are envisaged in public policy.

The European Court of Justice

The primary purpose rule reappeared in the European courts, this time in the ECJ in 1992. *Surinder Singh* challenged the policy as an encroachment on the right to free movement of workers that is part of European Community law. When the person settled in Britain had lived in another member state with her or his spouse, that person gained the right to live in Britain.

The British government argued *Surinder Singh* in March of 1992. It claimed that should the Court rule in favor of the claimants it would undermine national sovereignty. As the opinion of the Advocate-General put it, '[T]he United Kingdom states that every Member State has a legitimate interest in preventing its own nationals and their spouses from relying on Community law in order to evade the conditions laid down in national legislation' (*Surinder Singh*, 1992, 370). Britain also raised the concern of increasing 'risk of fraud associated with sham marriages' (at 373). The ECJ did not find either reason persuasive. Instead, the ECJ held that rights of free movement, granted under Article 48, required that Community nationals have the same rights in their own state that they would have in another state. European membership could bring rights for those who belonged, and belonging did not depend wholly on British definitions of assimilation.

However, the claim was not a right to family life, not least because there is no such claim possible under Community law. Therefore, it was not respect for family life that was important. Instead, Community law guarantees the free movement of labor. Employment was the baseline reason for allowing movement. The ECJ is in accord with national states in seeing immigration as about labor (Constable 1993). Marriage and family life, rather than being crucial to the decision as they are in the domestic courts, were secondary. Labor, rather than the association of family with femininity, was crucial.

Just before the ECJ announced its decision, the Home Office announced in June 1992 in Parliament that it had stopped enforcing the primary purpose rules where the couple had established a family life for five years or more or where there was a British child. The under-secretary stated that the choice was a response to judges' decisions about 'intervening devotion'. It had not published the change and did not intend to do so; neither did it intend to inform immigration advisers of the change (*Parliamentary Debates*, 1992). Indeed, they had only announced the change in response to a question. The question came up because immigration representatives had been finding for months that the Home Office was conceding cases it once would not have, raising suspicion that policy had changed. The announcement was grudgingly granted only after the policy was relatively well known among immigration representatives.

After *Surinder Singh* some of the conservative national papers played on the mistrust of Europe popular among some Conservatives in Britain. The government criticized the erosion of sovereignty which the decision meant (an issue governments in Britain raise every time they lose in a European court). A Conservative spokesman also raised the continued concern with immigration and its assumed link to race relations. In response to *Surinder Singh*, the Conservative chair of the Home Affairs Committee in Parliament, Sir John Wheeler, could still argue that good race relations required close investigation of marriages involving an immigrant (Hooley 1992). In particular, the government and the papers emphasized the sham marriages that would result from the decision (see, e.g., Hooley 1992; Kavanagh 1992). While lawyers and newspapers could and did publicize decisions from the courts because many of those cases were so sympathetic, those who were critical emphasized sham marriages (marriages in which the parties do not intend to live together).

As discussions of who has the whip hand might suggest, husbands are refused entry slightly more than wives even at the initial decision level, and despite the ruling from the European Court of Justice. In

1994 43% of the new applications for entry from the Indian sub-continent were from wives. Thirty percent were from husbands. The refusal rate for husbands was 40% while that for wives was 30% (Home Office 1995, 8–9). The refusal rate for husbands had been higher until the primary purpose rules were modified in 1992. In 1994, 12,100 husbands settled; 40% were from the Indian sub-continent. In the same year, 18,100 wives settled; 30% were from the Indian sub-continent. For husbands this was an increase from previous years; the Home Office ascribed that increase to the changes in the primary purpose rule (Home Office 1995, 5).

Individuals could strategize around *Surinder Singh*; those who worked with immigrants emphasized strategizing was necessary to counter the hostile immigration practices. *Q news*, a Muslim newspaper, heralded the decision by saying '[M]any Muslim husbands and wives separated by Britain's immigration laws can now legally unite their families by spending some time in an EC country and then move to the UK and seek right of residence' (Khan 1992). Some immigration advice centres, in response to *Surinder Singh*, have advised people to move to Europe if they could afford to do so. By doing so they can invoke their European rights (see, e.g., *The Observer,* 13 November 1994, 13). Representatives have noted that moving abroad is a difficult burden; however, moving can be a last ditch option. One representative told of a case where, after trying everything else imaginable, he did advise a couple to move to Ireland for a while and 'We'll see you when you come back.'

The government concession did not end the marriage cases. Adjudicators could continue to decide adversely for applicants based on the intention to live together, whether there was adequate housing and the adequacy of maintenance. Furthermore, rules similar to those governing spouses govern fiancé(e)s, providing another series of cases to contest. Litigators and applicants were also willing to continue challenging decisions by adjudicators. In a 1995 case in which Justice Schiemann held that the adjudicator had to clarify his decision, the judge concluded:

> In making these comments I follow a long series of cases over the years in which judges have expressed concern about the way in which adjudicators faced with trying to apply the primary purpose rule have appeared to leap to a conclusion which does not follow from the premises .... It may be that, in the light of these repeated comments by various judges, the Home Secretary would think it

appropriate to consider whether the relevant paragraphs in the Statement of Changes in Immigration Rules ... should be phrased in a way which makes the task of adjudicators, the Immigration Appeal Tribunal and this Court simpler. The application of the present rules is fraught with difficulty and liable to give rise to a sense of injustice in those affected. (*R.* v. *Immigration Appeal Tribunal ex p. Begum*, 1995)

The immigration law rumor mill did have it in 1995 that the government was considering changing the primary purpose rules (see, e.g., Gillespie 1995).

British politicians have had an extremely ethnocultural understanding of what the British community is (Gilroy 1987; Goulbourne 1991): that is, rather than formal citizenship status, what has mattered in terms of *legitimately* belonging has been ethnicity. Not surprisingly, that commitment to ethnocultural interpretations of what it means to belong is evident in legal cases regarding marriage as much as it is in cultural disputes over cricket. Politicians have focused on assimilation and support for Englishness as defining characteristics of what it means to belong (Gilroy 1994). When the courts have instead sometimes pointed out that people get married for a variety of reasons, no matter what their culture, or when the courts have recognized that people could possibly marry although the marriage does not fit either a stereotyped Asian or English script, they begin to recognize the cultural mixture and ambiguity that characterizes the world as people make their lives within it (Gilroy 1994; Modood, Beison and Virdee 1994; Tully 1995).

The 'intervening devotion' decisions raise questions of what cultural accommodation means. They sometimes move from the relentless pursuit of white Englishness defined by political elites. The possibilities that these interstitial challenges to the rules offer cannot be taken as a definitive opening-up of Britain in the cultural assumptions made in law. The British state has closed off these possibilities as much as it can. Appeals are not only limited by statutes and rules; appellants against unfavorable decisions do not receive legal aid, making it difficult for those who are least well-off to appeal (Dummett 1994). Yet even so, within the primary purpose rules lawyers, community activists and finally courts (including the ECJ), have simply made the rules not worth the cost of administering them in some cases. It was easier for the British state to concede cases with a child or in which the marriage had lasted for five years than to continue to fight them.

CONCLUSION

Courts in Britain do not have the authority to constitutionalize immigration in any sense. They can and do interpret within the rules, noting contradictions and impossibilities, such as allowing a spouse to apply for settlement but taking that as evidence that the primary purpose of a marriage was immigration. Those decisions have led to changes in policy by state administrators despite the limited authority of the courts. The court decisions often only remit the case back to the administrator to decide in accordance with the law, instructing an administrator to take the right things into account. In focusing on procedures the courts take an approach similar to that which shaped immigration procedures in the more explicitly constitutionalist USA in the supervision of administrative action (Stewart 1975; Shapiro 1988). In the early twentieth century immigration cases in the USA, addressing procedure also shaped immigration policy (Salyer 1995). Courts are relevant to governance even without substantive enforceable constitutional rights. In addition, in the broadest sense litigation of belonging is constitutionalist (Tully 1995).

Addressing the jurisprudence of the courts is helpful for understanding tensions within formal policy: that is, the primary purpose rules might seem relatively straightforward rules about family settlement until one addresses how the courts have disagreed with the Home Office, immigration adjudicators and the Immigration Appeals Tribunal regarding these cases.[14] Without confronting cultural complexity in the detail in which it appears in cases such as these, it would be too easy and wrong to continue to discuss problems of belonging today as ones of cultural clashes rather than ones of cultural connection.

Notes

1.   I am grateful to the Obermann Fellowship program at the University of Iowa, the Council for the International Exchange of Scholars and the Centre for Research on Ethnic Relations at the University of Warwick for support for this research. I am grateful to Sally Kenney, Bill Buss, Eric Heinze, Ken Holland, Bill Reisinger, John Reitz, Jeff Seitzer, Alec Stone, and several anonymous reviewers for comments on earlier drafts of this chapter.
2.   Some who have tried to interpret the rule of law in the USA from a rational choice point of view have had a difficult time explaining statutory interpretation. In rational choice language, courts are 'agents' of the central government. As such, their purpose could be to control administrators and keep them to central government purposes. A

problem this perspective addresses is how to keep agents, in this case the courts, from drifting away from the purposes of their principal, in this case the central government. From this framework McCubbins, Noll and Weingast have argued that the point of specific provisions in statutes is to control courts (1990, 315–17). As we shall see, seeing statutes as controlling makes statutory interpretation far too simple.

3. How often applicants win is difficult to assess. Judicial review is a two-step process. Applicants first apply for leave; if granted the case can go on to a substantive hearing. The Home Office withdraws cases after a court grants leave rather than lose the case in circumstances where it might think the applicant has a good attorney or a case with 'good facts', or when the case is assigned to a judge who tends to see immigration applications favorably. These withdrawals are not recorded as wins or losses. Overall in immigration cases during the first quarter of 1991, the latest period for which figures are available, 10% of cases granted a full hearing succeeded. Again, the 90% of cases that did not succeed included cases that were withdrawn, which includes cases in which the Home Office conceded. Of the applications themselves, 30% in the first quarter of 1991 were withdrawn without going to a substantive hearing (Bridges, Meszaros and Sunkin, 1996, 124, 127). By 1994, only 13% of all immigration applications were granted leave (Bridges, Meszaros and Sunkin, 1996, 121). Immigration representatives, including the government's Immigration Advisory Service, argue that these withdrawals by the Home Office should count as victories. These numbers provide a sense of what happens to cases, but in this chapter I want to focus on the doctrinal struggle over what it means to belong.

4. In discussing the marriage of the Princess of Wales after her death in August 1997, the media often called her marriage to the Prince of Wales an arranged marriage.

5. No one in Britain hyphenates ethnicity as Americans do. Gilroy (1994) has written of recognizing the importance of black British culture, but he needs to argue that point because it is not generally accepted. Those whose families were initially from Pakistan are called Pakistanis, which does not distinguish those who have lived in Britain their whole lives and those who live in Pakistan. The problem this chapter considers is the ambiguity of cultural practice and belonging, so it is important to make these distinctions.

6. For a discussion of the conflict, see Bhabha and Shutter (1994), pp. 71–8.

7. For a fictional discussion of the way that women can feel torn between the independence Britain offers and the sense of home that a country of origin can provide, see Emecheta (1989).

8. Applicants cannot win in these circumstances, which judges have noted. If the applicant had said it was his preference to live in Britain, with the woman claiming that she would only follow her husband's wishes, the adjudicator could readily conclude that the primary purpose of the marriage had been to immigrate. For a brief sketch of the catch-22s in the administration of immigration rules, see Grant (1995).

9.   As the administrators have agreed not to challenge the purpose of marriages in a wider range of cases, many representatives believe that they have challenged settlement under the maintenance and accommodations requirements more aggressively (interviews, 1995–6; see Hussein and Seddon (1996)).

10. Kureishi (1989) has provided a superb discussion of a sense of not entirely belonging anywhere having grown up in England and having family from Pakistan.

11. For this issue in Britain, see Sahgal and Yuval-Davis (1993).

12. Settlement of dependent children is another issue that has been challenged in the courts. The British Home Office has in recent years relied on DNA testing to see whether the children are related as claimed. Children are almost always related to at least one parent as claimed. When one child in a family is biologically related to only one of the parents as claimed and the others are related to both, the Home Office has decided that 'compassionate circumstances' mean that all the children should be allowed to settle in Britain. See Ihenacho (1991).

13. See, for example, the court's discussion of the couple's reproductive history in *Kumar* (1986).

14. Indeed, Calvo (1997, 385) in criticizing American immigration law for spouses, has argued for moving to a rule like the British one.

7 The Judges of the Court of Justice of the European Communities[1]

Sally J. Kenney

In view of the far-reaching significance which the Court has obviously assumed for governments and private individuals alike in the member states, one may be justified in asking who are the justices wielding such extensive power and responsibility? How are they appointed and under what conditions can they be removed from office? What are their duties and privileges, and what measure of judicial independence do they possess (Feld 1963)?

INTRODUCTION

This chapter attempts to systematically answer Feld's first question – a question that remains unanswered yet relevant more than 35 years after he posed it – and issues a call for scholars to answer the rest. Researchers in the USA have long pondered the following questions: how representative of the population should judges be, and what different groups need representation? Who should participate in the selection process? What should be the role of legislatures and interest groups in judicial appointments? What should the qualifications for judges be?[2] While many have debated the merits and legal reasoning of the ECJ's rulings, few have studied how judges are chosen or who they are (Kennedy 1996). Interestingly, the catalyst for such a discussion has come from the European Parliament. Parliament has demanded that it play a role in selecting members of the Court. Parliament has also criticized the member states' failure to appoint women.

Article 167 of the Treaty of Rome states that the judges and advocates general shall be appointed by common accord of the governments of the member states for a term of six years. In practice, each member state government follows its own internal selection procedure and simply announces the result to the Council when a vacancy occurs. Because the Court of Justice is a hybrid, a supranational court that is part international and part constitutional, member state judicial selection procedures display an interesting combination of conventional judicial selection procedures and systems for choosing European Community appointees more generally. There appears to be little public scrutiny of appointments to the Court within member states and there is none within Community institutions.

I begin by providing some background on the EU and how the Court operates. Comparisons with the US Supreme Court provide a context for understanding the ECJ for a North American audience but also stem from the greater body of social science literature on courts and judicial selection in the USA. After describing my sources, I analyze patterns in member states' appointments, review the issues surrounding judicial selection, outline the European Parliament's attempts to participate in the judicial selection, and end with a discussion of why it matters who participates in the process of selecting judges. The absence of women may provide the focus for Parliament's criticisms of member states, but elite domination of the Community, its democracy deficit, and the secrecy of its deliberations lie beneath Parliament's demand for greater participation. Despite the efforts of Parliament, there has been little demand for opening up the selection process either to greater public participation or even to greater public scrutiny.

BACKGROUND: THE EUROPEAN COURT OF JUSTICE

As of 1995, fifteen judges sit on the Court of Justice, one from each member state. The Council of Ministers officially appoints members for renewable six-year terms. The judges elect one of their members to be the President for a three-year term. The President assigns cases, is in charge of the administration of the Court, and leads the Court in its internal deliberations. Also sitting with the Court are nine (formerly six) advocates general (modeled on French practice) with one assigned to each case. The advocate general reads the briefs, attends oral argument, and writes an opinion setting out the facts, summarizing the legal arguments, and recommending how the Court should rule.

Despite frequent comparisons of the US Supreme Court and the ECJ (Stein 1981; Bridge 1982, Sandalow and Stein 1982; Rasmussen 1986; *The Economist* 1989, 48; Lenaerts 1990; Fernhout 1993), the two courts and the legal systems they head are very different. Treaties creating the Coal and Steel Community and the European Economic Community provide the legal basis of the ECJ, not a constitution (Mancini 1989). The Community is 'a distinct legal order of a novel kind, neither international nor national but more akin to an embryonic federation' (Brown 1989, 39). The ECJ has used its judicial power to promote greater European integration (Arnull 1985; Burley and Mattli 1993; Garrett 1995; *The Lawyer* 1995, 1). With the craftiness of the Federalist former Chief Justice John Marshall, it has turned the treaties into a constitution (Hallstein 1972, 35; Stein 1981). Through its doctrine of direct effect (holding that the Treaty is not merely binding on the governments of member states but legally enforceable by individuals in national courts), and by holding European Community law to be supreme, the ECJ has expanded its own power and transferred power to national courts at the expense of the executive and legislative organs of the member states. Shapiro (1987, 1008–9) concludes: '[N]o other court, including the Marshall Court, has ever played so prominent a role in the creation of the basic governmental and political process of which it is a part.' (See also Weiler 1986, 1103–42). The Court has resolved important policy questions when other Community institutions reached an impasse (Koopmans 1985a; Hartley 1988, 227; Brown 1989, 4, 7). The 'activist' nature of the Court and the 'juridification' of politics in the European Community has generated much commentary (Koopmans 1986; Rasmussen 1986, 1988; Weiler 1986; Cappelletti 1987; Smith 1990; Bzdera 1992; Volcansek 1992b; Rice 1995).

As the Court was created to hear cases about coal and steel and later to hear cases about the common market, its docket has little of the human rights cases that provide the mainstay of controversy and publicity about constitutional courts in the USA or Germany. The vehicles for its landmark decisions are cases on customs classifications, fisheries, equal pay for men and women, and the importation of foreign liquors (Van Hamme 1991; Volcansek 1993; Weiler and Lockhart 1995). (Although it has landmark cases, the ECJ is also asked to rule on matters that have little legal significance or are simply routine. Unlike the US Supreme Court, the ECJ does not have the power to refuse to hear cases, thereby setting its own agenda and controlling its workload through granting or denying *certiorari*.)

Perhaps most characteristic of its status as a hybrid international, constitutional or federal court is its procedure for deciding preliminary rulings. An individual may bring a case in a domestic court and ask for that court to apply Community law to the case. When a national court or tribunal concludes that the case before it raises a matter covered by European Community law, Article 177 permits it to submit questions and request that the ECJ give a preliminary ruling interpreting the Treaty. The ECJ answers the questions and sends the answers to the national court to apply to the facts of the case. Unlike the US federal system, the EU does not have independent trial courts (other than the Court of First Instance). The ECJ must rely on national courts to submit cases to it and to carry out its rulings (Volcansek 1986, 1992b; Stone 1994b; Stone and Brunell, forthcoming 1998).

Like many European courts, but unlike the modern US Supreme Court, the Court of Justice of the European Communities issues only one collegiate judgment; there are no dissenting or concurring opinions (Mackenzie Stuart 1983, 118–27). Speaking with one voice strengthens the authority of the Court's opinions. It also conceals disagreement within the Court (Bacon 1993, 29–32; Synopsis 1995, 93). As with the US Supreme Court, muddled or vague opinions may result from the need to compromise. The President assigns one judge to be *juge-rapporteur* of each case. The *juge-rapporteur* takes instructions from the conference (*délibéré*) and writes the judgment. The judgment, then, reflects the views of the formation as a whole, or the majority, rather than the *juge-rapporteur's* personal views (Mackenzie Stuart 1983, 120–1). The judgments themselves differ remarkably from US Supreme Court opinions. The European Court's opinions are terse and declarative in the tradition of civil law opinions rather than exercises in legal reasoning and persuasion (Rudden 1987; Helm 1996b). They are as Dawson describes French opinions: 'condensed and laconic ... [their] function could be equated with the flashing of a policeman's badge' (Dawson 1968, 375–6).The brevity of the opinions deprives legal scholars and future judges of access to or knowledge of the complexity and diversity that may have characterized the judicial debates (Bzdera 1992, 131–2). Often it is the advocate general's opinion rather than the Court's that more fully explicates the legal, public policy and political choices presented by the case.

Judges defend the need for secrecy and unanimity because their appointments are only for six-year renewable terms. If they signed separate opinions, member states could check whether their judges were voting for or against the national interest and refuse to reappoint judges who did not vote appropriately, thereby compromising their independence. President Mackenzie Stuart criticized the short, renewable six-year term as too short to provide enough continuity, and implied that member states have replaced rather than renewed a judge for political reasons (Dickson 1988c, 52). Judge Mertens de Wilmars described it as 'beneficent anonymity' (Synopsis 1986, 126). There is a high turnover at the Court for several reasons. Not all member states choose to reappoint a judge or advocate general when his or her six-year term expires. The additional judge (who was rotated between the larger member states) and the two (now four) advocates general from the smaller member states could never be reappointed because those positions go to a different member state to fill. Furthermore, not all the members view membership on the Court as the pinnacle of their careers or as a job they will do until retirement. After one or two terms, many members return to (or take up) judgeships in their member states, return to the professoriate, or return to private practice (Formal Sittings 1982, 62–3). The turnover of membership of the ECJ is thus higher and the length of service lower than at the US Supreme Court (9 years versus 15 years on the Supreme Court), but is consistent with the shorter fixed terms served by judges on European constitutional courts in Germany, Italy or France (Stone 1995, 293). In both 1988 and 1994 the same high number changed (five of thirteen judges and three of six advocates general)–nearly half of the members of the Court (Rice 1994, 20).

When thinking about judicial selection and appointments, it is important to recall that the ECJ is an international or supranational court rather than a simply a constitutional court. Its members are drawn from the fifteen member states. Their native languages vary. The working language of the Court is French. All written documents are available to members and *référendaires* (legal secretaries or law clerks) in the language of the case, and all are also translated into French. The advocate general's opinion is drafted in his or her native language and then translated into French. The *délibérés*, draft judgments, and correspondence between *cabinets* are in French. While all members need French to function at the Court, clearly the proficiency of the members varies from native speaker, to those who are truly bilingual, to fluency, to merely adequate (Feld 1963, 56, n. 74). It makes sense that those judges who are most skilled in French, as well as those who speak fluently several Community languages, will find it easier to interact with their colleagues on a professional as well as a social basis. Members and *référendaires* who are multilingual will also be able to work directly from the pleadings in the language of the case without waiting for translations as well as listen to oral proceedings without relying on interpreters. The linguistic skills of the members and their staffs is an important consideration which is not relevant at the US Supreme Court.

While many Supreme Court justices are drawn from the federal bench, there is no equivalent Community bench from which to draw members of the ECJ (with the possible exception now of the Court of First Instance [Kennedy 1989]). Members are drawn from the judiciaries of member states, judicial administration, the practising bar, and the professoriate. Members vary, then, in their depth of knowledge of Community law. A judge on the French *Conseil d'État*, a judge from the Irish Supreme Court, or a legal administrator from Denmark do not necessarily have a background in Community law comparable to the knowledge of federal law of a justice of the Supreme Court who may have served on the federal bench for 20 years. Members from countries who have only recently joined the Union may have few judges or legal academics trained in Community law. Thus knowledge of both language and Community law become important considerations in appointing members to the ECJ in a way that has no parallel in the USA.

It is clear from the speeches in formal sittings of members joining or leaving the Court that there are advantages and disadvantages to appointing members who have little knowledge and experience of European Community law. The Court has an evangelical mission, trying to educate and train (even coopt) judges, lawyers and the public about the details of, and the importance of European Community law. While the Court depends on some of its members being experts in Community law, it also benefits by educating and then exporting judges with little prior experience in Community law (Synopsis 1990, 189; Synopsis 1995, 93–4).

Like other international courts, members of the ECJ not only do not share a common native language, but they do not share a common legal tradition. A French judge and a German judge may have very different ideas about how to draft a judgment, just as common law and civil law judges will have very different notions about how to proceed. Similarly, the different member states have very different practices about the use of oral argument and the use of legal staff.

The ECJ has not received the same scholarly attention as has the Supreme Court, and neither has it received the attention its importance merits. The little we know about the inner workings of the ECJ compared to the US Supreme Court reflects its relative newness, oversight by scholars, and structural barriers to gathering information. We know little about how member states make their appointments to the

ECJ (Bzdera 1992, 128, 130) and little about members' legal and political backgrounds. Werner Feld's 1963 study looked closely at the appointment process in Germany and France, and assembled information about the judges in the first ten years of the Court. Stuart Scheingold's 1965 book on the early days of the Court also contains rich information on the judges, but there has been little scholarly study since. No journalists comprise an ECJ press corps who go beyond reporting the outcome of the cases to analyzing how the Court is operating (Formal Sittings 1984, 38; Carvel 1992, 27; Helm 1996b, 14). Like the founding fathers of the US Constitution, the drafters of the Treaty did not make available the record of their deliberations (Sandalow and Stein 1982, 17). Unlike their US counterparts, no James Madison came forward to offer individual documentation of the decisionmaking. Similarly, no written materials about the internal workings of the Court are available: no draft judgments, memoranda, or even the pleadings presented by member states or the Commission who have the right to intervene in cases they regard as of national importance.

This is not to suggest that scholars have ignored the ECJ. Scholarly journals and the press widely report and comment upon the judgments of the Court. Textbooks instruct future lawyers about procedure and doctrine. Legal scholars debate the merits of the ECJ's rulings. Others have examined the rise of judicial review (Cappelletti 1979, Shapiro 1987), the ECJ's status as a constitutional court (Hallstein 1972; Hartley 1988; Mancini 1989; Borchardt 1991), its role in policymaking (see University of Chicago Legal Forum 1992) and policing the boundaries of federalism (Lenaerts 1990; Bzdera 1992), and the impact of its rulings on judges in member states (Volcansek 1986; Stone and Brunell 1998, Weiler and Lockhart 1995; Stone, forthcoming 1998). Political scientists are now beginning to focus on the Court (Krislov, Ehlermann and Weiler 1986; Volcansek 1986; Shapiro 1990, Burley 1992; Alter 1994; Stone and Brunell 1998; Caldeira and Gibson 1995; Gibson and Caldeira 1995; Kilroy 1995). The governments of member states themselves have underestimated the extent of legal integration and the power of the European Court, to their peril. The Court's decisions may derail important legislative initiatives or result in costly financial awards against the government.

It is much more difficult to study the judicial selection process in Europe than in the USA. First, Europeans, especially officials at European Community institutions, accept and consider normal a higher degree of secrecy. Second, the line between law and politics is drawn in a different place.[3] (Drewry characterized the situation in

Britain as 'endemic academic apartheid between legal and political studies' [1991]: political science does not study courts.) Baum agrees (1977). Scholars and judges alike resist classifying and studying the Court as a political institution (Tate 1987). Members and staff at the ECJ, while friendly, accessible and helpful, are understandably cautious about betraying the confidentiality of the Court's decisions or saying anything that might disrupt the collegiality of the Court.[4] While they go out of their way to help those studying the Court, it is clear that many, but not all, view studying the political or internal aspects of the Court as inappropriate (Formal Sittings 1979, 31; Synopsis 1995, 18). Members of the Court would clearly prefer that scholars confine their research to studying its judgments and national courts' compliance with them.

SOURCES

Most of the biographical information on the judges comes from the Court's own publications. Many of the *vitaes* of the judges are printed in the *Annual Report* (*Synopses*) when they join the court, or are available in other documents such as the *Proceedings*. I gleaned additional information from reading the texts of speeches at formal sittings of the Court that occur when a new member joins the Court, leaves the Court, dies, or there is a special occasion, such as an anniversary of the Court. I perused *Who's Who* in its many European forms, as well as encyclopedias of EU officials. To the extent my linguistic abilities allowed, I searched European newspapers and other daily reporter services, such as *Agence Europe*.

In addition, I visited the ECJ, attended oral proceedings, and conducted interviews in 1989 and 1990. I interviewed seven current or former *référendaires*, two staff members of the Court, and several lawyers involved in litigation for the European Commission in Brussels. I also interviewed the former Dutch judge, Judge Koopmans. In 1994, I spent a month in Luxembourg conducting interviews, working in the Court's archives, library, and computerized database, and attending oral proceedings. I interviewed nineteen *référendaires*, and four former *référendaires*. I interviewed at least one person from eleven of the then thirteen *cabinets* of the judges, and four out of six of the advocates general. I spoke with three judges and one advocate general (who himself was a former *référendaire*).[5]

Some volunteered information about how judges were picked in their countries; others said they did not know. In any case, it is

difficult to verify what was reported as 'the' method. Because
European social scientists have been less interested in studying courts
as political institutions, and because European countries neither elect
judges nor require their legislatures to confirm them, little information exists about how member states pick their judges for the ECJ.
The Court's own extensive database contains little on judicial selection, apart from the occasional discussion about whether judges should
serve fixed or life terms, and whether they should represent each legal
system in the Union rather than merely one for each member state
(Jacobs 1981, 11; Schockweiler 1993; *Proceedings* 1995). Most comparative law texts or books on the ECJ say little about judicial selection
(Freestone and Davidson 1988, 133–5; Abraham 1993, 85–92; Brown
and Kennedy 1994, 43–69; Merryman, 1994, 912–13, 1091–93) or
merely quote the Treaty provisions.

For many member states, it is safe to say that there is no clear
pattern and practice. A member state such as Britain, which has made
five appointments (counting Sir Gordon Slynn who served as both
judge and advocate general as one), may alter its procedure slightly as
it 'learns' what it seeks in a judge, or as there is a larger qualified pool
from which to draw. New members of the EU may have few scholars
or lawyers well versed in EU law and fluent in French and willing to
leave their professorships, practices or the bench to move to
Luxembourg. With such small numbers of appointments, it is difficult
to state definitively, let alone generalize, about how each member
state picks its judges. Nevertheless, I did discover who the member
states appointed, and can describe their characteristics.

JUDGES

The Court has had 76 members since 1952, of whom 54 have served as
judges, and 28 as advocates general (six men have held both position).
Plotting who succeeded whom is somewhat complicated by the presence of an additional judge when the number of member states was an
even number and the existence of additional advocates general (see
Tables 7.1 and 7.2). The original six member states of the European
Coal and Steel Community appointed one judge each and one additional judge to prevent a tie. Van Kleffens (Netherlands) served for
one term, followed by two Italian judges, Catalano and Trabucchi,
who served until 1973. The enlargement of the six to nine necessitated
no additional judges until Greece joined in 1981. Judge Grévisse

*Table 7.*1   Judges of the European Court of Justice, 1952–97

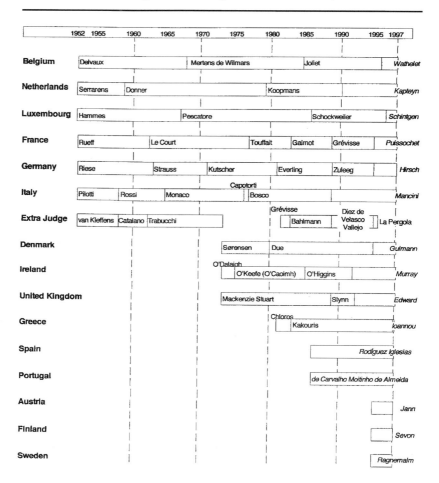

(France) served as an extra judge for one year followed by Judges Bahlman (Germany), Diez de Valesco Vallejo (Spain) and La Pergola (Italy). Spain's appointment of Bahlman's replacement was contested by Italy who denied that Spain was promised the next extra judge. This dispute delayed the appointment (Dickson 1988 a, b; Brown and Kennedy 1994). The latest enlargement to fifteen has eliminated the need for an extra judge.

Table 7.2   Advocates General of the European Court of Justice, 1952–97

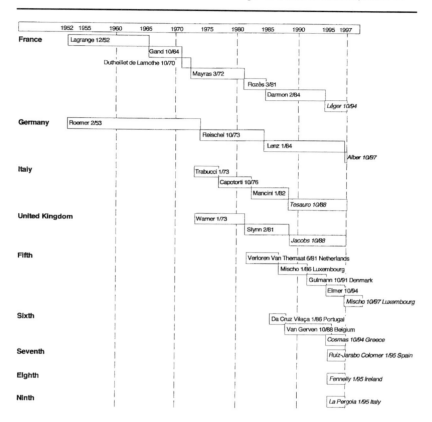

Initially there were two advocates general, Maurice Lagrange (France), who is credited with defining the role (Synopsis 1988, 202) and Karl Roemer (Germany). In 1973, two additional advocates general were added from Italy and the UK. When Greece joined in 1981, a fifth advocate general was added, and a sixth added in 1986. The fifth and sixth positions are rotated among the smaller states. As of 1997, there are nine advocates general. Italy, France, Germany, and the UK each have one, and the remaining five are now filled by Denmark (Elmer), Greece (Cosmas), Spain (Ruiz-Jarabo Colomer), Ireland (Fennelly) and Italy (La Pergola). Advocate General La Pergola was the extra judge for two months until the new members of the Court were added in January 1995.

In the nomenclature of the Court, members refers to both judges and advocates general. Six men have held both roles (four of them Italian), but the movement between the two positions has been in both directions. Slynn, Gulmann and Mancini were advocates general before becoming judges, whereas with Capotorti, Trabucchi and La Pergola it was the other way round. Two men, Edward and Schintgen, served first on the Court of First Instance. Da Cruz Vilaça became President of the Court of First Instance in 1989 after completing what remained of a term as advocate general to the Court. Jacobs and Gulmann appear to be the only members who were first *référendaires*.

Of the 53 members who are no longer serving, the average length of service was 9.24 years.[6] Dutheillet de Lamothe served the shortest time (1.42 years), followed by Chloros (1.84) and O'Dalaigh (1.92) while Roemer served the longest (21.8 years) followed by Donner (20.47) and Pescatore (18). Justices on the US Supreme Court, by contrast, served an average of just over 15 years (n = 111). Although it is difficult to tell why members left the Court, at least eight members left the Court to take up important judicial posts in their own countries. Another left to become President of Ireland. The average age of the 79 appointments I could calculate who joined the Court was 54.81 (compared with 53.13 for US Supreme Court Justices). Rodríguez Iglesias was the youngest man (of those for whom I obtained birth dates) to join the Court at 39, followed by Donner (40) and da Cruz Vilaça (41). Pilotti was the oldest appointee at age 72, followed by Bosco (70), Touffait (69), and O'Higgins (69). Not surprisingly, then, Bosco was the oldest ever member of the Court, stepping down at the age of 83.

At least thirty-four members had doctorates in law. Five others had advanced degrees (LLM, LLD, PhD, D Phil and LLB). At least seventeen had studied abroad. At least eighteen had education or experience in economics, a number that would be larger if I included those lawyers specializing in competition law. Defining the occupations of the members is difficult since the vast majority of them had at least two occupations. Twenty-one were chiefly professors, often professors of Community, comparative or international law. Forty-one had some 'judicial' experience (including the *Conseil d'État*, administrative tribunals and prosecutors). At least 22 had served on the bench for more than 10 years. At least 10 had argued cases as advocates before the ECJ; eight had helped negotiate the treaties (or their country's accession, or rules of procedure). At least ten had experience as legislators, two had been members of the European Parliament (four others had worked for the legislature as staff to committees or as Ombudsman). At least 56 had had substantial executive branch appointments in their own governments, most commonly the Ministry of Justice, but including Cabinet positions or legal advisers to the government. The Court has been led by nine different Presidents. President Pilotti (Italy) served for six years from 1952 to 1958. Judge Donner (Netherlands) also served two three-year terms as President but remained on the Court after stepping down as President in 1964 for fifteen more years (the only President to stay on the Court after serving as President). He was succeeded by President Hammes from Luxembourg who served the shortest period of time: only three years. President LeCourt from France served the longest term: nine years. Presidents Kutscher (Germany), Mertens de Wilmars (Belgium) and Mackenzie Stuart (UK) each served four years. President Due (Denmark) served two three-year terms before his retirement from the Court and from the law in 1994. President Rodríguez Iglesias (Spain) replaced him.[7] Thus, the Presidents have served on average nearly two terms each (5.25 years). Although there is no strict rotation, and the judges choose the President themselves (since 1964), all of the original six member states have provided a President for the Court. Ireland, Greece, Portugal and the three newest members (Austria, Sweden, Finland) have yet to fill that position.[8]

The President has many important duties (Brown and Kennedy 1994, 49–50). He alone has the power to decide on interim measures. He assigns the *juge-rapporteur* to the case and he and his staff oversee progress on all cases. He chairs the Court, when he sits on a case (usually only in cases involving the full court) and formal sittings. He chairs the general meeting which determines the formation of the case: that is, how many judges will hear and decide the case. Along with the registrar, he is responsible for the administration of the Court. Although staff at the Court occasionally referred to President Due's special suitability for the position because of his long experience in judicial administration at the Department of Justice in Denmark, it appears that rotation between the member states has been an important factor along with any individual's leadership skills, in determining who shall be President. This may explain in part why the judges chose Judge Rodríguez rather than Judge Mancini to be the new President. The test is whether he will be succeeded by an Irish, Portuguese, Greek, Austrian, Swedish or Finnish judge, or whether another country will have a second president.

Each country faces its own set of interests and cleavages to represent on the Court: party, language, region, legal system, governmental department. Among the member states, leadership of Community institutions may be balanced. Within a member state, a different balancing process occurs. Parties or languages may have to be balanced across ECJ appointments: advocate general, judge, judge at the Court of First Instance, or across 'international' courts such as the ECJ, ECHR, and International Court of Justice. Appointment to the Court in some cases in some countries displays many of the same mixed features of ambassadorships: exile for a party luminary who is in trouble, a retirement prize for exemplary public service, the removal of a competitor within a party, or a consolation prize for a failed judicial appointment. This chapter is only the beginning of a full account.

Belgium has appointed five members to the Court: Louis Delvaux, Jos Mertens de Wilmars, René Joliet, Walter van Gerven (advocate general) and Melchior Wathelet. Belgian judges stay on the Court until retirement or death, serving several terms. Belgium parcels the appointments out, balancing party, region and language.[9] Rather than appointing judges with either domestic or international experience, Belgium appoints either high-ranking politicians or professors of EC law. The appointment of Belgium's sitting judge, Melchior Wathelet, generated much controversy in the press, apparently both on the grounds of his judicial abilities as well as concern about events during his tenure at the Ministry of Justice (Helm 1996a, 11; *Agence France Presse* 1997). It is hard to tell whether the increased public attention at Wathelet's appointment represents a protest over some unspoken balance being tilted, controversy over a particular unpopular individual, or greater attention to judicial appointments to the Court in general.

The Netherlands appoints professors who specialize in Community law and reappoints them to serve until they choose to retire or assume another office. Luxembourg natives must leave the country to study law, and many study in France.[10] Luxembourg appoints knowledgeable international lawyers with substantial experience as governmental ministers and reappoints them.

France tends to appoint administrative judges mainly from the *Conseil d'État*,[11] but also appoints judges from the *Cour de Cassation*, or the Court of Appeals in Paris, or from 'eminent personalities with legal background' (Feld 1963, 45).[12] All of its judges have also had experience in governmental administration, chiefly the Ministry of Justice. The Foreign Minister has primary responsibility for selection, in consultation with the Minister of Justice. The final decision is made by the Cabinet without consultation of parties or professional organizations. After its initial two appointments, France has appointed judges for only one term (half of its advocates general have been reappointed once). France's first appointment of an advocate general was Maurice Lagrange, who had served for more than 21 years at the *Conseil d'État* and had been part of the negotiations for the Treaty of Paris, as well as an important drafter of the Protocol on the Statute of the Court. Lagrange more than any other shaped the position of advocate general, and President Mackenzie Stuart referred to the position as effectively holding 'one of the most eminent professorial chairs of Community law' (Synopsis 1988, 202). France has appointed the only woman member of the Court, Madame Rozès, as advocate general. Rozès left the Court after only three years to serve as First President of the *Cour de Cassation*.

In Germany, the overriding concern in distinguishing among well-qualified and suitable appointments is political party.[13] When I asked a *référendaire* for a German judge if he had aspirations to sit on the ECJ his first reply was, 'I don't have a party card.' Appointments in Germany are an eclectic mix of distinguished professors of law, judges, high-ranking administrators in the Ministry of Justice, and legislators. Germany's practice of alternating the appointments among the political parties means that sitting members who want to stay on may not be allowed to. According to Rice, Everling – a Christian Democrat and reported 'Euro-enthusiast' – wanted to stay on the Court longer than his eight years, but he was replaced by Zuleeg, a Social Democrat, in 1988 (Rice 1995, 10). While Germany may have regularly failed to reappoint sitting judges so as to rotate parties, its first advocate general served nearly 21 years. Like Lagrange, Roemer was a true architect of the edifice of European Community law (Synopsis 1986, 161).

Italy's chronology of appointments is perhaps the trickiest to plot because it moves its appointments around between extra judge, advocate general and judge. When Mancini was appointed, President Mertens de Wilmars referred to 'the best Italian tradition' of appointing a respected professor (Formal Sittings 1984, 27). Italy draws less on judges for its appointments than France and Ireland, and tends toward distinguished professors who have also had considerable public service as legislators, administrators or in international affairs.

Federico Mancini replaced Capotorti as Italy's advocate general in 1982 and then replaced Bosco as its judge in 1988. Mancini was a professor of labor law who also wrote on comparative private law. Like Bosco, he served for six years prior to his appointment at the *Consiglio superiore della Magistratura*. Then Socialist Prime Minister Craxi attempted to appoint Mancini to the constitutional council in Italy but could not get that appointment through Parliament. Although Craxi was willing to attempt the appointment again, Mancini withdrew and received a posting in Luxembourg. Mancini was reappointed by Italy in 1994, the same year that he narrowly missed being elected by his colleagues to serve as the Court's President.

The UK has appointed three judges and three advocates general, but only five men since Sir Gordon Slynn served as advocate general before his appointment as judge. Nominees are usually judges, or professors who are also practicing barristers (who are likely to have argued cases for the government). The Foreign Office selects them with the advice of the Lord Chancellor (Rice 1994, 20).[14] It appears to be the Treasury Solicitors Department (which has responsibility for presenting the UK's arguments to the ECJ), in conjunction with the Scottish office, and not the Lord Chancellor who forwards the UK's nomination. (Warner, Slynn and Jacobs argued cases for the Treasury Solicitors Department before they were selected to serve on the Court.) Britain's first appointment as a judge, Mackenzie Stuart, was Scottish, and its first appointment as advocate general, Jean-Pierre Warner, was bilingual. The UK's current judge, David Edward, is also Scottish.[15] President Due commented:

> It is not without reason that Scottish lawyers have played an important role as interpreters of Community law. The law of Scotland forms a link between the Common Law and continental law. It is therefore only natural that Scottish lawyers are attracted by the symbiosis of different legal cultures and traditions presented by the new legal order which is Community law (Synopsis 1995, 97).

Edward was Britain's first appointment to the Court of First Instance and was appointed as a judge when Slynn left for the House of Lords in 1992.

Denmark's first appointment, Max Sørensen, was a professor of public international law who had also served as legal adviser to the Ministry of Foreign Affairs. Sørensen had chaired the European Commission on Human Rights. His replacement, Ole Due, was President of the Court for two three-year terms. In 1979 when Denmark appointed him, Due at 48 was the Court's youngest member

(Formal Sittings 1979, 35). Due was a twenty-year veteran of the Ministry of Justice who had served on the commission to prepare for Danish accession. Due was thus one of several men who helped negotiate the Treaty or their country's accession and then went on to serve on the Court.

Little more than anecdotal evidence exits for which governmental department or departments is responsible for selecting the member state's nominees. In the UK, the Treasury Solicitor's Department coordinates the representation of the UK before the ECJ, and thus, has the largest say in who shall be judge or advocate general, in consultation perhaps with the Scottish Office, whereas it is the Lord Chancellor who has responsibility for the appointment of domestic judges. Appointments to the ECJ could be the purview of the departments of Foreign Affairs, Economics or Justice, or all three, depending on the member state. Due was clearly a creature of the Danish Ministry of Justice. Interdepartmental wrangling became public as Denmark settled on Due's successor in 1991, Claus Gulmann. He had not only assisted the Ministry of Foreign Affairs in the field of Community law and pleaded on behalf of the Danish Government before the ECJ, but he had served as a *référendaire* for Max Sørensen.

Ireland has appointed four judges.[16] Three were Supreme Court Justices (two Chief Justice) and all four had been Attorney General. None was a professor. Ireland's early appointments were neither well-schooled in EC law nor French, although its later appointments have been. Ireland's first appointment, O'Dalaigh, was a senior counsel,[17] twice Attorney General, a Supreme Court Justice for nine years, and Chief Justice of the Supreme Court for eleven. After nearly two years on the ECJ, he was appointed President of Ireland.[18]

Greece not only faced the challenge of finding jurists qualified in European Community law but those untainted by military rule. Its first appointment, Alexandros Chloros, had spent his professional life as an academic in the UK. He served as the legal expert on the five-person negotiating team for Greek accession. Chloros died at the age of 56 after serving less than two years on the Court. His successor, Constantinos Kakouris, was a judge on Greece's highest administrative court, the State Council. When he took the oath, President Mertens de Wilmars commented, 'during the period when liberty was restricted in your country, you, both as a citizen and as a judge, stood up for the defense of liberty and you paid the price for that act of courage' (Formal Sittings 1984, 50). Due's first comment welcoming Greece's first advocate general, Georgios Cosmas, was to express his pleasure that 'for the second time, [Greece has chosen] a Member of the Greek State Council who opposed the dictatorship of the Colonels in 1967' (Synopsis 1995, 162). Like Kakouris, Cosmas had studied European Community law in Paris before taking up his position at the Council of State and rising through its ranks.

Both of Spain's appointments as judges have been professors of public international law. Spain's first appointment to the Court in 1986 was Gil Carolos Rodríguez Iglesias, a chaired professor in European Law. Before earning his appointment at the University of Granada, Rodríguez also taught in Germany. He is fluent in Spanish, English, French and German.[19] In 1994, the judges elected him President to succeed Due. Diez de Velasco Vallejo was the thirteenth judge from 1988 to 1994, after much wrangling over whether Spain's accession meant Spain (España) should precede Italy in the rotation based upon alphabetical order.

Portugal has appointed only one judge, José Moitinho de Almeida, upon accession in 1986. Moitinho had risen through the ranks of the judiciary to become public prosecutor for the Lisbon Court of Appeal. He served as Principal Secretary at the Ministry of Justice, where he served as its representative to the Committee for European Integration as well as to several committees for the Council of Europe, and then he became the President of the Ministry's Department of European law. He then became a chaired professor of Community law at the Catholic University of Lisbon. Portugal re-appointed Moitinho in 1992.

After the enlargement of 1986, a sixth advocate general post was created and Portugal appointed José Da Cruz Vilaça to serve for the two years and nine months before the position rotated to Belgium. A year after leaving the Court, he became President of the Court of First Instance in 1989.

Austria's first and only appointment is Peter Jann. Jann earned his doctorate of laws at the University of Vienna and then passed his qualifying exams to enter the judiciary. He served as a magistrate, then as a 'Referent' at the Ministry of Justice, and then as the Secretary to the Parliamentary Committee on Legal Affairs. From 1978 until his appointment as a judge on the ECJ, Jann served on the Austrian Constitutional Court. His mandate ends in October 2000.

Finland's first judge, Leif Sevon, earned a doctor of laws degree and began his career as an assistant professor. The bulk of his career, however, was spent in the Legislation Department in the Ministry of Justice (with a brief stint as a judge of the City Court of Helsinki in

1979). In 1991, Sevon became a judge on Finland's Supreme Court of Justice. In 1994, Finland appointed him to serve on the European Free Trade Area Court, where he became that Court's President. Finland renewed Sevon's appointment in 1997 (he had drawn one of the short terms).

Sweden's first appointment was Hans Ragnemalm, a Chair of Civil Law at Stockholm University and former Parliamentary Ombudsman. From 1992 until his appointment in 1995, Ragnemalm served as a judge on Sweden's Administrative Court. His mandate expires in 2000.

JUDICIAL SELECTION

Why does it matter who judges are and how they are selected? The literature and debates over judicial selection revolve around four themes. First, what should be the relationship between the courts and the other branches of government? In particular, how can judicial independence be assured? In Britain and France, debates over judicial selection concerned how to ensure that judges and courts would be independent of the monarch (Volcansek and Lafon 1988). Debates at the founding of the USA concerned the question of how to ensure that judges were independent from the President (Abraham 1992; Berkson 1980, 1992; Goldman 1997). State constitution writers grappled with the issue of how to secure the independence of judges chosen by the legislature. The relationship of the judicial branch to other branches becomes more important as the welfare state's administrative power grows and parliaments are seen as less able to provide a system of checks and balances (Cappelletti 1989, 4). Judges at the ECJ, like Commissioners, are to be independent of the governments who appointed them rather than representatives (in the sense of delegates – like members of the Council) from them. The issue of independence arises because members are appointed for short (six-year) renewable terms rather than a single nine-year term or for life.

Second, how responsive should judges be to popular opinion (Caldeira 1986, 1987; Marshall 1989; Caldeira and Gibson 1995; Gibson and Caldeira 1995, 1996)? Are judges the bulwark against democratic excess, or dangerous exercisers of countermajoritarian, unchecked power (Cappelletti 1985)? Constitution writers grapple with how to ensure that judges are both independent and responsive. Life tenure and near irremovability is thought to ensure independence, but raises the possibility of incompetent or irresponsible judges wielding unchecked power. The salience of this debate often hinges on the extent to which judges exercise legislative or administrative judicial review. Discussions of this issue in the EU have centered around the length of term, and, to a lesser extent, the European Parliament's role in judicial selection. One defense of the short (less than life) terms of judges on the German and French Constitutional Courts is that they are then more responsive to changes in political power as well as public opinion.

The third issue is the nature of judging, especially judging in constitutional cases. Is judging something that requires integrity and common sense, or something that only experienced legal professionals are competent to do? Is judging the application of complex legal rules and precedents or is it participating in constitutional debate over intrinsically political rather than solely legal questions? Cappelletti describes the recognition of the law-making power of judges as the decline of legal formalism (1989, 9–14). In Britain, judges take a posture of deference to parliamentary sovereignty and adopt literalist rules of construction to maintain the narrative of mere implementation of the legislative will. In Germany, France and Italy, the 'regular' courts have been saved from 'contamination' by the separation of 'political' courts (constitutional or administrative) from 'judicial' courts (but see Chapter 2 in this volume). Once judging is construed as making choices of public policy rather than applying legal rules, less justification exists for allowing only a narrow segment of the legal community to serve, rather than also those who bring different kinds of expertise to public policy – political or economic rather than merely legal, for example – which leads to demands for greater public accountability. In fact, the more you question whether what the US Supreme Court, the French Constitutional Court or the GFCC are doing is different from what legislatures do, the more you call into question the legitimacy of transferring this power to judges at all. Member states of the Community differ in how they think about this question. Britain is no doubt the extreme in the small number of people eligible to be judges at higher levels (Griffith 1981). In other member states, judges are more like career civil servants, although members of constitutional courts are often drawn from a wider pool and serve shorter, fixed terms. Appointments to the ECJ have included professors, judges, and politicians. The recognition of the powerful policy making role of the ECJ has led member states to call not for greater public participation in judicial selection, but for curtailing the role of the Court as a whole. This subject was discussed in the briefing papers for the 1996 Intergovernmental Conference.[20]

Lastly, how representative should the courts be? Should the bench reflect the diversity of the population in terms of language, religion, race, gender, class, region, political party, or other important divisions in society? Perry analyzes how the idea of representativeness of the US Supreme Court has changed over time (1991). Geography, particularly a balance between northern and southern states was perhaps the overriding issue of representation for at least the first 100 years of the USA. Rather than mirroring the society's racial, religious or gender composition, at different periods of the Court there has seemingly been a Jewish seat, an African-American seat, and now possibly one (if not two) women's seats.

The representativeness of the ECJ has emerged as an issue with respect to member state, legal system and gender (although language is always lurking beneath the surface). In its report for the 1996 Intergovernmental Conference, the Court seeks to draw the attention of the Council to 'the problem of maintaining the link between the number of Judges and the number of Member States, even though the Treaties do not provide for any link between nationality and membership of the Court (paragraph 16)'. Mackenzie Stuart raised the issue of representativeness when discussing the three-judge chambers (1983, 126).

To the extent that these issues have generated public or academic discussion, the most salient issue has been the powers of the Court as a whole rather than the length of term of members or the method of judicial selection. Before turning to a discussion of the European Parliament's activities with respect to who chooses judges and how representative they are, it is worth repeating that there appears to be little public or legislative involvement in the selection of judges or advocates general at the ECJ within member states (Scheingold 1965). In Britain, for example, there is no equivalent of the Senate confirmation proceedings: the decisions all take place behind closed doors and all documents are secret. Kennedy and Brown describe the American process of confirmation as 'unseemly', and everyone at the Court is well aware of Robert Bork and Clarence Thomas and anxious not to emulate the US example. The European Parliament's demand for a more substantial role in all matters of EU affairs extends to a claim to participate in the selection of judges. The European Parliament is one of the few voices demanding a consideration of judicial selection of the ECJ, and it has been joined by the *The Economist,* which recently called for either the European Parliament or national parliaments to play some role (1997), the occasional editorial writer (Carvel 1992, 27), and the Bavarian Minister for European Affairs, Thomas Goppel (*Agence Europe* 1993). The Court is adamantly against such involvement. In its report for the 1996 Intergovernmental Conference, the Court wrote:

> a reform involving a hearing of each nominee by a parliamentary committee would be unacceptable. Prospective appointees would be unable adequately to answer the questions put to them without betraying the discretion incumbent upon persons whose independence must, in the words of the Treaties, be beyond doubt and without prejudging positions they might have to adopt with regard to contentions issues which they would have to decide in the exercise of their judicial function (paragraph 17).

Of the 54 judges at the Court of Justice and 28 advocates general (76 appointments), only France has appointed a woman, Madame Rozès, as advocate general. All members of the Court are currently male. When the *Financial Times* reported on the new members in 1994, for the first time and in the opening paragraph of the article, it stated: 'None of the appointees, announced last week, were women, leaving the Court once again all male' (Chambers 1994, 13). Perhaps the gender of the judges is beginning to appear on the public's agenda. The body most concerned about the gender of judges and judicial selection generally has been the European Parliament.

THE EUROPEAN PARLIAMENT

The European Parliament is a weak body with little legislative power (*The Economist* 1991, 1994; Westlake 1994). The Single European Act provided it with a greater role in legislation, the Maastricht Treaty further expanded its role, and the Court has interpreted the Treaty to give Parliament greater power to challenge actions of the Commission and Council. Legislative functions are shared largely by the Council and the Commission. Parliament has sought a greater role for itself; this demand intensified once Parliament became directly elected in 1979 (Westlake 1994, 44). Greater European integration and an expanded scope of activity led to concerns with the Union's democracy deficit (Westlake 1994, 106–9) since the most important decisions are made by non-elected bodies (the Commission, the Council, or the Court of Justice) and these decisions are made in secret. In European Community parlance there is a lack of transparency. One of the ways Parliament would like to increase its power is to participate in appointments to the ECJ.

From the outset of the Community, different possible methods of selecting judges were floated (Feld 1963, 53 n. 68). Parliament has called for a greater role through individual questions to the Council, through resolutions and committee reports, and through a draft constitution. As early as 1980, MEPs Sieglerschmidt and Glinne submitted written questions[21] to the Council asking why Parliament did not have a greater role in selecting judges and why the process differed from the Council of Europe's selection of judges to the European Court and Commission of Human Rights (Jackson 1993, 220). When the Council merely restated the Treaty Provisions (Article 167) and made the profound observation that the two systems were different, a testy Sieglerschmidt responded that the refusal to answer was inconsistent with the great importance supposedly attached to the activities of Parliament. The Council reply noted no such inconsistency, and pointed out that: 'Member States do not think the institutional balance which underlies the Treaties establishing the Communities should be changed.' The Council then reiterated that the Communities differ from the Council of Europe.

In 1985, Dieter Rogalla submitted a written question asking the same question (Feld 1963, 42). Commission President Delors replied simply that it was not for him to comment on how the Council of Europe conducts its business and that the current arrangements seemed to work just fine. Rogalla next posed the question to the Council of why Parliament could not play some role in judicial appointments? The Council merely noted that changing the role of Parliament in the appointment of judges would require amending the Treaty.

As early as 1982, as part of proposed reform of the Treaties, Parliament called for greater participation in the process of judicial selection. In 1993, the European Parliament passed a resolution calling for Parliament (by majority vote), in conjunction with the Council, to appoint judges to the Court of Justice for non-renewable nine-year terms. This is then included in Parliament's proposed Constitution for the European Union. In 1993, the fullest exchange occurred in a response by Council President Pangalos to an oral question by MEP Alber on behalf of the Committee on Legal Affairs and Citizens Rights. Alber (who is now himself an advocate general on the

Court) pointed out that the Community was now constitutionally different from when the Treaty of Rome established an economic community, and that the Court of Justice was now a constitutional court. While Alber was not willing to go so far as the Parliament's draft constitution to call for Parliament to appoint judges, he thought that Parliament should at least be consulted. Pangalos replied by emphasizing that the Treaty provisions do restrict member states in their choice of appointment to the Court by requiring them to be eligible for the highest judicial office and to be independent.

MEP Medina Ortega then spoke. He observed that no one was challenging the independence, stature, or importance of the Court. Nevertheless, he argued, the method of selection (intergovernmental) is outdated given this stage of European integration. After noting the procedures at the Council of Europe (for the Court of Human Rights) and in the USA (for the Supreme Court), Ortega commented about the judges at the Court of Justice: 'their appointment is lacking in something which is currently receiving particular emphasis in the process of European integration: transparency and democratic accountability'. Ortega called for some consultation, for example, with the Committee on Legal Affairs and Citizens Rights. Pangalos suggested that the appointment of judges might be a suitable topic for the 1996 Intergovernmental Conference.

In 1989, with the creation of the Court of First Instance, four members obtained 261 signatures for a written declaration that member states appoint women to the Court of First Instance. None did, although two members are now women, appointed by Austria and Sweden. Perhaps the most hard hitting challenge to member states' absolute discretion with respect to appointments to the Court came from a written question by Jaak Vandemeulebroucke in 1995. Vendemeulebroucke suggested that Belgian's recent appointment, Wathelet, was unqualified because he lacked independence. According to Vandemeulebroucke, fifteen years of government service without any 'de-lousing' ensured that Wathelet could not be independent of the appointing government. Furthermore, he questioned whether Wathelet would have met the standards the Treaty sets down that judges meet the standards for high judicial office within the member states. Lastly, Vandemeulebroucke questioned whether Wathelet had sufficient knowledge of EC law. The answer is typical, in that the Council merely restated the Treaty provision. Parliament clearly wants some role in judicial appointments[22] and may use the slowness of member states to appoint women as the vehicle for demanding a greater role. When member states appoint members of the Court who are under a cloud of controversy, they provide Parliament with the opening it may need to press the issue further. In addition to the Court's recommendation against a role for Parliament in its paper for the 1996 Intergovernmental Conference, at least two former members of the Court have taken public positions against it. While still a judge, Fernand Schockweiler wrote in *Rivista di diritto Europeo* that Parliament's participation would undermine judicial independence. Gordon Slynn, too, spoke out against involving Parliament in the process, arguing that member states knew best who was well qualified, and that although 'non-legal, non-judicial factors' do come into play, involving the Parliament would 'politicize' the process (Bacon 1993). The former judge, Koopmans, however, took a different position. He pointed out that Parliament's current proposal of dividing appointments between the Council and the Parliament might be unworkable because politicians' belief that the nationality of the judge is very important would lead both bodies to appoint one judge from each member state, making the Court too large to be workable. Unlike Schockweiler and Slynn, however, Koopmans was less negative about Parliament playing some role, suggesting that a system modeled on the US Senate's powers of 'advice and consent' might be more appropriate (1985, 46–7).

CONCLUSION

Now that I have described the Court and its members, made some tentative generalizations about patterns of appointment, discussed judicial selection, and highlighted Parliamentary proposals, I must return to the question asked at the outset: why does it matter who the judges are and how they are selected? First, such a project has historical value. Describing who the judges are is part of telling the story of the development of an interesting court. Social scientists who study the US Supreme Court take such information for granted as they flip to appendices in constitutional law textbooks.

Second, who the member states select to sit on the Court determines how effectively the Court functions. We might want to investigate whether a member of the Court must be fluent in French and knowledgeable about EC law to be effective. Do professors or experienced judges make better appointments? Should member states appoint younger members, who will return to domestic courts and bring with them knowledge of EC law, or older members who can bring their knowledge and experience and are no longer worried about future judicial or political appointments? What specialties of law best serve members of the court: public international law, comparative law, EC law, or others? Is it useful to have members who have experience of holding public office? Should members have a background in economics as well as law? Given the complexity of EC law, the difficulty in producing consensus among judges of different languages and legal traditions, and the serious backlog of the Court, concerns about the Court's efficiency lead us to examine whether member states are serving their own interests and the interests of the Community well in their appointments.

Third, such a descriptive historical project lays the foundation for the larger project of disaggregating the court. Although the Court speaks with one voice, and we may never be able to (or consider it desirable to) study the individual jurisprudence of each separate member, all of its judges do not agree on every issue. Because I do not believe that judges, particularly constitutional judges or interpreters of a general treaty, are discovering the right answers to legal questions but rather are making difficult decisions about policy, I would argue that who those men and women are matters. We already know anecdotally that member states may investigate a prospective judges' party and position with respect to European integration (Euro-skeptic as opposed to Euro-enthusiast), although they do not always do so. I think even the judges themselves would concede that they differ with respect to economic philosophy, political philosophy (how should the institutional structure of the EC operate and how should power be shared between the EC and member states, as just one example), and canons of legal interpretation. The main reason, however, why it matters who the judges are and how they are picked is because the Court wields enormous power. It makes policy, even if the manner of its policymaking is constrained by law and differs from legislatures. In the past, the Court has been the engine of European integration and its decisions affect huge numbers of people.

Judges at the European Court are interested in protecting the power of the Court to interpret the Treaty and maintaining their independence from member state control. They are also concerned about representing the legal traditions within the community and concerned with making the Court work with so many languages and legal traditions. The European Parliament stands virtually alone in calling for public participation in selecting judges, and sometimes couches its call in terms of the absence of women on the Court. Although I would argue that it has been the representativeness of the Court that has prompted what little discussion has occurred to date, and that Parliament may be conveniently using the underrepresentation of women as a vehicle for expanding its own power *vis-à-vis* other Community institutions, more fundamental issues lurk beneath that call.

European legal elites may prefer to maintain the position that judges merely apply the law agreed to by member states. They may prefer that decisions as to who applies that law stay in the hands of elites (in Britain, 'the great and the good') and that the criteria for choosing and method of choosing remain secret and invisible to the public. Indeed, they may be right in thinking that such a system has produced largely outstanding judges and furthered European integration. Exploring the biographical history of the members of the Court reveals no scandal of incompetence or patronage, although some members have served more effectively than others. Yet I argue that public scrutiny within the member state and the Community as a whole is more democratic and, ultimately, therefore, more legitimate. Citizens are rightly concerned that they are transferring power from their member state to elite-dominated, secret and unaccountable institutions. As they become more informed about the importance of the Court as a community institution, and each member state appoints more members, informed citizens and the legal community will, I predict, show a greater interest in the men and women on the Court. This chapter is a first step in contributing to an informed discussion.

Notes

1. Thanks to Susan Curry for her research assistance as well as Amy Lynch, Ding Li, Didi Wendel-Blunt, Jennifer Pruszynski and Vinita Jethwani who also worked on the project. Thanks to Tom Kennedy for his extensive comments. Thanks, too, to the contributors to this volume for their helpful comments.
2. For an overview, see Slotnick (1988), *Journal of the American Judicature Society* (1994) and Goldman (1997). See also Carp and Stidham (1996, 229–90); Slotnick (1992); Cook (1978); Cook *et al*, (1988); Graham (1990); Perry (1991); Schmidhauser (1979); Goldman (1978, 1993); Goldman and Saronson (1994); Stumpf (1988); Abraham (1992, 1993); Grossman (1965); Chase (1972); and Jackson (1974).
3. I would argue that Europeans are more apt to characterize law as what Martin Shapiro describes as the prototype of courts: 'an independent judge applying preexisting legal norms after adversary proceedings in

order to achieve a dichotomous decision' (Shapiro 1981, 1). David
Kairys refers to: 'an idealized decisionmaking process in which the law
on a particular issue is pre-existing, clear, predictable, and available to
anyone with reasonable legal skill; the facts relevant to disposition of a
case are ascertained by objective hearing and evidentiary rules that reasonably ensure that the truth will emerge; the result in a particular case
is determined by a rather routine application of the law to the facts;
and except for the occasional bad judge, any reasonably competent and
fair judge will reach the 'correct' decision' (Kairys 1990, 1). See the
exchange between former President Mackenzie Stuart and MPs in the
May 1997 *Times* arguing about whether the European Court of Justice
is political.

4.   Rightly so, based on the US experience with *The Brethren* ('Comment',
     University of Pennsylvania Law Review 1981).
5.   Karen Alter has also generously shared her findings about judicial
     selection based on nine interviews of judges and a review of judicial
     selection in France and Germany.
6.   Judges averaged 9.02 years, advocates general 7.18.
7.   Rodríguez's election as President was somewhat of a surprise, accord-
     ing to commentators. He is one of the Court's younger members and, at
     48, its youngest ever President. Mancini was the 'unofficial deputy'
     President and Kakouris was the third candidate. There were two rounds
     of voting (*Reuter European Community Report* 1994; Smyth 1995).
8.   Donner describes the process as 'triennial periods of embarrassment
     and secrecy' and prefers the previous method (that left him as
     President) of having the appointment of President made by member
     states rather than the judges themselves, as was the case with both
     Donner and Pilotti (Mertens de Wilmers 1988, 16). See also Hammes'
     views on why he was chosen over a German, so that Hallstein could be
     President of the Commission. Feld describes a similar balancing of the
     Presidents of the different EC institutions, arguing that Reise was
     the most likely Presidential candidate to follow Donner, but a German
     was already then President of the Commission (1963, 44).
9.   Interview with Lenaerts (1993). The balance is made including appoint-
     ments to the Court of First Instance. Hermann comments that Joliet,
     who teaches European anti-trust and intellectual property law at the
     University of Liège, was chosen by French-speaking liberals who were
     allotted the slot to fill (1984, 43).
10. Such a small country may at times have difficulty staffing all its interna-
     tional positions. There has been some difficulty finding *référendaires*
     from Luxembourg to staff the Luxembourg *cabinet*, for example.
11. Lagrange, Gand, Dutheillet de Lamothe, Mayras, Grévisse, Galmot and
     Puissochet. Mackenzie Stuart refers to the *Conseil d'État* as the 'breed-
     ing ground of distinguished members of the Court' (Synopsis 1990, 172).
     Judges may strictly speaking be the wrong term for administrators
     (schooled at the prestigious ENA) who spend their careers at the
     Conseil d' État and ultimately rise to the position of *Conseiller*.
12. At the swearing in of Advocate General Léger, President Due referred
     to the tradition 'and it is a good tradition [of drawing] one of the two

French Members ... from the administrative courts and the other from the ordinary courts' (Synopsis 1995, 163).

13. Feld reports the parties in 1963 as only one group consulted, along with the Federal Guild of lawyers. Feld identifies the Ministries of Justice, Economics, and Scientific research as the principal players (although the Cabinet decides: 1963, 43). Interviews with *référendaires* suggests the Ministry of Economics was now the most important.

14. Slynn refers in Bacon (1993) to vetting by the Lord Chancellor's Office. Blom-Cooper (1991) comments on the selection of judges overall 'without so much as a whisper from the public'.

15. McKain (1993, 11) describes Edward as 'one of the top earners at the Scottish bar, appearing in a series of major planning inquiries and medical negligence cases'. Edward clashed with the Conservative Government over Foreign Secretary Malcolm Rifkind's proposal to reform the Court (MacDonald 1996, 8; Meade 1996).

16. The Irish Constitution (Article 35) provides for judges for Irish domestic courts to be chosen by the President, although the decision rests with the Government (Murphy 1977, 90; Kelly 1984, 353). The initial two appointments appear to have gone to Fianna Fail, and the next three to Fine Gael.

17. Senior counsel, like the British Queen's Counsel, indicates that a barrister has served for ten or fifteen years and is at the top of the profession. All judges are chosen from this small pool (Bartholomew 1971, 22–4; Murphy 1977, 89).

18. O'Dalaigh became President without an election, since he was the only candidate (Kelly 1984, 58). He resigned in mid-term after declining to sign an emergency anti-terrorist law without having it first scrutinized by the Supreme Court (UPI 1983).

19. Newspaper accounts referred to him as a Germanophile (*Reuter European Community Report*, 1994).

20. The tone of the Report of the Court of Justice on Certain Aspects of the application of the Treaty on European Union for the Purposes of the 1996 Intergovernmental Conference reveals its grave concern over a possible reduction in its powers (*Proceedings of the Court of Justice and Court of First Instance of the European Communities*, 15/95, 22–6 May 1995, 8–11). The main impetus seemed to come from Britain, and a change in its Government has probably rendered that threat moot for the time being (Adonis and Rice 1995, 17; Peston 1996, 1).

21. The Treaty grants to all members of the European Parliament the right to table written questions to the Commission and the Council (Westlake 1994, 174). The responses are then part of the *Official Journal*. See European Parliament, *Rules of Procedure* (June 1994).

22. The Treaty gives the European Parliament greater role with respect to appointments to the Court of Auditors (Article 188b). Parliament has made far greater progress modifying its powers to participate in the selection of the President of the Commission (*The Economist*, 21 May 1994, 24).

8 Legal Orientations and the Rule of Law in Post-Soviet Russia[1]

William M. Reisinger

> The business frenzy and the legal anarchy that color life in post-Soviet Russia began with the fall of the older order .... As things have worked out, the police state has turned into what Russians call *bespredel*, meaning anarchy, lawlessness, limitless greed .... It is this shadowland of legal chaos, the overlap of commerce and government, that is less understood and at least as important as the presence of organized crime .... Millions of Russians feel that they are worse off now than they were before .... The sense of visceral alarm in Moscow about the rise of the new rich spreads across the political spectrum .... One speaker after another [business people from across Russia] made the same series of points: no matter what the rest of the country or the world might think, the new wave of Russian entrepreneurs craves a legal order; chaos is bad for the country and bad for business (Remnick 1995, *passim*).

The critical role that law and legal institutions play in establishing a successful democratic state is obvious in post-Soviet Russia. Seven years into Russia's post-Soviet statehood, the prospects for ameliorating a range of frightening problems rest in one way or another on the functioning of the Russian legal system. During that same period, observers have paid the most attention to maintaining democratic institutions, the trials of economic change and the prospects for peace. Yet the proper functioning of Russia's judicial system is essential to all three.

Russia's recent problems did not arise because it inherited no legal machinery from the Soviet Union; rather, the challenges have been of two sorts. First, Russian leaders have had to reform the country's legal institutions and law codes given the switch to liberal, competitive constitutional rule and market economics. Moreover, they had to think through carefully and politically craft the changes despite pressure to get the new system in place as quickly as possible. By 1997, they had made a fair amount of progress, with much left to do. The second set of challenges stem from the heritage of Soviet-era attitudes toward the law and courts. To some extent, the alterations that have been made to the formal rules of the country's legal system will shape behavior, as individuals respond to new rewards and punishments. Yet institutions never operate in a vacuum. The new legal codes and court reforms will not produce the effects desired of them if Russians, on a broad scale, distrust, ignore, evade or subvert the legal system. In particular, Russians of influence – political leaders, prominent figures in the mass media and popular culture, commercial elites, judges, prosecutors and other legal officials – must view law and legality in ways that support the rule of law, and their actions must evince such a supportive posture. The Soviet legacy would seem to be very worrisome on this score (see discussions by Wortman 1976; Sharlet 1990; Huskey 1991; Solomon 1992). To trace and explain Russia's movement (or lack of movement) toward the rule of law, therefore, sustained attention needs to be paid to Russians' legal orientations.

Russians' legal orientations are, naturally, quite complex. Many points of view are highly controversial and many seem contradictory. Russians often believe both that bureaucrats are too powerful and that bureaucrats are not powerful enough to maintain order. Scholars must measure and analyze legal orientations broadly among Russian legal experts, judicial officials and commentators across the gamut of legal institutions, and then set the resulting patterns in contrast to past Russian patterns and to patterns in other societies. In this chapter, I argue that a content-analytic approach can reveal patterns of legal orientations across a wide array of individuals and settings. After making this argument, I illustrate the technique with the results of a content analysis of Russian writings about the concept of the rule of law.

LAW AND THE LEGAL SYSTEM IN THE SOVIET UNION AND POST-SOVIET RUSSIA

Before turning to the chapter's theoretical and methodological discussions, I need to sketch the background against which Russian commentators discuss legal issues. The 1993 Russian constitution and the formal statements of top Russian leaders commit the country to respecting the rule of law and, specifically, to reforming Soviet-era institutions and practices so as to make possible the creation of a 'law-governed state' (in Russian, *pravovoe gosudarstvo*; as explained below, this phrase is used rather than the English formulation 'rule of law'). Those Soviet-era institutions and practices arose through the melding of the Czarist legal system (primarily influenced by the continental legal tradition, with some common-law elements) and Marxist views of law and its role in a socialist state. In the immediate aftermath of the 1917 revolution, the Bolsheviks disbanded much of the Czarist legal apparatus (Sharlet 1990). They saw law as a weapon that had been used by the upper class to control the lower class. Popularly elected local courts and revolutionary tribunals were set up to handle disputes. Fairly soon, however, it became clear to Bolshevik leaders that they could not do without regular courts, trained legal counsel and fleshed-out legal codes. They, like other governments, needed this instrument of statehood. Under Stalin, the earlier Russian view that law was a means of strengthening the state and not of limiting the state in favor of individuals, re-emerged with a strong emphasis on state power (Solomon 1987). The show trials of the late 1930s – in which former leaders of the 1917 revolution who had been tortured confessed to ludicrous charges – represented the low point of this trend. Even with the courts so subservient to Stalin's regime, the regime bypassed the formal judicial system in important ways. Thousands of Soviet citizens were sentenced to death or imprisonment in camps not by courts of law but by *troikas* (tribunals) set up to expedite the processing.

In the post-Stalin era, the worst features of the purges and mass terror came to an end. Soviet courts were divided into two branches: those handling cases of economic disputes among Soviet enterprises, called courts of arbitration, and those handling other criminal and civil matters. The former hierarchy was headed at the all-union (highest) level by a Supreme Court of Arbitration and the latter hierarchy by the Supreme Court. At the lower levels, for minor offenses, the Soviet Union had a system of 'people's courts' for which the judges were popularly elected. Comrades' Courts handled even more minor offenses. At all levels, judges were vetted by one or another organ of the Communist Party. Both legal consultants and defense attorneys had limited powers and very low prestige in the Soviet Union (Kaminskaya 1982). The most influential and prestigious among legal positions was that of procurator, a state official who acted as prosecuting attorney but who also conducted investigations and had broad responsibilities for supervising legality (Smith 1978). The Soviet procuracy had more extensive powers than the French procuracy on which it was patterned.

Although the Soviet legal system had well-developed rules of procedure that were followed in most cases and although Soviet leaders saw law as an important tool of governing, political authorities, whether high-level or low-level, were able to influence the outcome of important cases. The fact that most trials were fairly conducted without politicians being involved does not offset the fact that, when the stakes were high, the legal system was not independent and neutral. This was most clearly demonstrated by the judicial system's acquiescence in the KGB's efforts to eradicate a small community of citizens who challenged the regime from a variety of points of view. Known in the West as 'dissidents', many of these individuals became famous through writings circulated from individual to individual (*samizdat*) within the Soviet Union and then brought out of the country to be published in the West. The most prominent dissidents, such as Alexander Solzhenitsyn and Andrei Sakharov, were handled gingerly: police flew Solzhenitsyn out of the country and revoked his citizenship and sent Sakharov into internal exile in a city off-limits to foreigners. Many others, however, were imprisoned, sent to labor camps or forced into insane asylums and treated pharmaceutically (Reddaway 1972; Tokes 1975; Barghoorn 1976; Rubenstein 1988).

From 1987 on, the Soviet leader, Mikhail Gorbachev, who had received his undergraduate degree in law from Moscow State University in the 1950s, frequently spoke out against Party officials' interference with the courts, saying that 'our past experience' shows the dangers of doing so. He was referring not just to the Stalin era but also to increasing corruption during the late Brezhnev period. He introduced the term 'law-governed state' into debate and gave it his imprimatur. It was not easy for all Soviet legal scholars to adjust to using positively a term that previously they had treated as a fig leaf for bourgeois domination of the legal system (Griazin 1988 states this). Still, a literature relating the conception to the political transformation of the Soviet Union soon sprang up (Berman 1991). Democratic political forces also rallied behind the concept. By forcing through in 1988 a reduction of direct Communist Party control over the Soviet legislature and government, Gorbachev took the crucial first step toward the rule of law. These reforms included the establishment of a Constitutional Commission to review the constitutionality of legislation.

Russia became a somewhat autonomous governing unit within the Soviet Union following the March 1990 legislative elections. These elections allowed Boris Yeltsin to assume leadership of Russia, first as the legislature's chair and in 1991 as elected President. Yeltsin and other Russian leaders decided, as had Gorbachev earlier, to create an institution for judicial review of legislation and executive rulings. Instead of a Constitutional Commission, however, amendments to Article 165 of the Russian Republic's constitution established a Constitutional Court of 15 judges and called for a federal law to elaborate on the Court's operations. This law was promulgated on 12 July 1991. By 31 October of that year, 13 of the 15 positions had been filled, permitting the Court to begin operating. Within just a few weeks, the Soviet Union came to an end and the newly independent Russian government undertook the economic reform measures that sparked political turmoil. Russia's Constitutional Court would not have an easy job navigating the turmoil (Hausmaninger 1992; Smith 1996).

In late 1992, the Court's chair, Valerii Zorkin, became involved in the legislative-executive power struggles (Vedernikov and Vedernikova 1994; Rumyantsev 1995; Sharlet 1995). By March 1993, Zorkin was an outspoken critic of Yeltsin. In the eyes of some, this harmed the credibility of the Court to serve as an impartial arbiter between other branches of power. This early phase of the Court's existence ended with the tragic violence in Moscow in early October 1993.[2] Soon after these events, Yeltsin suspended the Constitutional Court's activities.

This raised the prospect that the Court might never be resurrected. It was, however, although with a delay. Russia's present constitution – adopted by popular referendum on 12 December 1993 – retains the Constitutional Court of the Russian Federation, with minor changes from the earlier constitution (Article 125). The previously chosen members of the Court were not removed. Justice Zorkin lost his position as Chief Justice but remains on the Court (for more details, see Smith 1996). A new federal law on the Constitutional Court came into force in July 1994, superseding the 1991 law (more on the Court's powers and procedures can be found in Korkeakivi 1994b). By February 1995, the upper house of the legislature had confirmed the Court's new members, and the Court resumed operation (Rakhmilovich 1996).

The rest of the Russian judiciary (outlined in Articles 126–8 of the 1993 Constitution) has the two-track structure of the Soviet system. The Supreme Court of the Russian Federation is the highest judicial organ for civil, criminal, administrative or other cases.[3] The Supreme Court of Arbitration of the Russian Federation is the highest judicial organ for resolving economic disputes. Both of these Supreme Courts supervise a network of lower-level courts. Legislation detailing the interrelationship of all federal courts was promulgated only at the end of 1996 with President Yeltsin's signing of the Federal Law on the Judicial System (1997).

For the most part, the Russian legal system bears more resemblance to continental European civil-law traditions than to the Anglo-American common-law traditions (Hazard 1994a). This means, for example, that judges are supposed to apply the wording of statutes to the circumstances of a case as precisely as possible without being influenced by other similar cases and precedents set in the judgment of those cases. Some Russian legal scholars, however, are beginning to advocate an increased role for case law in the new post-Soviet Russian judiciary (Hazard 1994b). Another common-law institution that has appeared is trial by jury, which was introduced on an experimental basis in nine Russian regions in 1994 (Henderson 1994; Thaman 1995). Although difficulties occurred in implementing jury trials, the government considered the experiment a success. A deputy minister of justice announced in March 1995 that gradually jury trials would be introduced throughout Russia (BBC, 5 March 1995). The present constitution also continues the institution of the Procuracy, headed at the federal level by the Procurator-General of the Russian Federation.

Although Russia's courts have taken some positive steps since 1991 (Hazard 1994a; Ruble 1995, 82–6), virtually everyone concedes that massive work remains if they are to meet the demands that have been placed before them. Legislative and executive bodies at different administrative levels (federal, regional and local) must clarify the division of labor and delineate the jurisdiction among different courts. An additional area needing serious attention is safeguarding the independence of the judiciary (Solomon 1995). Challenges yet to be overcome include securing adequate pay for justices and their aides without placing them under the control of political authorities, devising effective rules for selecting justices, and implementing guidelines about appropriate behavior of judges off the bench. Solomon (1995, 98) notes that:

Work as a judge conferred low status and gave low pay compared to legal work in the new private sector, where demand was growing. Worst of all, though, was the sheer physical danger of working as a judge. Courthouses were burned and judges murdered when they dared to confront the interests of serious criminal elements.

In addition, because the Russian Procuracy possesses quite strong prosecutorial powers by comparative standards, its officials must have salaries and working conditions sufficient to minimize corruption.

Also pressing is the need to train judges, lawyers and other legal experts to be familiar with new legal practices and new laws. There are estimated to be 50 000–65 000 trained lawyers in Russia (counting both *advokaty* [trial lawyers] and *yuriskonsulty* [legal consultants]). This works out to about 330–450 per million population. In other countries, the available estimates (from the early 1970s) of comparable figures are 417 per million in the Federal Republic of Germany, 390 per million in Belgium, 890 per million in Canada, 606 per million in England and Wales, 206 per million in France and 2348 per million in the USA (Reitz 1996b). So Russia has more lawyers than a few Western countries, but it is near the low end of the scale. It is likely, though not certain, that the current number of Russian lawyers is inadequate. Moreover, most Russian legal experts received their training prior to 1988. Even though many are scrambling to adapt to new conditions, this is not simple. Numerous programs are underway to remedy this, but it will take some time. In the meantime, Russia's expanding market economy and increased international trade will create a growing demand. Also, the many rights granted to Russian citizens by the 1993 constitution – the protection of which Article 18 places at the feet of the judiciary (Korkeakivi 1994a, 1994b; Smith 1994) – cannot be protected adequately without lawyers able and willing to undertake rights cases. Presumably, the eventual number and quality of lawyers in Russia, as well as the speed with which new training takes place will depend much on the potential income of lawyers in a market economy.[4] Finally, corruption among administrators is, by all accounts, particularly severe in Russia at present. Officials whose decisions can mean hundreds, thousands or millions of dollars in profit for private firms or individuals receive monthly salaries equivalent to a few hundred dollars. The salaries, moreover, are frequently not paid.

HOW A LEGAL COMMUNITY'S ORIENTATIONS INFLUENCE THE ESTABLISHMENT OF THE RULE OF LAW

The formal rules governing judicial institutions, like those of other social institutions, only partially reveal how the institutions work and the outcomes they produce. One must also understand the orientations of those who occupy roles within judicial institutions as well as of those who appeal to or are affected by them. Krygier (1990, 646), for example, has argued that the essence of the rule of law is 'a widespread assumption within society that law matters and should matter'. Judicial institutions will not achieve such fundamental goals as peacefully resolving interpersonal conflicts and protecting the citizenry from violence unless the cases they handle form only a tiny percentage of the potential cases. Deterrence must outweigh punishment, by some large factor. This in turn depends on most citizens respecting judicial institutions as well as the law (in the abstract and, preferably, each concrete law). For the rule of law to be effective and stable, supportive legal orientations should run throughout a society, from the highest officials down.

In other words, Russians need to develop legal orientations that are supportive of the rule of law (analyses of Russian legal orientations include Bonk 1986; Solomon 1992; Mikhailovskaia 1995; Reisinger, Miller and Hesli 1997). Scholars can and should study Russians' legal orientations so that the country's course toward or away from the rule of law can be properly described and understood. My use of the term 'orientations' is meant to include various psychological characteristics of individuals (highly abstract 'values', more grounded 'attitudes' as well as very specific 'opinions') but to exclude (at this point) actual behavior toward or within legal institutions. The broader term that incorporates both orientations and behavior is 'legal culture' (e.g., Hendley 1995). Even though legal culture is a much-mentioned term in comparative legal scholarship (an early treatment is Friedman 1975), very few studies of any country examine the components of legal orientations and document them with empirical evidence. Moreover, seeking to characterize an entire society's legal culture presents daunting challenges, both theoretical and practical. Indeed, focusing on that as the objective might lead one to obscure important differences among types of orientations. For these reasons, I describe in this chapter a way to depict not Russia's entire legal culture but the pattern of more concretely specified legal orientations.

Certainly, it is common among current Russian commentators to decry the lack of legal orientations that support the rule of law. For example, the legal scholar Anatolii Sobchak (1995, 7), a former mayor of St. Petersburg, asserted in a 1994 speech before an audience of Western officials and scholars that 'In Russia today, many problems relating to crime and political instability are largely due to the continuing domination of the [judicial and police] structures ... by people

appointed in the days of yore with the approval of the party committees concerned.' President Yeltsin, in his 'state-of-the-federation'
speech to the legislature in February 1995 argued that:

> The old technology of power based on ideological and political
> coercion is giving way with difficulty to modern methods and
> approaches. *Rule by directive rather than the rule of law still prevails*
> .... Last year Russia continued to live in a rarefied legal area. *The*
> *number of laws which the country needs exceeds many times over the*
> *number that have been adopted.* The legislative process is often over-
> whelmed by political struggle. *New legal customs have not taken*
> *shape and legal culture is poor. It is important to realize that respect for*
> *the law in society will only take root once the authorities respect the*
> *law.* The judicial system has not yet become an equal, truly inde-
> pendent and authoritative branch of power (BBC Summary of
> World Broadcasts, 20 February 1995; italics added).

Note that Sobchak and Yeltsin are fundamentally criticizing
Russia's elites, its 'authorities'. Westerners, by contrast, tend to see
the Russian public as the main obstacle to the rule of law. Some go
beyond the public's unfamiliarity with many Western rule-of-law institutions by stressing nihilist or anti-legal outlooks among the Russian
public (Wortman 1976; Sharlet 1978; Huskey 1991).

Whether the problem lies primarily with the general public is an
empirical question that scholars can answer through research. It will
require analyses of legal orientations both among Russian society as a
whole and among its political leaders. Yet a third social category
should be distinguished. Scholars of public opinion have long distinguished between the bulk of the public in democratic societies and the
minority which is more attentive and more politically active (Almond
1950; Milbrath and Goel 1977). Similarly, the outlooks of the minority
in a society that pays more attention to legal issues and is more active
in the judicial sphere should prove disproportionately influential. I
refer to this minority as the society's 'legal community' (following
Reitz 1996a). Judges, prosecutors, legal consultants, trial lawyers, lawmakers (or those contending to win office), administrative officials
upon whom the state relies to implement policies legally, and others
influential in the legal realm (such as journalists who write specialized
opinion columns), collectively form the legal community. Not only are
they disproportionately important in the evolution of a legal system,
they serve as a bridge between the legal orientations of politicians and
the public. Efforts to identify the legal orientations prevailing among

the members of a country's legal community are particularly likely to shed light on progress toward the rule of law.

Russians' legal orientations can be expected to vary along several key dimensions (and later research can examine how the patterns of legal orientations in Russia differ along these dimensions from the patterns existing in other societies).[5] First, how do Russians understand key terms such as 'the law', 'a law' or a 'law-governed state'? Second, to what degree do Russians believe that law matters and should matter? Such a belief is the opposite of legal 'nihilism': contempt for the law (Sharlet 1978). A belief that law matters also implies, in the case of Russia, the acceptance of what Huskey (1991) calls 'legalism': that law is a 'universal value of human development'. In addition, it implies that law must have primacy over extra-legal factors, such as patronage ties, in resolving a conflict (Huskey 1991, 63).

Third, what provides a judiciary with legitimacy? Is it procedural probity? Or is it the courts' substantive performance? If the latter, do Russians expect their courts (1) to resolve conflicts, (2) to protect society from the state (tyranny), (3) to protect society from its own members (crime), or (4) to promote desirable societal changes? A fourth relevant dimension is litigiousness (Jacob 1996). Do Russians believe that bringing claims before a court is an effective and broadly appropriate way of resolving demands or adjudicating disputes?[6]

Fifth, to what extent do Russians show acceptance of a civil-law perspective as opposed to the common-law orientations prevalent in the Anglo-American tradition? Over several centuries, Russia has been influenced primarily by continental civil-law approaches, although Anglo-American legal ideas had a larger impact than in Central Europe (Reitz 1996a). One practical issue relevant to this dimension is the degree to which legal statutes must be in written form and published, carefully crafted, and prioritized such that statutory law has precedence over substatutory law. (Huskey 1991 discusses how these issues ran through Soviet scholars' debates.)

Sixth, what is the preferred role for law in regulating state-society relations? How deeply do Russians believe that individual rights should be broadly defined and strictly protected? Who do they believe should provide rights protection, courts or state bodies? Huskey (1991, 58, 64–6) points to Soviet-era debates about this issue. Some Soviet legal scholars used to argue against rights protection since socialism had eliminated any contradictions between state and society. A group of scholars emerged in the 1970s who argued for a better balance between state and society, in particular, for greater guarantees for criminal defendants and greater power and independence for the courts. This group gained ground rapidly under Gorbachev and now holds sway in official post-Soviet Russian doctrine. Even so, attachment to the idea of limiting the state might not be widespread outside the elite.

Finally, to what degree is there acceptance of the idea that judicial institutions should be strong: that legal training must be broad and high-quality; that the legal profession must have adequate working conditions; that judges and others should have physical security, adequate offices and courtrooms, and soon; and that the judiciary must be independent from political pressure?

ANALYZING A SOCIETY'S LEGAL ORIENTATIONS

How, then, can one go about answering such questions? No method can be entirely satisfactory because of the inherent unknowability of any individual's values and preferences. Even what an individual says or writes about his or her own views cannot be taken entirely at face value. Nevertheless, differences in how people *present* these views are measurable and serve as effective indicators of actual differences in outlook. (Substantial and important differences in outlook showed up in speeches and writings during the Soviet period despite quite close official monitoring of the content of all publications, as Western scholars demonstrated [among many others, Linden 1966; Tatu 1968; Lodge 1969; Gustafson 1981; Breslauer 1982; Willerton 1992].) So it is vital that scholars pose questions about legal issues either to members of the legal community themselves or, in a sense, to their writings.

Posing the questions to the individuals themselves – that is, interviewing them – might seem the best approach because it is the most direct. It does have several drawbacks, however. Because of the time and expense involved in identifying and locating relevant interviewees, gaining permission for the interview (not possible at all for some individuals who are central to the legal community, such as high court justices) and conducting the interview, it is not possible to interview more than a sample of the legal community. Neither would it be easy to interview a sample sufficiently representative of the entire legal community that one could generalize from patterns in that sample.

Content analysis of the writings of members of the legal community is an alternative technique that can produce a very rich pool of information about these individuals' outlooks.[7] Even given the relatively broad understanding of the legal community presented above, a society's legal community will constitute a small and reasonably well-defined proportion of the populace. The outlets by which members of this community communicate with each other and with the mass public can be identified fairly exhaustively. This makes it possible to analyze something near to the universe of pertinent documents. For example, by carefully choosing the time periods under study (which I discuss below), and even given the need to include different categories within the legal community (see below), the number of documents for analysis becomes manageable.

In addition, content analysis is unobtrusive, whereas the presence of the interviewer can potentially alter answers to surveys (e.g., North *et al*. 1963, 17; Weber 1990, 10). Content analyses need not be strictly quantitative or qualitative in gathering information. A combination appropriate to the object of study can be devised. As with other methods, ensuring the validity and reliability of the conclusions drawn is a key challenge for content analysis. However, much work has gone into devising procedures to test the reliability and validity of content-analytic data (Weber 1990). When properly done, systematic large-*n* content analyses are clearly superior to anecdotal evidence.

I have begun a project to carry out content analyses of Russians, legal orientations. Before describing the first set of findings below, I will now describe in slightly more detail the methodology of this project. It will involve analysing a range of documents from three periods: (1) 1980–1; (2) from mid-1988 to 1991; and (3) 1992–6, the first years of post-Soviet Russia. The first period was the height of the late-Soviet period of 'stagnation' under Leonid Brezhnev. The second was when Mikhail Gorbachev called for debates on the meaning and applicability to the Soviet Union of the concept of the rule of law. Documents from these two periods will provide crucial comparisons to current orientations.

Within each time period, I will be analyzing documents from different sources. It is useful to subdivide the members of the legal community since the writings of each serve different functions. These subdivisions are judges, lawyers (especially legal scholars), informed non-lawyers (e.g., journalists) and political elites. Hence, the categories of relevant writings include: (1) judicial rulings, (2) books and articles by legal scholars, (3) commentary by informed non-lawyers in the mass media, (4) commentary by political elites in speeches and testimony, and (5) mass-oriented books, periodicals and television and radio shows.

Two 'passes' will be made for all documents during the first part of the project: (1) using the document as a 'respondent' and conducting an 'open-ended interview' of the document; and (2) conducting a more quantitative content analysis. The former method has the advantage of allowing careful readings in search of nuances, details of interpretation, and so on. The person coding a given document identifies its answer, if there is one, to each of a series of questions based on the dimensions along which legal orientations are expected to vary. Assumptions or assertions in any document that do not pertain to a specific question yet seem pertinent are also recorded to contribute to my characterization of the author's treatment of the rule of law.

The quantitative approach involves examining the documents for (1) how frequently if at all the author mentions key concepts (measured as the proportion of the document's paragraphs in which reference to the concept occurs); (2) in which affective direction, positively or negatively, the concept is mentioned; (3) any words or phrases of emphasis surrounding the mention ('the *language of insistence, accusation, urgency, and/or defensiveness*' in Breslauer's words [1982, 17; italics in original]); and (4) what other ideas are linguistically linked to the use of the concept. This can be done for a large number of documents with the assistance of textual analysis software now available. The resulting data can then be examined for central tendency, spread and patterns across types of sources, date of publication or social groups.

In sum, the prospect that this approach holds out is to produce both a 'broad' and a 'deep' empirical picture of Russians' legal orientations. In the next section, I illustrate the interview technique discussed above by presenting results from analyzing a small set of pertinent documents.

RUSSIAN LEGAL COMMENTATORS AND THE LAW-GOVERNED STATE

Reflecting the first approach described above, I had native Russian speaking coders read articles from Russian legal journals and books and chapters written by legal scholars and legal professionals during the periods 1980–1, 1988–91 and 1992–6. The journals included *Gosudarstvo i Pravo* [*State and Law*, formerly *Soviet State and Law*], *Zakonnost'* [*Legality*, formerly *Socialist Legality*], *Rossiiskaia Iustitsiia* [*Russian Justice*, formerly *Soviet Justice*], *Vestnik MGU* [*Moscow State University Herald*, Law Series], as well as others.[8] Together, these capture well the range of debate current among the Soviet and later Russian legal community. All articles, chapters and books were coded that dealt with issues of defining law, the place of law in society, or the proper role for the judiciary as a whole or its constituent parts. I use results from 217 sources herein. They include both scholarly articles, in which ramifications for judicial reform may be noted or implied but general arguments are primary (for instance, O.E. Leist, 'Pressing Problems of the Interrelationship of Law and the Statute', *Vestnik MGU*, no. 5 [1988]), and articles by legal practitioners, who more straightforwardly address a matter of judicial practice (such as E. Smolentsev [the Chair of the Russian Republic's Supreme Court], 'Tasks Facing Courts in Modernizing the Judiciary', *Sovetskaia Iustitsiia*, No. 20 [1988]). The coders were asked to determine each document's 'answer' to a series of questions. In some cases, closed-ended options were available for a question. In other cases, the coders characterized the author's probable response based on the arguments in the document.

As I noted earlier, many observers fear that Russia's transition to rule of law will be hindered by the presence of cynicism or disrespect toward the law in the outlooks of either the populace or elites or both (the problem of 'legal nihilism'). So one question I asked of each document was 'Does the author signal any nihilism toward law?' Four possible answers were coded: (1) exclusively nihilist: the author clearly asserts that law and/or legality does not play a role or plays a negative role [possibly because law is a weapon of a ruling class]; (2) relatively nihilist: the author considers law and/or legality temporarily necessary in a socialist state until communism can be reached; (3) relatively anti-nihilist: the author asserts the importance of law and/or legality in Soviet or Russian society but primarily as a tool of statehood and not as a tool of control over the state; or (4) sharply anti-nihilist: the author stresses that legal nihilism must be fought and considers that legality and a culture supportive of law must exist throughout society. The coders were able to ascertain positions in 103 of the 217 sources. The results show that, among this sample of the legal community, legal nihilism is absent. Over 96 per cent of the sources took an exclusively anti-nihilist position. This pattern was the same in all three time periods: nine out of ten coded documents in 1980–81 were exclusively anti-nihilist; 67 out of 69 from 1988 to 1991 and 23 of 24 from 1992 to 1996. As observers of the Russian legal profession have noted, the legal nihilism that came to prominence in the early years of Soviet power was displaced in the post-Stalin era. This pattern does not disprove the concern about legal nihilism in Russia: very different results could emerge when I expand the sample to include writings from non-legally trained politicians and other elites. It is worth noting, however, that members of the Soviet and post-Soviet legal community share this concern for heightening attention to law despite their disagreement on many other fundamental matters.

An issue related to, but distinct from, legal nihilism is whether lawyers see law as solely a reflection of the society's class structure and not as something more autonomous: not, for instance, a 'universal value of human development', in Huskey's (1991) terms. So another question was: 'How class-oriented is the author's view of law?' The possible codings were: (1) exclusively class-oriented: the author argues that the essence of law consists of the will of a ruling class (of the working class in a socialist society); (2) relatively class-oriented: the author argues that in any society law reflects the will of a ruling class yet general human values existing in a given epoch also influence the content of law; or (3) non-class-oriented: the author argues that law flows from general human values that do not inherently favor one class or another. Overall, only 18 per cent of the documents took a codable position on the relationship of law and class. Of those, one-third were exclusively class-oriented, but over half explicitly sought to de-couple law from a class understanding. Not surprisingly, there is a sharp difference across periods. In 1980–1, 10 of the 18 documents made clear a position on the relationship of class and law, and all 10 were class-oriented. In the transition years of 1988–91, when calls for reinvigorating law and the judiciary were ubiquitous, 81 per cent of the documents do not take a class position. Of the 19 that do, two take a pro-class position and 11 are anti-class oriented. After 1991, 90 per cent do not take a position and only one of the ten that do sees law as reflecting social class. In short, statements linking law to the social class structure shift from prevalent in the early 1980s to virtually non-existent from the late 1980s on. The Soviet-style Marxist position on law seems to have few proponents among the Soviet legal community, with pre-Gorbachev statements of belief in that position being part of a necessary posture for publication. In a couple of cases in this sample, the same author's answer to this question changes between the 1980–1 period and later periods.

A third issue, which is highly relevant for understanding the course of Russian legal reform and constitutionalism, is the degree to which Russian lawyers view law in the positive-law manner as the sum of the legally adopted statutes and other rules. The Russian legal tradition stems primarily from the civil-law tradition, which originally took a positivist approach to understanding law. The opposing position, which came to prominence first in common-law traditions, holds that law should be understood as having sources beyond (or perhaps prior to) the statutes, decrees and other rulings that give law enforceable form. An implication of this position is that legally adopted rules can be challenged if they violate an aspect of law in the larger sense, such as certain individual rights. Without denying the complexity of these different perspectives among lawyers in both common-law and civil-law systems today, I believe that these different positions form a spectrum along which individual commentators can be placed. The Soviet official position on the matter was fairly strictly positivist though, as noted above, debates arose in the 1970s.

I therefore asked: 'How positivist is the author's view of law?' The possible answers were: (1) exclusively positivist: law consists of the entirety of the correctly promulgated statutes and other normative instruments; (2) positivist: law consists of the set of statutes but only if those statutes satisfy certain conditions; (3) mixed: the author expresses both positivist and rights-oriented views; or (4) rights-oriented: law flows from common human values that have priority over any statute. Ninety documents took a clear position. Of those, only 19, or 21 per cent, took an exclusively positivist or positivist position. Those taking a rights-oriented position constituted 64 per cent of the total. Again, the change from the pre-Gorbachev period to later periods is dramatic. Six of seven documents in 1980–1 take one of the two positivist positions, with the other being mixed. No rights-oriented position appears. In 1988–91, seven positivist or exclusively positivist arguments appear in the 47 documents (15 per cent), contrasted with 33 (70 per cent) rights-oriented arguments. The percentages from 1992–6 are 17 per cent and 69 per cent.

This pattern is surprising on several counts. Whereas many lawyers could be expected to be uncomfortable with the Soviet-era official view that law stemmed exclusively from the class basis of a society, a positivist position toward law is less clearly an imposition by politicians on expressible legal views. A lawyer can take a positivist position without denigrating law or the importance of legal practitioners. Moreover, the positive view of law has adherents in contemporary Western societies. There was a perceived need in many areas of the Soviet elite, especially during the late 1980s, to reform in a Western, more modern, more 'civilized' direction. Legal reform was no exception, and the search for Western exemplars was common. Yet that trend did not necessarily commend a rights-oriented view of law rather than a more positivist one. (Of course, protection of individual rights has been a critical feature of civil-law systems since the second World War: see Chapter 2, 3 and 4 in this volume.)

The final issue I will discuss is how Russian commentators interpret issues of the rule of law. *Pravovoe gosudarstvo* is the Russian term that comes closest to the English 'rule of law'. Even in Western societies that esteem the rule of law, much debate surrounds the concept (e.g., Dahrendorf 1977; Babington 1978; Neumann 1986; Hutchinson and Monahan 1987; Sejersted 1988; Krygier 1990; Schauer 1991; Shapiro 1994). Whereas in the Anglo-American tradition, the phrase is rule of law, a situation,[9] in the German tradition, the phrase is a noun, *rechtsstaat*, referring to a particular type of state.

> *Rechtsstaat* meant that not the nation, the *volk*, in its historical development, and not natural reason and conscience, but the will of the supreme political authority, the will of the lawmaker, was both the ultimate source and the ultimate sanction of law. Nevertheless, the supreme political authority was to be law-based; the state was to constitute a 'law-state', and not a state ruled by the arbitrary will of an absolute monarch as in earlier centuries. Nor was it to be a *Polizeistaat* – a 'policy' or 'welfare' state ruled by a benevolent autocrat. The *rechtsstaat* was to govern by law and was to be bound by, and not absolved from, the law which it makes. It was not to apply its law inconsistently or otherwise abuse it (Berman 1991, 3).

Yet, after the development of this coherent meaning in the nineteenth century, varieties of interpretations ensued:

> Throughout this century we consequently find *rechtsstaat* is interpreted by the various authors: a) as an equivalent of the constitutional state for its formal guarantees of civil rights; b) as an equivalent of the state recognizing a system of administrative justice; c) in the formalist meaning (made famous by Kelsen) whereby state and law coincide so that each state is a law-governed state; d) as a synonym of rule of law; e) as a notion founding the entire activity of the organs of the state on the principle of 'supremacy of law' (*gospodstvo zakona*) (Berman 1991, 5).

Note that interpretation (a) has become, even in Germany, ascendant since the Second World War II (see Chapters 2 and 3 above).

Pravovoe gosudarstvo, like the German *rechtsstaat*, refers to a type of state and is often translated as 'law-governed state'. Naturally, however, *pravovoe gosudarstvo* developed shades of meaning among Russian legal scholars such that it should not be understood as being exactly similar to the German term. (Arguments about the meaning of *pravovoe gosudarstvo* in Russian legal scholarship can be found in such works as Quigley 1990; Berman 1991; Ajani 1992; Shelley 1992.) The official Soviet approach to the concept was to view it as one of the concepts that capitalist states employ to mask how law maintains the upper class's dominance over the lower. It was a term of denigration that was avoided when referring to the Soviet Union or other socialist systems. It would appear in critiques of Western legal systems, often in quotation marks to convey a sneer.[10] Yet, less than a decade later, the 1993 Russian constitution used the term as a designation of the type of state to which Russia aspired.

I therefore asked 'How does the author understand the term *pravovoe gosudarstvo?*' The possible answers were: (1) *pravovoe gosudarstvo* is a bourgeois conception/lie; (2) *pravovoe gosudarstvo* implies the superiority of statutes, whose content is not limited; (3) *pravovoe gosudarstvo* has a mixed meaning; or (4) *pravovoe gosudarstvo* has a rights-oriented understanding: a law-governed state depends not only on the superiority of statutory law but also the country's statutes must answer to human rights and/or constitutional norms. Of the 82 documents that took a clear position, only one took the hard-line ideological position (it appeared in 1980–1, of course). Eight documents (10 per cent) took a positivist position. Twenty-eight (34 per cent) had a mixed view. A majority of 45 (55 per cent) understood the term to mean the protection of rights. None of the documents in the latter group appeared in 1980–1. While 50 per cent of the documents from 1988 to 1991 took this position, 73 per cent did in 1992–6. As with the previous question, a particular perspective on law and society gains increased prominence over the past decade, one at odds with prevalent positions in the Soviet and pre-Soviet eras.

The rights-oriented perspective becomes predominant in post-Soviet Russia, but the level of attention to the concept of a law-governed state declines during this same period. The number of documents taking a position on the meaning of a law-governed state averages two per year in 1980–1, 13 per year from 1988 to 1991 and five per year from 1992 to 1996. Whereas during the Gorbachev era, all legal issues seemed to be discussed in relation to the need to develop a law-governed state, the popularity of the term in legal writings falls off after 1991. To use the leading journal, *Gosudarstvo i Pravo*, as an example, the phrase appears as part of an article title not at all in 1980 and 1981, 16 times from 1988 to 1991 and once from 1992 to 1996. In the organ of the Ministry of Justice, *Sovetskaia Iustitsiia* (later *Rossiiskaia Iustitsiia*), the phrase does not appear in an article title in 1980–1, appears nine times from 1988 to 1991 and appears only once from 1992 to 1996.[11] Reference to *pravovoe gosudarstvo* has disappeared from the rhetoric of politicians and legal reformers (Solomon 1995, 107). In part, no doubt, this reflects the enshrinement of the law-governed state in the Russian constitution. That Russia should be a law-governed state is no longer a case that needs making. A more important interpretation, though, is that Russian legal scholars have turned to the urgent tasks of legal reform and judicial progress and do not see a need to be guided by general theoretical considerations as much as by practical concerns.

CONCLUSIONS

Content analysis of the writings of Russia's legal community shows promise as a tool for understanding the intersection of legal theory and institutional reform in a post-communist country. Even the preliminary look at these writings presented in this chapter illustrates some surprising features of the Russian legal debate. The degree to which general theoretical positions held by Russian lawyers depart from official outlooks under both Soviet and Czarist regimes is surprising. It is less unexpected, though, in light of post-war international trends. Russian lawyers' views reflect new ways of thinking about the nature of law and the role of the state and of individual rights that have become dominant in the West in recent decades. They also reflect a practice of comparing their country's practices to those of the USA which stemmed from the Cold War rivalry and extended to matters of economics, culture and politics as well as law.

The differences in expressed views among the three periods is also noteworthy. The patterns presented here suggest that legal theorists were quite constrained in presenting their views during the Brezhnev era in the early 1980s. The official perspective on questions of legal theory was not actually deeply held by Soviet lawyers since when they gained permission in the late 1980s to depart from the previous orthodoxy, virtually all of them opposed it. After the initial euphoria of legal reform and discussion of basic issues in legal and political theory, Russian lawyers have tended to focus on practice. Still, the theoretical debates of the middle period, 1988–91, paved the way for fundamental reforms in Russia's judicial institutions. That these reforms are struggling to meet the challenges of post-Soviet legality is not surprising. The struggle is now occurring amid a wide commitment to the importance of a law-governed state and of protecting individual rights.

Notes

1. I thank Peter Solomon as well as the other authors in this volume for helpful comments on an earlier draft. John Reitz and I were able to begin investigating issues of Russians' legal orientations in the summer of 1993 due to an Interdisciplinary Research Grant from the University of Iowa's Obermann Center for Advanced Studies. I thank the Center's director, Dr Jay Semel, and its staff for their support. Coding of Russian texts was made possible by a grant from the University of Iowa's Central Investment Fund for Research Enhancement as well as by grant #SB-9602031 from the National Science Foundation. I thank Tatiana Aleksentseva, Marina Kostina, Lusya Plesskaia, Anastasiia Prianikova and Maria Sokolova for their work coding and entering data, as well as Andrea Morato-Lara for her research assistance.

2. Yeltsin issued a decree on 21 September 1993 that disbanded the Russian legislature with little pretense of constitutional justification but with a clear appeal to the need to resolve the highly polarized deadlock between the legislature and the executive. Many legislators, as well as Vice-President Aleksandr Rutskoi, remained in the legislative building (the 'White House') and called for resistance to Yeltsin's actions. Little changed over the next two weeks, as negotiations facilitated by the Russian Orthodox leadership failed to produce concessions. On Sunday 3 October demonstrators marched to the White House to show support for those inside. In mid-afternoon, Rutskoi gave a speech to these supporters that provoked some to form armed bands and attack the nearby Moscow city government building. Trucks were seized and used to transport more armed people to the central television station and fight to seize control of it. In response, Yeltsin was able to win support from top military leaders to have military units put an end to the attacks and to end the holdout inside the White House. Early the next morning, tanks and artillery surrounded the White House and shelled it, while elite troops entered and fought their way from floor to floor upward to regain control. This action, as well as the fighting in the other buildings in Moscow, caused numerous deaths. Rutskoi and other resisters were arrested (though they would be released six months later in a general amnesty).

3. This court did not have a high public profile until it was called upon in late October 1995 to review the decisions made by Russia's Central Electoral Commission about which political parties would be placed on the ballot for the December parliamentary elections. In a series of decisions, the Court required the Commission to approve several prominent parties whose absence from the ballot would have cast doubt on the fairness of the elections.

4. A recent government resolution specified rules for licensing individuals and firms who provide legal services (Russia and Commonwealth Business Law Report, 24 May 1995). It requires a law degree and three years' experience. Those with a foreign law degree are qualified to offer advice on the law of the country from which they received their degree.
5. For discussions of how single-country case studies may contribute to comparative knowledge, see Campbell (1975); Eckstein (1975); George (1979); George and McKeown (1985); Jervis (1990); Teune (1990).
6. An article in the *Observer* (London) from 27 November 1994 described lawsuits as 'all the rage in Russia's top circle'. Particularly common have become libel and slander suits. Those facing such suits include President Yeltsin, for writing in his autobiography that a legislator in the old Supreme Soviet was a fascist.
7. The outlets for individuals' discussions of legal issues will, of course, have editorial perspectives and preferences. With a large number of documents available, the analyst can examine variation across authors and outlets to assess how strongly the publication source matters.
8. A full list of sources is available from the author.
9. 'The premise or decisive element of the rule of law is not the state, but rather an autonomous, extra-state law – case law or *Juristenrecht*. Rule of law thus exists above all without the state, or, more precisely, where the state does not take the production of law upon itself.' '[C]ivil law terminology does not possess a satisfactory term to translate and express the notion of rule of law. All the translations that include the term "state" (*Rechtsstaat, état de droit, pravovoe gosudarstvo*) are inappropriate in that they misinterpret the essence of the idea of rule of law' (Ajani 1992, 5).
10. Note, though, that critiques of Western practice published in Soviet journals were frequently vehicles for introducing Western ideas into the Soviet debate. Certainly, the explosion of treatments of *pravovoe gosudarstvo* after 1987 suggests that Russian legal scholars had previously been well exposed to the various facets of the concept.
11. The journal does, however, have a periodic rubric, 'The Law-Governed State: Theory and Practice', under which articles of general institutional issues appeared during the latter period.

9 The Success of Judicial Review

Martin Shapiro

COMPARATIVE LAW

Comparative law as practiced by academic lawyers is typically a sterile taxonomy saved by a pragmatic experimentalism. The legal doctrines of two countries are exposed through a careful sifting of statutes, judicial opinions and scholarly commentary. Similarities and differences are noted. For most areas of law in most countries, or at least most post-tribal or post-feudal countries, similarities overwhelm differences. Noticing the dominance of similarity, some authors may then seek the grail of universal legal principles derived from a universal moral or natural or categorical law, or international human rights, or the holy progress of the law, to meet universal human needs. To the less sanguine, the dominant similarities point only to the human concerns for security of person, mine and thine, and family that are indeed universal but are not necessarily moral, progressive or unifying. Others, more struck by the legal differences they observe, turn to adumbrating a global law divided into a number of families: common, civil, Islamic, Socialist, Confucian. These families of law scholarship bear a striking resemblance to the anthropological scholarship of race. First crude, but readily observable, morphological differences served as the basis for building the fundamental or ideal type for each family. Then successively more sophisticated and subtle analyses indicated that certain ranges of variation between the members of each family exceeded that variation between families, that many observable entities exhibit a mix of the basic features of two or more families and that phenomena, which at one level and technique of observation appear strikingly different, at another appear quite similar. The seeming clarity and simplicity of families of law, like races of men, slips back into a chaos of detailed similarities and differences here and there.

This whole exercise also is played out at the level of legal institutions or processes with the same results. Comparative law becomes one of two things. Either it is a kind of curious cultural adornment worn to amuse and amaze the mundane, or it is a catalogue of bits and pieces rather arbitrarily, but nonetheless usefully, arranged to serve the legal bricolateur. If our garden wall of law seems to be crumbling or our door to be sticking, we may leaf through the catalogue to see what we can borrow from some other legal system to mend our legal collapse or friction. Of course, to each call: 'It worked there, it might work here,' comes the response: 'But there is different from here.' Chorus: 'Yes, but not so different. Let's try it and see if it works.' And it does work often enough that a small group of legal scholars keep at it. No doubt the illustrated catalogue will go on-line one of these days.

Social scientists doing comparative law are often up to something different. The comparative method is used as a substitute for the typically unavailable experimental method of theory construction and testing. A general proposition that appears to predict outcomes correctly in one legal environment is tested to see whether it also successfully predicts outcomes in another. Or, put differently, will some causal hypothesis account for the similarities or differences observed in two legal systems? At a more modest level, the social scientist may be content with garnering merely serendipitous understandings. For some reason or other we think we pretty well understand how a certain legal doctrine, device, process, institution, technique or discourse operates in one country. When we stumble on a seemingly similar legal phenomenon in another country, we are led to inquire whether it works similarly there. Or encountering the same problem in two societies we are led to inquire whether the response to it in one society is similar to that we already know occurs in another. Or upon encountering a proposal for legal change in a foreign land, the wise traveler can say, 'Been there. Done that,' and add some cautionary wisdom. As with the lawyers, a kind of *ad hoc* pragmatism is often the best we can hope for but is not to be sneezed at.

The studies in this volume variously mix and match all these comparative methods and motives. They are all concerned with Europe and/or North America. They are mostly about one or another kind of constitutional judicial review, but, taken as a whole, the volume is concerned with statutory as well as constitutional review and with stuff called rights and rule of law.

CONSTITUTIONAL JUDICIAL REVIEW: THE FEDERALISM-ENGLISH HYPOTHESIS

That a volume mostly about constitutional judicial review can be produced with its balance point somewhere in the Atlantic, and pretty far east in the Atlantic at that, tells us something not quite obvious and also leaves us with a central problem of causation. Until after the Second World War, constitutional judicial review (that is, the power of a court to invalidate a statute or other action of government because it is in conflict with the constitution) really flourished[1] in only three countries: the USA, Canada and Australia. This obvious finding of comparative law led to a number of causal hypotheses. First, successful constitutional judicial review is caused by and may be requisite to successful federalism. At the time these three countries were, with one more, the only really working federalisms among the nations of the world. And the one extra, Switzerland, also had a form of judicial review, albeit a much weaker one. This hypothesis was supported by the argument that a federalism required some institution to police its complex constitutional boundary arrangements. In more contemporary, public choice terms, the member states of a federalism have entered into a joint contract, each because it sees more benefit from entering than not entering. Even though each will wish to violate specific terms of the contract from time to time, each will see that it is to its benefit that all others always obey the rules of the contract. Thus each, in spite of its own urges to deviate, will continuously support the creation and maintenance of some institution designed to spot and deter non-compliance by the others.

Against the federalism hypothesis runs the argument that an arrangement which places the third-party conflict resolver between the member states and the central government within the central government itself can hardly make sense to the member states. Why should a state involved in a dispute with the central government support the creation and maintenance of an arm of the central government itself to resolve the dispute, for such an arrangement makes the central government the judge in its own case?

This apparent flaw in member state self-interest as an explanation of constitutional judicial review leads to a second hypothesis. Judicial review is caused by a peculiarly English allegiance to the rule of law plus the peculiar evolution of the British Empire in the eighteenth and nineteenth centuries. Because of the firmly held beliefs in judicial independence, neutrality and fidelity to law prevalent in English-speaking cultures, citizens were prepared to vest the enormous power of constitutional review in courts, and/or member states were willing to allow a court nominally a part of the central government with which it was disputing to resolve the dispute. England itself did not have constitutional judicial review because it was not federal and/or because its seventeenth-century revolutions had not sufficiently disrupted the English political traditions working against judicial review, traditions that had been disrupted by the movement of Englishmen abroad. New Zealand was not federal and South Africa was not English.

The post-Second World War period provides a good but flawed opportunity for substituting comparison for experiment to test the federalism-English hypothesis. A flawed opportunity, of course, because three of the four large nations that moved toward judicial review after the war (Germany, Italy and Japan) did so more or less at the point of a gun. While some will dispute my evaluation, constitutional judicial review has not really worked in India or Japan. It has in Italy and Germany. Neither is English-speaking, and one is federal while the other is not. The pre-war dual hypothesis appears to be disproved. As usual in comparative work, however, the n is so small that the two disconfirming cases may be special exceptions. Germany's long *rechtsstaat* tradition may have substituted for English rule of law ideology so as to give member states confidence in a federal constitutional court. An even more special explanation may apply to Italy. Because of its formal switch of sides in 1943, Italy was not a conquered nation at the end of the war. It was not required to dismantle its old law and start over. It avoided that massive task by keeping its existing body of statutory law but writing a new constitution providing for judicial review. Instead of the massive, concentrated in time, task of rewriting all the accumulated Fascist laws, the Italian constitutional court could and did winnow them case-by-case over time. The success of judicial review in Italy may be attributed to this peculiar Italian situation and so not necessarily undermine the federalism-English hypothesis.

THE DIVISION OF POWERS HYPOTHESIS

The next comparative test was France, neither federal nor English, and indeed with a very vivid anti-judicial tradition. It is here, of course, that Alec Stone's and John C. Reitz's contributions to this volume are crucial. Stone depicts the French Constitutional Council as an enormous success that has become a very powerful participant in the French legislative process. If Stone is correct, then either we must denote France a special case like Italy or modify our federalism-English hypothesis. With France piled on Germany and Italy, and Spain and Hungary to come, it is probably time to abandon the

English portion of the hypothesis entirely. Clearly judicial review can flourish in non-English-speaking environments. It is also time to modify the federalism portion of the hypothesis. Although the US Constitution involved both federalism and a division of powers at the capital (what Americans call separation of powers), Canada and Australia, following the mother country, espoused unified government at the capital, 'parliamentary sovereignty'. Put the USA, England, Australia and Canada together and you appear to get the irrelevancy of the organization of power at the capital to the flourishing of judicial review. The pattern of concentration versus division of capital power does not correlate to the pattern of judicial review. Germany and Italy are parliamentary sovereignty states where review came to prevail. Nevertheless, as Stone has shown, France clearly adopted review in the face of a somewhat hostile political culture precisely because in the Constitution of the Fifth Republic it had chosen to move from parliamentary sovereignty to a system of dividing power between Parliament and presidency. The Constitutional Council is invented for no other purpose than to patrol the boundary between the two. Thus, still content to leave Italy an anomaly, we move to the modified hypothesis that judicial review is caused by a division of powers either federal or at the capital. Because not only division at the capital but also federalism are associated with judicial review our modified hypothesis is saved from too tight a tautology. For if the hypothesis simply read division of powers at the capital causes review, it would not only be disproved by Australia and Canada but would be the proposition 'judicial review causes itself' because judicial review is itself an element of capital division of powers.

There remains the alternative of treating France as a second anomaly along with Italy. There might be two reasons for doing so. The first involves turning Stone's own findings, both those of his own book (Stone 1992) and of his chapter in this book, on their head. In stressing the phenomenon of dialogue between the French legislative chambers and the Constitutional Council, what Stone may be depicting is not a constitutional court but a specialized third legislative chamber. Indeed he himself inclined in that direction in his book on the Council but has tended to drift away or be distracted from that argument as he places the French Council in the context of judicial review in other Western European states. It is easier to make such European comparisons if all the constitutional review institutions are treated as courts. But if what the French have actually concocted is an innovative institutional arrangement that strengthens the capacity of the legislative body to make *bona fide* constitutional decisions about its own legislative initiatives, then France has constitutional review but not judicial review and does not arise to trouble our federalism hypothesis for judicial review. Serious thought must be given to this possibility.

The other route to French exceptionalism lies along the distinction between abstract and concrete review. A distinction long familiar to continental analysts, it is quite strange to those raised in the common law. Perhaps abstract review is so peculiar that it cannot be thrown in with other judicial reviews. Thus as the extreme instance of pure abstract review, France might be entirely excluded from the data used to construct and test hypotheses concerning the causes of successful judicial constitutional review. Indeed, to combine the two routes to French exceptionalism, one might argue that pure abstract constitutional review is what makes the Constitutional Council a third branch of the French legislature rather than a court.

Professor Reitz's treatment of abstract review takes a rigorous and conventional form. Abstract review is treated as the dependent variable, political economy as the independent. However well this research strategy may work for Reitz, it may not help much in regard to our more general judicial review hypothesis for a number of reasons. First the USA does have abstract judicial review well beyond the disguised abstract review cited by Reitz. It has it, however, not in constitutional but administrative law. Pre-enforcement review of agency rules is the norm in federal administrative law. Although such review is not characterized by automatic standing for official parties which is central to Reitz's concerns, it does involve a reviewing court in testing the legal validity of a written norm 'on its face' rather than as applied to a particular set of facts. American academic lawyers raised in the common law tradition do not really have the category 'public law' in their minds, and can easily treat administrative law as irrelevant to constitutional. That is not so easy for American political scientists or continental lawyers. For them the neat division between concrete review in the USA and abstract review in Europe is not so easily maintained.

Second, *from the point of view of fixing the place of judicial review in the whole scheme of constitutional powers*, abstract review in France and Germany may well be seen as *part of* opposing, not complementary, phenomena. Reitz notes, of course, that France employs abstract constitutional review exclusively while Germany mixes abstract and concrete review. In France the exclusivity of abstract review was deliberately employed as a means of limiting review. In Germany the combination of abstract and concrete review was deliberately employed to expand judicial review. Professor Seitzer tells us that Hungary also uses the combination to expand review. A court, conceding for the moment that the Constitutional Council is a court, that is forever debarred from considering the constitutionality of a statute once it is enacted, and entirely debarred from ever considering the constitutionality of government action implementing statutes, is severely handicapped. Indeed the fierceness of the Assembly–Council dialogue that Stone depicts may result largely from the Council's knowledge that it gets only one time at bat. The GFCC, on the other hand, is secure in the knowledge that it gets as many turns at bat as it wants and gets to review the whole range of government actions from statutes through rules and down to individual government decisions implementing rules.

Thus treating the USA as a non-abstract review state and lumping France and German together in the abstract review camp is helpful for some purposes, *especially Professor Reitz's*, but not others. In the context of hypotheses about review, I am inclined to submerge the distinction between abstract and concrete review in Germany, treating Germany as simply having very strong review. Abstract review in France may be treated as either strengthening the third legislative chamber argument or as a purely strategic move to limit the judicial review introduced by the Fifth Republic sufficiently that a hostile French political culture could accept it.

All things considered, I would opt for claiming that the French indeed have achieved a flourishing judicial constitutional review, peculiarly limited by its abstract only character but still roughly comparable to constitutional judicial review elsewhere. If this is so, then I would also opt for modifying the federalism hypothesis for review to a more general division of power hypothesis.

Spain is the next test of the hypothesis. The peculiar regional autonomies of Spain do not rest easily in a federalism formula. And it may well be that the ethnic character of those autonomies undermine the confidence in judicial autonomy and independence that allow the members of most federal systems to have their disputes with central government resolved by a judicial arm of that government itself. Spain has more or less conventional parliamentary sovereignty. The consideration of Spain also makes it imperative for the first time to consider the dreaded topic of rights.

THE RIGHTS HYPOTHESIS

From a purely contemporary perspective, it would appear more than a bit odd to shape hypotheses concerning the flourishing of constitutional judicial review with no consideration of individual rights or civil rights and liberties or human rights. That point is central to Stone's and Seitzer's chapters. Nevertheless the original English-speaking judicial reviews concerned themselves little with individual rights until long after they had achieved institutional legitimacy. The German Court obviously was founded in part to protect individual rights and has done a flourishing rights business from the beginning. Yet Germany's highly complex federalism would have necessitated constitutional judicial review even if there had been no concern for constitutionalizing individual rights. The French Constitutional Council and the ECJ have miraculously found bills of rights in constitutions that clearly do not contain them, but both did so in the context of an already firmly established division of powers jurisprudence. Only in Israel might it be fairly said that constitutional rights have generated judicial review. Indeed, in Israel the Supreme Court has generated a constitutional law of rights and judicial review to enforce those rights in the face of a dramatic failure even to promulgate a constitution. Israel can join Italy in our anomalies bag.

Spain, then, becomes crucial. The Spanish Constitution clearly grew as much or more from a concern for post-Fascist individual rights as from division of powers concerns. As already noted, constitutional judicial review is not especially promising as a tool for containing the centrifugal forces of regional, ethnically-based, autonomy. The SCT has done a flourishing rights business from the beginning. Unfortunately, not enough is known about Spanish judicial review, at least by me, to say whether Spain is the straw which, along with Italy and Israel (and the ECHR which I shall take up shortly), breaks the back of the division of powers hypothesis. It may well be that we must now entertain two, not necessarily mutually exclusive, hypotheses. Division of powers systems generate judicial review. Ideological commitments to individual rights generate judicial review. But for the ECJ, we might even time-stage these hypotheses. Those polities which first adopted judicial review did so because of division of powers. Right concerns engendered recent judicial review. More probably: rights-generated judicial review now takes its place beside division of powers-generated judicial review with the expectation that both kinds will be found in the future. Most probable: a conjunction of division of powers and rights concerns is most likely to generate successful review.

It must be noted that while the ECHR is chock-full of rights and morals, it is also chock-full of division of powers. The ECHR is not part of any conventional state. It is an organ of the 'Council of Europe' which itself is a loose association of a number of European states, some kind of international organization; but, even in that amorphous realm, one with little concrete existence or day-to-day operation besides the Convention system itself. Technically speaking, the Convention lies in the realm of international not constitutional law, so that the Court does not do constitutional judicial review. It is not quite right totally to ignore this technicality. The basic question we are really asking when we ask what causes successful constitutional judicial review is 'Why do politically powerful entities obey the orders of constitutional courts?' The ECHR is successful precisely because the obligation to obey of the member states is reduced to the level prevalent in international law from that prevalent in constitutional law. Essentially the Court must negotiate with an aberrant member state with the aim of persuading it to change its practice or its legislation. While to some degree member states feel some compulsion to defer to the Court's judgments, those judgments are directed to admittedly sovereign states. Yet the Court has rendered enough judgments that have caused enough changes in state practices so that it can be counted to a rather high degree as a constitutional judicial review court in the light of the realities, as opposed to the technicalities.

The Court of Human Rights does not follow the pattern of a court established to police division of powers which later takes on rights jurisdiction. It was indeed established to do rights business and only rights business. On the other hand, it is entirely a creature of a division of powers system with extremely weak powers given to the centre and most powers reserved to the periphery. If the question being tested is, 'Does division of powers or rights ideology generate judicial review or do older judicial reviews depended on division of powers and recently established ones on rights?', the Court of Human Rights is simply a bad test. It too thoroughly conflates division of powers and rights, in too peculiar a context, to help us much in constructing a theory of successful constitutional judicial review.

For a number of obvious reasons it is convenient to turn next to the ECJ which is the subject of Professor Kenney's chapter. It is a remarkably successful constitutional judicial review court. Indeed it picked itself up by its own bootstraps having, by self-proclamation, converted itself from an international law to a constitutional law court. It has created a large body of constitutional jurisprudence that has become largely, if not entirely, a part of routinely enforced law of the forum of the fifteen member states of the EU. Established in the 1950s and reaching full bloom by the late 1960s, this Court certainly tends to confirm the division of powers hypothesis. Although it has also self-proclaimed an individual rights jurisdiction, clearly the overwhelming bulk of its business has been division of powers. And while, like the USA and Germany, from its origins it has done both areal[2] and capital division of powers cases, like both of them, too, areal division of powers cases far, far outnumber capital cases. Although it is frequently and correctly claimed that the EU is not a conventional federal state but *sui generis*, it is also frequently and correctly claimed that, unlike the European Convention on Human Rights, the EU treaties are constitutional not international law, and the ECJ unlike the ECHR is a constitutional not an international court. There is no question that the ECJ fits the model of a constitutional court which is successful because it assures each member state that the others will obey the rules.

Next we may turn to the UK. It is typical of a volume on European judicial review that everyone else will be talking about constitutions and/or treaties while the commentator on the UK will be talking about statutes, for we all know that the UK has neither written constitution nor constitutional judicial review. Professor Sterett's contribution to this volume and other work of hers (Sterett 1997) shows the degree to which administrative judicial review and statutory interpretation are a kind of quasi-constitutional review in the UK. Indeed, basing ourselves in Sterett's work, and what Stone's chapter has to say about the duty of member state courts of the EU to interpret domestic law in the light of EU law, and following the vogue of speaking of 'soft law', we might begin to speak of a 'soft constitutional judicial review' whose vehicle is purported statutory interpretation. The American rule that a statute must be interpreted if possible so as to save its constitutionality is familiar to most constitutional scholars. Various pronouncements of the House of Lords that English law is to be interpreted in light of the assumption that Parliament intended to conform itself to the European Convention on Human Rights may be less familiar. Such judicial practices boldly employed can sometimes veto a statute just as much as an outright finding of unconstitutionality.

No matter how strong a face may be put on soft constitutional judicial review in the UK, however, that polity can hardly be counted as an instance of successful constitutional judicial review. Admittedly the matter is one of degree, but not in form, substance, quantity or quality of policy influence do British courts yet come up to legitimate and effective constitutional judicial review powers. No matter what the past and future arrangement for the various Celtic lands, the UK is a land of Parliamentary, not divided, government. And it is a land in which self-satisfaction about the rights of Englishmen under common law has dampened ideological concerns for independent constitutional guarantees of private rights.

Insofar as the UK has been feeling external pressures toward soft constitutional judicial review, they have come from the rights-based, but anomalous, European Convention on Human Rights and from the division of powers-based EU. Perhaps the most important UK phenomenon for our purposes has been the organized and vocal sentiment there in favor of a written constitution. While some of that sentiment sounds in pro division of powers antipathy toward Parliamentary sovereignty, clearly central to the movement has been the urge for a written, judicially enforceable bill of rights. In this sense the UK might be taken as evidence for the rights hypothesis: that is, that contemporary constitutional judicial review is based in rights rather than division of powers concerns. On the other hand, the movement in the UK has not succeeded, which may be taken either as evidence that rights concerns there are not strong enough to generate review or that, *contra* the rights hypothesis, rights concerns are not enough to trigger successful review.

POST-LENINIST REVIEW

It is this proposition, that rights concerns are not enough to trigger successful constitutional judicial review, on which the newest developments in constitutional construction allow us to get some comparative handle. In relation to hypothesis testing we face the following situation at the point that the post-Leninist states[3] appear to allow us our next round of comparisons. The federalism hypothesis, modified after France into the division of powers hypothesis, remains our best hypothesis. Italy, Israel, the ECHR and perhaps Spain lead to an alternative individual rights hypothesis. It is also possible to state the two hypotheses not as mutually exclusive alternatives but as a time-staged, branching pair: all older, and some newer, successful constitutional judicial reviews are caused by division of powers but tend to add individual rights-based legitimacy over time, and some more recently established successful, constitutional judicial reviews are wholly rights-based. The post-Leninist states present us with an interesting mix of division of powers and rights concerns.

It might be tentatively offered as a general proposition that constitution drafters will divide what they fear most in the central government. In earlier times legislatures were feared most, and where new constitutions were to be federal, a legislative house for the member states was also used. So in the USA and Germany we get the dual purpose two-house division. The post-Leninist states come out of an experience of an excessively concentrated executive but one in which the excessive concentration usually existed behind constitutional forms involving both Prime Minister and President titles. When they write their new constitutions, such states naturally – but paradoxically – adopt the French model and divide their executive authority between President and Prime Minister. I say paradoxically because the French division between President and Prime Minister was intended to strengthen, not weaken, executive authority. Nevertheless when the post-Leninist states opted for a division of executive authority, in my view at least, they virtually were constrained also to adopt constitutional judicial review, just as the French were. The constitutional judicial review being adopted by the post-Leninist states seems to me a major confirmation of the division of powers hypothesis.

Professor Seitzer tells quite a different story about Hungary. It is clear, of course, that fear of concentrated power and concern for individual rights are an indivisible package in the post-Leninist states. Thus they will not easily allow us to separate division of powers from rights as bases for judicial success. Moreover, we do not yet know whether constitutional judicial review will flourish in most of these states. The Russian Constitutional Court self-destructed in circumstances that make *Dred Scot* look like a self-inflicted scratch. Perhaps sometime or other it will reconstruct. Only in Hungary do we have what appears to be a clear-cut post-Leninist judicial success story. No doubt that is why Seitzer chose to write about it. You cannot write much about things that have not happened. But, from all accounts I have read, the Hungarian case breathes peculiarity. The political relationship between the legislature and the executive in Hungary remains highly tense and uncertain. There is an understandably chaotic quality to partisan politics which for the moment makes the Constitutional Court appear to be an attractive alternative. The Court's most significant decisions really have been neither about division of powers or rights but about a populist resistance to World Bank pressures to end the fiscal insanity almost inevitable in the radical economic shifts taking place. This move may well be a strategically wise one for the Court in terms of establishing long-term legitimacy, and certainly wiser than the early political moves of the Russian Court. But its very wisdom lies in avoiding any test of whether a committed legislative or popular majority will yield to judicially imposed rights constraints. Ordering the Hungarian Government not to obey the World Bank is equivalent to Marshall's great *Marbury* move of ordering his own court not to exercise some of the powers given it.

It may take comparativists a long time to discover whether the post-Leninist states as a whole will tend to confirm the hypothesis that rights ideology can generate successful constitutional judicial review. As Seitzer carefully notes, the situation in Hungary is very peculiar and complex. Standing alone and now it simply may not help us much in theorizing about judicial review.

Theorizing about review, however, may help us a good deal in dealing with the situation in the post-Leninist states. The rivalry between the division of powers and rights hypotheses alerts us to the problematic nature of ideological commitment to rights as a basis for a flourishing judicial review. The three most successful and extensive judicial reviews are those of the USA, Germany and the EU. All three are division-of-powers based. Two of the three also do have major rights components which may indeed well have outstripped their division of powers concerns. And there is a special reason why the third, that of the EU, does not: the parallel existence of the ECHR. For the USA and Germany, however, the basic story may well be not one of review standing equally on the two legs of division of powers and rights, but of economic and political elites and institutions being compelled to accept judicial protection of rights in order to get the judicial review needed to make a division of powers system work. Certainly that is what has happened in France. Judicial review courts in those countries have the security of constantly saying tacitly that no matter how much you dislike our rights decisions, you cannot do without us if you want to keep the basic institutional processes running.

There are two underlying assumptions here. One is that ideological rights commitments tend to be diffuse and relatively disinterested, and thus to yield to the more focused and self-interested policy needs of the moment. The other is that division of powers commitments are powerfully institutionalized and may be heavily freighted with economic interest. Germany truly may have a two-legged review or even one in which rights have been the stronger leg from the very beginning. A number of very special factors, however, complicate the German situation. Obviously the immediate pre-history of German review is one. A second is the continuous presence of the armies of foreign states interested in imposing a rights regime on the Germans. (This factor tends to be ignored by admirers of German political development.) A third is the Cold War division of Germany that rendered West German individual rights and liberties a display piece against the rival East German regime. And most importantly German judicial review flourishes against the background of the German economic miracle. People who are getting rich find it easy to love rights.

If, then, of the three greatest judicial review success stories we stick to the USA and the EU, the story is fairly persuasively one of economic and political elites accepting judicial review for the protection of rights as a minor cost of the benefit of review in the maintenance of the division of powers. Both the USA and EU were established largely to achieve the benefits of a large free trade area that, for political reasons, can only be achieved by creating a federal or transnational political regime. In both, the judicial review court spends almost all of its energies in the institutional formative years of that regime in backing the very interests in free trade that were sufficiently dominant to create the regime in the first place. Both do so by review that quells sporadic member state resistance and generally strengthens the hands of the new central institutions. Neither does any substantial individual rights business during the period in which its judicial review powers are being firmly established and legitimated. The ECJ is only dragged into the rights business as a kind of compelled addenda to keeping its essentially economic division of powers business going successfully.[4] The US Supreme Court takes itself out of most rights business in a Marshall Court decision (*Barron* v. *Mayor and City Council of Baltimore*, 1833). After the Civil War, when the Court, along with all the other institutions of American government, has to rebuild its legitimacy, it does so by a vigorous defense of corporate power against populist government regulation. (The Court of Justice has exhibited similar tendencies.) The New Deal and Warren Courts, which turned review into a rights ratchet machine, did so on the basis of a stored legitimacy for review that had been built up through over a century of service to free trade and corporate growth.

The point for the post-Leninist states is obvious. The rights successes of the Warren Court that have so colored international thinking about human rights, and the major successes of review in Europe, should not make us overly sanguine about the capacity of new courts armed with new judicial review to act as a primary force in the initiation of new rights. Hungary is an interesting testing ground and worth the attention that Seitzer and a number of other political scientists are giving it, but it may be a very special place.

RUSSIA

The key case, not so much for social science as for the world, is of course Russia. Professor Reisinger's contribution to this volume is not specifically about constitutional judicial review in Russia, in part for the very good reason that as yet there is none. It remains to be seen whether the second constitutional court will shoot itself in the foot as badly as the first one did. Reisinger focuses on the rule of law as the foundation for any and all future Russian legal developments. And he rightly differentiates between various aspects or definitions of the rule of law and the *rechtsstaat*. The failure to do so confuses much scholarly commentary on rights and judicial review. The evolution of judicial review in Russia clearly depends initially on the redevelopment of the whole system of law and courts in that country. Reisinger's pioneering efforts remind us that a number of pitfalls lie in our way in studying that redevelopment.

The most important stem from our general lack of skill as comparativists. As Reisinger points out, Russia lies in the civil, not the common, law tradition. American lawyers and political scientists are likely to have a hard time with civil law, tending to fall back on clichés almost unconsciously even though at some level they know better. Common law systems are case law systems. Civil law is statutory. The common law traditions emphasizes suprastatutory or natural legal rights. Civil law is positivism. The statutes are the source of rights. Common law judges and lawyers employ the common law method of *stare decisis*, case-by-case inclusion and exclusion and analogy. Civil lawyers work from the statutory text. Common law is adversarial. Civil law is inquisitorial. All of these statements are far more false than true. Americans who specialize in the study of Western European law know all this and use it constantly in their daily work. Americans who now begin studying Russian law are not really doomed to spend a whole generation repeating the mistakes common lawyers made about civil law two or three generations ago. Get up to speed in civil law before studying Russian law.

A number of other obsolescences are likely to hamper our entry into Russian law. I can only briefly enumerate a few of them here. In general, out of our particular concern for rights and because of Soviet terror practices, we are likely to have an excessive concern for Russian criminal law and courts. The Soviet arbitrage system was the one truly socialist feature of Soviet law. It was almost unknown to Americans. As Reisinger points out, the division between arbitrage and civil and criminal law is being maintained in post-Soviet Russia. It is in the arbitrage or commercial courts that the really important law of Russia will be done (Hendley, forthcoming). The business of law is business. If real respect for the rule of law is to emerge in Russia, these are the crucial courts. If ten times more Americans are not studying the arbitrage courts than the criminal courts, we are just being stupid.

Similarly the normal English translation of procurator is prosecutor. That translation is wrong. The procurators' offices do criminal investigation and prosecutions, but they also exercise general oversight of the lawfulness of all activities of government. Even when privatization is much further along than at present, the procurators will be performing major oversight of many large economic enterprises. The main job of the procurators has been, and apparently will continue to be, in the realm of administrative law, overseeing the lawfulness of the activities of government administrative agencies. Let us not commit the foolishness of setting our too numerous criminal justice specialists on to the procurators, leaving out of account their vast administrative oversight jurisdiction.

More generally let us not make the mistake again of caring too much about constitutional law and too little about everything else. This point returns us to Reisinger's useful distinctions among the various rules of law. The most primitive meaning of rule of law is that government should obey its own laws until it chooses to change them. As legal theorists or constitutional scholars we are far more concerned with a more advanced notion of rule of law that contains an element of individual rights above and beyond the everyday law. Indeed we are so much more concerned that we frequently forget that the more advanced meaning is entirely dependent on the more primitive one, and that unless the government is prepared to obey its own laws, higher law rights are not going to make any difference. The first and most fundamental rule of law problem is Russia is not about higher law rights but about the most mundane and routine obedience of government officers to regular laws. That is, Russia's biggest problems are in the realm of administrative, not constitutional, law.

In this sense Reisinger's quotation about the Russian problem being that it is a government of directives rather than statutes is informative but has a tendency to misdirect. The key problem is that Soviet administrative directives were not subordinated to statutes. The problem today is as much the administrative law problem that Russian administrative agencies' rules, regulations and decisions are not adequately grounded in and controlled by the statutes that do exist, as the more constitutional problem that government often acts without bothering to pass a statute.

These areas of commercial and contract law, procuratorial administrative oversight and administrative law more generally are important to us as scholars not only because they are intrinsically important in the real world but for another reason as well. I return here to my distrust of the rights hypothesis. I remember that as an undergraduate I came upon Dwaine Marwick, for whom I worked, laughing as he refereed a paper for the then-titled *Western Political Quarterly* which began something like, 'Out of the desire of the citizens of Logan [or maybe it was Ogden or Provo], Utah, for places of beauty and family recreation came the municipal public park system.' Dwaine's comment was, 'Or out of the desire of someone to unload some land on the city at a profit.' It seems to me unlikely that a strong general affection for individual rights is either a necessary or sufficient condition for constitutional judicial review or the rule of law. Echoing Locke, Weber and many others, it appears more likely that triadic conflict resolution is established for the convenience of potentially conflicting economic interests, that the triadic figure finds it convenient to announce (discover, make) substantive rules on which to base his or her decisions, and that the parties find themselves willy-nilly conceding the legitimacy of the rules as the price of enjoying the conflict resolution services.

In Russia it may matter far less whether the scholars or the political classes or the elites proclaim fidelity to law than that economic elites find a working court system with reliable verdicts and remedies essential to their own economic well being. Fidelity to law is likely to emerge, if it emerges anywhere, in the arbitrage courts. Rule of the law in the more primitive sense is likely to emerge, if it emerges anywhere, in the procurators' government regulation jurisdiction and the courts the procurators invoke. The fate of Russian constitutional judicial review is more likely to depend on the general success of the legal system in providing the services economic elites want than on a general commitment to individual rights.

If the constitutional ought not to blind us generally to the other areas of Russian law that Reisinger begins to uncover for us, neither should we fall into one of the special blind spots of constitutional scholarship. What for many years has been a commonplace of the more advanced political science teaching on constitutional law, and is now enshrined in a striking new volume on the subject (Hoffman 1997), is that constitution writers and readers normally skip the two most crucial institutions of modern industrial democracies: parties and bureaucracies. Given the historical background, no student of Russian affairs is likely to miss bureaucracy even if his or her starting point is an orientation in American constitutional law. Academic lawyers are so enamored of judicial independence that typically they avoid seeing any connection between courts and political parties and denounce any connections they do see. The fact that all successful, domestic, constitutional judicial review systems (but not the ECJ and the ECHR) are associated with more or less democratic competitive party systems may help to remind us that the political parties court connection is not always and necessarily a negative one. Russia, the other former Soviet pieces, the eastern European states, Mongolia, Taiwan, South Korea, Mexico, Chile and other states are currently possibly on the move from non-competitive to competitive party systems. It may well be that competitive party systems are a necessary condition to constitutional judicial review. (The curiously muted nature of judicial review in Japan may be partially a result of the curiously muted nature of electoral competition there (Ramseyer 1994).) In spite of our distaste for party bosses calling judges on the phone, we ought now to undertake the direct investigation of the relation between parties and judicial review that has been missing from most American constitutional scholarship, and this need is particularly pressing in Russian studies.

JUDICIAL SELF-DEFENSE

The general story of successful constitutional judicial review is one of other powerful political actors accepting some level of judicial policy-making as an inevitable cost of getting what they want from courts, namely third-party conflict resolution of particular kinds of dispute. I have argued here that division of power boundary disputes are those most likely to motivate such actors, but that a plausible case can also be made out for rights disputes. The political world is unlikely to be as simple as this. Major phenomena tend to be overdetermined, the product of multiple causes. And long-term fundamental human motivations are frequently perturbed by shorter-term considerations that may destroy relatively quickly what has been built up slowly over time. It is unlikely that long-term needs for conflict resolution would sufficiently protect constitutional judicial review from the crises of opposition that it almost inevitably engenders from time to time in any polity in which it operates. Indeed, we can hardly deem constitutional review to be successful in a particular polity unless it has sufficient impact to engender heated opposition from time to time.

So we must consider the institutional self-defense capacities of courts as well as the basic motivations of other political players if we are to account for successful review. Obviously the first such defensive resource is precisely that constitutional judicial review is wielded by things that are usually called and act like courts. A lot of the resources that have been poured into creating the vision of the independent, neutral, law-serving rather than law-making judiciary create a kind of fund of legitimacy that a judicial review court attacked for its policy interventions can draw on. The concentration of Seitzer on rule of law reminds us of this defense, but the contributions of Stone and Reitz indicate that some polities fairly clearly differentiate constitutional 'courts' from other courts and constitutional review from routine judicial decisions. In those polities constitutional courts have less ability to call upon general judicial legitimacy for protection. The *Marbury* formula of concrete review obviously packs the most punch. 'We judges do constitutional review only because we cannot help doing so in the routine disposition of ordinary cases and precisely because it is part of our judicial routine we do it impartially, neutrally and as the law dictates just as we do everything we do.' Abstract review, particularly where concrete review is not present, most clearly strips reviewers of their judicial cover. Yet it may be possible to build up the judicial image even under such circumstances, as the French Constitutional Council has shown.

In the contemporary world the identification of constitutional judicial review with rights may itself provide a powerful defense. While I have voiced my doubts about rights as a foundational cause of successful review, there is no question that on any given day in many contemporary polities, judicial review gets as much support from rights as rights get from judicial review. This theme of the mutual, interacting support of rights and courts and of rights-oriented interest groups and judges, with much post-modern talk of constituting *autopoesis*, fields, and whatnot, is central to much contemporary legal scholarship. The capacity of constitutional judicial reviewers to depict themselves as rights preservers rather than interest servers is an important one. It is often difficult to isolate, however. In Seitzer's Hungarian case, for instance, it is difficult to tell whether the Court's kudos derives from popular loyalty to rights or from the popular perception that in the face of paralysis in the Parliament and executive, the Court is the only port in the storm, that judicial policymaking is preferable to no policymaking.

The most fascinating self-defense resource, long obvious to (but lacking systematic analysis by) judicial scholars, is the proclivity of courts to make low visibility, incremental, case-by-case, cumulative, seemingly 'technical' decisions exhibiting a particular capacity to manipulate short- and long-term outcomes. Although occasionally constitutional judgments are high visibility, most are not. Many that are involve a lot of misdirection in which controversy is concentrated on immediate minor matters, while the big judicial policy initiative remains more or less in hiding. Here again Reitz's discussion of abstract versus concrete reviewer is highly relevant, as is the limitation to institutional parties of access to review discussed by Stone, Seitzer and Reitz. Most of the decisions of the judges that Kenney studies, which have literally 'constituted' the legal order of the European Communities (that is, converted it from a field of international to a field of constitutional law), were made in cases involving private parties and trivial stakes.

Individual judicial decisions are inherently low visibility ones, but judges can work to make them more so in many different ways. Perhaps the most important of these is the judicial strategy of favoring one interest in the immediate outcome of a case and quite a different one in its long-term effect, particularly its cumulative effect in conjunction with other equally unheralded decisions. Judges are past masters at awarding immediate victory in a particular case to one party while planting doctrinal seeds that will eventually favor the other. And when the seeds sprout, the judges can quiet the complaints that finally arise by pointing out that their new policy is really no change at all, or only a tiny change from long established law (namely the seeds they planted earlier). One way of putting this is in terms of time horizons. The politicians who potentially oppose judges are satisfied with short-term victories, or at least 'not on my watch' defeats. The judges can, through a host of legal techniques, award immediate victory or non-defeat to their most dangerous potential opponents while moving the legal doctrine toward an eventual outcome that would have engendered highly destructive opposition if incorporated in actual results the day it was announced. *Marbury* itself is a classic example, but any constitutional scholar can provide dozens of others.

Low visibility policymaking may be particularly successful in the current hyperpluralist state of democratic politics. It may always have been a key to the survival of judicial policymaking in polities where other political actors had superior political resources.

Yet we are not at all certain that judges really have longer policy time horizons than other politicians. I am not talking about the law working itself clear. Least of all am I talking about the virtues of the common law because this kind of constitutional case-by-case manipulation is as prevalent among civil as common law constitutional judges. What is involved here is the great, although admittedly not unique, capacity of judges to manipulate the relationship between which party wins how much in a particular case, against the legal significance of that case for later cases. Not only is this manipulation difficult for outsiders to spot, but it is incredibly difficult to get the public interested in. Rather like incremental budgeting, by the time the public is aware, it is too late both because the final outcome is by then a *fait accompli* and because there has been time for the proponents of the new policy to recruit a support coalition.

All of this is only partly a matter of smoke and mirrors. Incrementalism is, by and large, a pretty good decision strategy. It certainly does not guarantee success. But it does allow the decisionmaker a high level of risk reduction and the improvements in policy and reduction in unanticipated consequences yielded by feedback. Again, these are certainly not uniquely judicial virtues. Other policymakers follow incremental strategies too. And judges, particularly constitutional judges, sometimes do go too far too fast. Nevertheless, the whole loading of the judicial process toward case-by-case policy making probably ensures for the judges a relatively high batting average for workable outcomes.

There is much talk these days of epistemic communities and their power in policymaking. Such communities are powerful both because of the knowledge they have and the knowledge others do not. Judicial decisions are low visibility to most of us, high visibility to lawyers; incomprehensible to most of us, native tongue to lawyers. Political science has had a lot of trouble getting to the study of lawyers, usually leaving them to sociologists. Academic lawyers have had similar troubles because they have trouble studying anything but law as such. All this is now changing,[5] but it is still not easy to persuade those in comparative politics that lawyers are so politically significant an elite that they ought to be permitted admission to the purview of comparative politics studies in a way engineers and architects are not. Yet one very important dimension of the self-defense armory of constitutional judicial reviewers is their embeddedness in the epistemic community of lawyers, and particularly academic constitutional lawyers.

It is not so much that such lawyers provide defenses for particular constitutional decisions. After all, they provide attacks as well. Rather it is that the constitutional law community provides a continuous and spirited defense of judicial review, although a peculiar kind of defense. We all know that the most prominent spokespersons against the general institution of judicial review as well as those in favor are constitutional lawyers. Yet constitutional lawyers, both practitioners and academic commentators (often both at the same time), by the very nature of their daily occupation, turn what judicial review judges say into the constitution. In countries that have constitutional judicial review, it is constitutional law and not the constitution that is the operative force. And in all such countries constitutional law is the case law. The constitution is what the judges say it is and what the commentators say the judges say it is. Here again this is as true in civil as common law countries. Nothing could be more clever than the production by French constitutional lawyers of a volume that melds the language of the constitution and the language of the cases into a book that presents itself as a quasi-official French constitutional code (Renoux and de Villiers 1994).

Academics are important to the extent that the subjects they teach are important. European constitutional law teachers went from the bottom of the pecking order as teachers of something like Freshman civics, to near the top of the order as constitutional judicial review came to flourish on the Continent. And just as that particular body of law made more of them, they made more of it. For it or against it in general and in particular outcomes, the professors made it important, made it law and made it the special esoteric domain of lawyers. And practitioners, who suddenly discovered a new source of income and prestige in constitutional litigation, joined in. (On the Continent many prominent practitioners are academics as well or primarily.)

Along with support, of course, comes the implicit claim to monopoly and the practices that will make good the claim. Constitutional law – that is, the decisions of the constitutional judges – like other law, is for the lawyers. No one else can understand it. But more important, it may not be spoken of except in the language of the law. Judicial review gets relatively little public attention not only because it is a low visibility, small stakes case by small stakes case, decision but because it is lawyers' business not the public's business.

The epistemic community that surrounds the constitutional courts may be cantankerous and ideologically divided on many issues, but it is united in the belief that the law is important, the law belongs to them and ultimately the law is what the lawyers say it is. Even at the height of the New Deal and liberal academia, the USA never experienced an epistemic executive sycophancy equivalent to the constitutional judicial review sycophancy that has continuously marked American life. The role of a relatively small group of academic lawyers and specialized practitioners in promoting the ECJ has been enormous and, as Kenney indicates, there is considerable overlap between the ring and the membership of the Court itself. Similar stories could be told in Germany and Italy, and most particularly in France. To go back to an earlier theme, there is no reason why the comparative study of judicial review should go through the same stages of selective blindness as did the study of American review. We should be after the lawyers from the start. And we should be aware that we are encountering one of the most politically powerful of the epistemic communities.

JUDICIAL WILL

No doubt there is much more to be said about the institutional defense mechanisms of constitutional judicial review, and no doubt much more will be said as comparative judicial review studies mature. Even if we were firmer in our hypotheses about the causes of review, and more systematic in our understanding of its self-defense mechanisms, however, we still would have a devilishly hard time predicting precisely when and where large-scale judicial policymaking would take place. No doubt it is true that the refusal to make new policy or change existing policy is itself a policy decision and one that often has enormous policy impact. Policy initiation is, however, what we are bound to be most interested in. And, no matter what their institutional strengths and defenses, with very rare exceptions, judicial review judges do not have to initiate new policies unless they want to.

The contributions of Professors Buss and Kenney to this volume bear on this question of judges' volition to make policy.

Kenney's work gives us a great deal about both why the ECJ attempted so much and why it got away with so much of what it attempted. If the ECJ had been used by the member states as an honorific retirement for senior career judges, its whole history might well have been quite different. Instead its judges have been a mix of politicians, experienced administrators, law professors and practitioners, as well as career judges. Moreover many of those with administrative experience had spent their time in their country's foreign ministry or ministry of justice, and many of the professors have been international or comparative law specialists. Nearly all have been public rather than private law specialists. When a French appointment comes from the French judiciary, it is typically from the Council of State rather than the regular courts. As Kenney also notes, political party affiliation plays a major part in many of the member states' appointments and, reading between her lines, it is pretty clear that a substantial number of the judges who have not been professional politicians have been politically active and strongly identified with party stances on legal issues. From her work it is also clear that a large number of those appointed had been active proponents of European integration before their appointments. This in a set of people unlikely as judges to sit back and let the world roll by. I think further extension of her work would show that the proportion of active proponents of integration was highest in the early period of the Court and the proportion of relatively routine former senior members of national judiciaries is highest now. Whether successful institutionalization of a constitutional court tends to lead to its incorporation into routine civil-service style judicial personnel systems, and consequently into less policy activism, is an interesting research question in Europe. Such an argument may be made about the GFCC and might account for some of the tendency toward judicial self-restraint evident in the more recent years of the ECJ.

Professor Buss's contribution to this volume proceeds largely at the level of culture and its effect on legal doctrine. But of course judges must be the carriers of culture if it is to become a key determinant of legal doctrine. Buss makes out a fair case for the proposition that the Canadian Supreme Court justices chose not to be judicially active in the hate speech case; that is, they chose not to strike down the statute involved because they liked that statute. No matter how potentially active a court may be, it does not act if its judges do not want to. In fact, the Canadian Supreme Court has been a particular consumer of fashionable legal chatter from south of the border. It frequently buys American-made goods that the natives have rejected. And more generally the Canadian legal academy tends to buy American critical legal scholarship much faster than the American academy. Ever since Skokie, with a few notable exceptions,[6] American free speech specialists have been peddling not freedom of speech but speech regulation. In the McCarthy period, when it was conservatives who wanted to limit speech in the interest of national security, the legal academy provided a thousand reasons not to. In a later period when it is liberals who want to limit speech in the interest of assorted underdogs, legal academics have found a thousand reasons in favor. For the last twenty years US free speech literature largely has been a hymn to stopping the speech of the bad guys, although a different set of bad guys from those who so alarmed us in the 1950s. Canadians read American law reviews too much.

All this is not necessarily to disagree with Buss. It may well be that American judges have been less eager and Canadian judges more eager to buy the new enemies list (racists, sexists, pornographers, homophobes, tobacco advertisers, pedophiles) touted so vigorously by the critical thises and thats of the American legal academy precisely because American culture in general is more resistant than Canadian to anti-speech moves. Certainly Canadian culture, perhaps more than any other in the world, is dedicated to being boring, and free speech is surely a threat to boredom.

Perhaps an additional dimension might be added to the cultural analysis of the Canadian scene. Until the new Canadian charter replaced (sort of) the old constitution (the British North American Act), Canadian judicial review was mostly federal division of powers review. In this area British judicial experience was irrelevant, indeed non-existent, because England is a unitary state, and American experience was dominant. The Charter suddenly injected a huge individual rights component into Canadian constitutional law. I think Canada is the more or less standard story of a court that built the legitimacy of constitutional judicial review by contributing to the sound workings of a division of powers system seeking to transfer that legitimacy to judicial determinations of rights policies. Here again American experience is dominant. Recent American rights experience, particularly as reflected in leading court opinions and academic writing, is one with a particular slant: a slant toward equality rather than liberty as the primary value. Underdogs have rights, overdogs have interests to be

The Success of Judicial Review

balanced away. But the American judiciary, in part because of the persistence of established doctrine and in part because of Republican appointments, is still anchored (impeded? – choose your side) by older negative or liberty regarding rights notions. The Canadians judges, relatively new to the rights game, are more open to the current fashions in rights discourse which favor government intervention in order to achieve equality. Given that most of the current rights discourse really opposes free speech, as usual not good guys' free speech but bad guys', the Canadian judges do the same. In any event, the Canadian situation reminds us that it is not only what judicial reviewers can do that counts but what they want to do. And as Baum has recently reminded us (Baum 1997), for all our quantitative and qualitative work, why they make the decisions they do is still something of a mystery.

Of course a volume titled *Constitutional Dialogues in Comparative Perspective* is bound to make my little heart go pit-a-pat given my own long-ridden hobby horses. Given the vitality of both constitutional and statutory review in Western Europe and a few other assorted foreign places, it has gotten harder and harder for constitutional law scholars, both lawyers and political scientists, to take a completely American view. So long as judicial review was a peculiarly American phenomenon, it seemed sensible to try to explain it in peculiarly American terms. Why did Americans let their judges get away with a level of policymaking that no other people in the world would tolerate? Now we have to ask, why do so many people in so many parts of the world entrust so much of their governance to judges? My own answer is because they cannot help it. Another answer is because they want to. Both answers may be too simple, but simple can be nice (Teagarden 1942).

Notes

1. I speak in this chapter of successful or flourishing judicial review. Such terms are both inexact and relative. I mean roughly judicial review in which judges manage to make a relatively large number of relatively important policy decisions that are relatively fully implemented.
2. The term areal division of power is taken from Maass (1959). It is convenient because federal is an inflammatory word in the EU context.
3. I use the term in a post-Leninist sense to describe states seeking to move from a one-party to a competitive-party system. The term includes all of the former Soviet bloc and Taiwan which had single parties directly inspired by Lenin's teachings and by analogy South

Korea, Mexico, some other Latin American and African countries and perhaps Japan.

4.   The ECJ discovered that the Treaties contained individual rights provisions by implication in response to opposition to its assertions of supremacy from the German and Italian constitutional courts which raised the specter of ECJ economic decisions abridging individual rights guaranteed by the German and Italian constitutions. The ECJ was in effect saying we will not abridge individual rights in the process of integrating the European economies. See Hartley (1994, 242–6).

5.   Among the political scientists who have done pioneering work on lawyers are the late Herbert Jacob; Austin Sarat, Lynn Mather and Herbert Kritzer. Post Watergate, the American Bar Association pressured the law schools to teach legal ethics and there is now much writing, a tiny bit of it empirical, on that subject from academic lawyers. Academic lawyers who participate in the law and economics movement produce some work on the economics of law practice, particularly the large law firms.

6.   See the many writings of Robert Post and Lillian BeVier.

Cases and Official Documents Cited

These are arranged by country, then by court or type of document.

AUSTRALIA

High Court of Australia

Australian Capital Television Pty Ltd. v. *Commonwealth of Australia*, 1992, 177 Commonwealth Law Reports 106.

CANADA

Supreme Court of Canada

Irwin Toy v. *Quebec* [1989] 1 Supreme Court Reports [SCR] 927.
Regina v. *Keegstra* [1990] 3 SCR 697.
Regina v. *Oakes* [1986] 1 SCR 103.
Zundel v. *Regina* [1992] 2 SCR 731–844

State Courts

Regina v. *Keegstra* 1991 63 CCC (3d) 110, 116–17 (Alberta).

Constitutions and Statutes

Canadian Bill of Rights (1960), Sections 1 and 2.
Canadian Charter of Rights and Freedoms, Sections 1, 2(b), 15, 27, 33.
Canadian Criminal Code, RSC, 1985 c. C-46 § 319(2).

FRANCE

French Constitutional Council

Decision of 18 November 1982. Case No. 82–146. 1982 *Recueil des decisions du Conseil constitutionnel* [Collection of Decisions of the Constitutional Council], 66.

GERMANY

Federal Constitutional Court

Decision of July 30, 1952. *Bundesverfassungsgerichtsentscheidungen* [Decisions of the Federal Constitutional Court, hereinafter 'BVerfGE'] Vol. 1, 396.
Decision of 16 January 1957. BVerfGE 6, 32.
Decision of 15 January 1958. BVerfGE 7, 198 (*Lüth* case).
Decision of 26 Febrary 1969. BVerfGE 25, 256.
Decision of 24 February 1971, BVerfGE 30, 173 (*Mephisto* case).
Decision of 18 July 1972. BVerfGE 33, 303 (Numerous Clausus case).
Decision of 29 May 1973. BVerfGE 35, 79.
Decision of 31 July 1973. BVerfGE 36, 1.
Decision of 25 February 1975. BVerfGE 39, 1 (First Abortion Decision).
Decision of 18 April 1989. BVerfGE 79, 311.
Decision of 28 May 1993. BVerfGE 88, 203 (Second Abortion Decision).

Constitutional and Statutory Instruments

Constitution (*Grundgesetz*) Articles 20, 93 (1)-(4).
Constitutional Court Law (*Bundesverfassungsgerichtsgesetz*) § 64.

HUNGARY

Hungarian Constitutional Court

First Compensation Case, Nr. 21/1990. (X.4.) AB
Paternity Case, Nr. 57/1991. (SI.8.) AB
Retroactive Justice I, Nr 41/1993. (X.13.) AB
Retroactive Justice II, Nr. 53/1993. (X.13.) AB
Second Compensation Case, Nr. 16/1991. (IV.20) AB
Second Compensation Case, Nr. 27/1991. (V.20.) AB
Welfare Case, Nr. 43/1995 (VI.30) AB

ITALY

Italian Constitutional Court

Decision of Italian Constitutional Court, Case No. 11, 1965a. *Giurisprudenza costitutionale* [Constitutional Decisions] Vol. 10, 91.

Decision of Italian Constitutional Court, Case No. 52, 1965b. *Giurisprudenza costitutionale* Vol. 10, 699.

Decision of Italian Constitutional Court, Case No. 133, 1984. *Giurisprudenza costitutionale* Vol. 29, 852.

Decision of Italian Constitutional Court, Case No. 220, 1988a. *Giurisprudenza costitutionale* Vol. 33, 862.

Decision of Italian Constitutional Court, Case No. 1146, 1988b. *Giurisprudenza costitutionale* Vol. 33, 5565.

Decision of Italian Constitutional Court, Case No. 243, 1993. *Giurisprudenza costitutionale* Vol. 38, 1756.

NEW ZEALAND

Court of Appeal

Ministry of Transport v. *Noort* [1992] 3 NZLR 260.

RUSSIA

Constitutional and Statutory Instruments

Federal'nyi Konstitutsionnyi Zakon Rossiiskii Federatsii O Sudebnoi Sisteme Rossiiskoi Federatsii [Federal Constitutional Law of the Russian Federation on the Judicial System of the Russian Federation] of 31 December 1996, *Rossiiskaia Iustitsiia* 3 (1997), 54–8.

SPAIN

Spanish Constitutional Tribunal

Decision of Spanish Constitutional Court, Case No. 80, 1982. *Boletin oficial del Estado* [Official State Bulletin] Vol. 4, 519.

Decision of Spanish Constitutional Court, Case No. 104, 1986. *Boletin oficial del Estado* Vol. 15, 559.

Decision of Spanish Constitutional Court, Case No. 159, 1987. *Boletin oficial del Estado* Vol. 19, 134.

UNITED STATES OF AMERICA

US Supreme Court

Adarand Constructors, Inc. v. *Pena*, 1995, 515 US 200.
Barron v. Mayor and City Council of Baltimore, 1833, 32 US (7 Per) 243.
Board of Education, Island Trees Union Free School District v. *Pico*, 1982, 457 US 853.
Bob Jones University v. *United States*, 1983, 461 US 574.
Brandenburg v. *Ohio*, 1969, 395 US 444.
Chaplinsky v. *New Hampshire*, 1942, 315 US 568.
Cohen v. *California*, 1971, 403 US 15.
Coleman v. *Miller*, 1939, 307 US 433.
Fullilove v. *Klutznick*, 1980, 448 US 448.
Flast v. *Cohen*, 1968, 392 US 83.
Lamont v. *Postmaster General*, 1965, 381 US 301.
Marbury v. *Madison*, 1803, 5 US (1 Cranch) 137.
Metro Broadcasting, Inc. v. *FCC*, 1990, 497 US 547.
NLRB v. *Gissell Packing Co*, 1969, 395 US 575.
Powell v. *McCormack*, 1969, 395 US 486.
Raines v. *Byrd*, 1997, 117 S.Ct. 2312.
RAV v. *City of St. Paul, Minnesota*, 1992, 505 US 377.
Regents of Univ. of California v. *Bakke*, 1978, 438 US 265.
Richmond v. *J.A. Croson Co.*, 1989, 488 US 469.
Roberts v. *Jaycees*, 1984, 468 US 609.
Sierra Club v. *Morton*, 1972, 405 US 727.
Simon & Schuster, Inc. v. *New York State Crime Victims Board*, 1991, 502 US 105.
Stanford v. *Kentucky*, 1989, 492 US 361.
United States v. *Lopez*, 1995, 514 US 549.
United States v. *Richardson*, 1974, 418 US 166
Watts v. *United States*, 1969, 394 US 705.
Wygant v. *Jackson Board of Education*, 1986, 476 US 267.

US Federal Appellate Courts

Cary v. *Board of Education*, 1979, 598 F.2d 535 (10th Cir.).

US Federal District Courts

Baxley v. *Rutland*, 1976, 409 F. Supp. 1249 (D.C. Ala.).
Doe v. *University of Michigan*, 1989, 721 F. Supp. 852, 856 (E.D. Mich.).
Post v. *Board of Regents of the University of Wisconsin*, 1991, 774 F. Supp. 1163 (E.D. Wisc.).

US State Courts

In re Welfare of RAV, 1991, 464 N.W.2d 507 (Minnesota).

Statutes and Constitutions

St. Paul Bias-Motivated Crime Ordinance, St. Paul, Minn. Legis. Code § 292.02 (1990).
United States Constitution, Amendments I, XIV.

UNITED KINGDOM

House of Lords
Council of Civil Service Unions v. *Minister for the Civil Service* [1984] 3 All E.R. 935.

Court of Appeal

Immigration Appeal Tribunal v. *Hoque and Singh, Immigration Appeals (Reports)* (1988), 216.
Masood v. *Secretary of State for the Home Department, Immigration Appeals (Reports)* (1992), 69.
R. v. *Immigration Appeal Tribunal, ex p. Kumar, Immigration Appeals (Reports)* (1986), 446.

Queen's Bench

R. v. *Immigration Appeal Tribunal ex p. Amin, Immigration Appeals (Reports) (1992)*, 367–75.
R. v. *Immigration Appeal Tribunal, ex p. Begum*, (Crown Office List). *The Times* (15 February 1995) (Queen's Bench Division).
R. v. *Immigration Appeal Tribunal ex p. Iqbal, Immigration Appeals (Reports)* (1993), 270.
R. v. *Immigration Appeal Tribunal ex p. Singh*, (Crown Office List CO/1787/88) (16 March 1990).

Court of Session

Mohammed Safter v. *Secretary of State for the Home Department*, [1992] Imm. A.R. 1.

INTERNATIONAL AND SUPRANATIONAL

European Convention of Human Rights, Article 10.
International Covenant on Civil and Political Rights, 1966.
International Convention on the Elimination of All Forms of Racial Discrimination, 1965.
Universal Declaration of Human Rights.

European Court of Human Rights

Abdulaziz, Cabales and Balkandali v. United Kingdom. 7 *European Human Rights Reports* (1985), 471.

Jersild v. Denmark (Freedom of Expression). 19 *European Human Rights Reports* (1994), 1.

Sunday Times v. United Kingdom, 1979, 2 *European Human Rights Reports* (1979), 245.

European Court of Justice

'Report of the Court of Justice on Certain Aspects of the Application of the Treaty on European Union for Purposes of the 1996 Intergovernmental Conference', *Proceedings of the Court of Justice and Court of First Instance of the European Communities* 15/95 (22–6 May, 1995), 8–11.

R. v. Immigration Appeal Tribunal and Surinder Singh ex p. Secretary of State for the Home Department. Case C 370/90 *Common Market Law Reports* 3 (1992), 358.

Court of Justice of the European Communities, *Formal Sittings of the Court of Justice of the European Communities, 1978 and 1979* (Luxembourg: Office for Official Publications of the European Communities, 1979).

Court of Justice of the European Communities, *Formal Sittings of the Court of Justice of the European Communities, 1980 and 1981* (Luxembourg: Office for Official Publications of the European Communities, 1982).

Court of Justice of the European Communities, *Formal Sittings of the Court of Justice of the European Communities, 1982 and 1983* (Luxembourg: Office for Official Publications of the European Communities, 1984).

Court of Justice of the European Communities, *Synopsis of the Work of the Court of Justice and of the Court of First Instance of the European Communities, 1984–1985* (Luxembourg: Office for Official Publications of the European Communities, 1986).

Court of Justice of the European Communities, *Synopsis of the Work of the Court of Justice and of the Court of First Instance of the European Communities, 1986–1987* (Luxembourg: Office for Official Publications of the European Communities, 1988).

Court of Justice of the European Communities, *XXXV Anni: 1952–1987* (Luxembourg: Office for Official Publications of the European Communities, 1987).

Court of Justice of the European Communities, *Synopsis of the Work of the Court of Justice and of the Court of First Instance of the European Communities, 1988–1989* (Luxembourg: Office for Official Publications of the European Communities, 1990).

Court of Justice of the European Communities, *Synopsis of the Work of the Court of Justice and of the Court of First Instance of the European Communities, 1992–1994* (Luxembourg: Office for Official Publications of the European Communities, 1995).

European Community Documents

Debates of the European Parliament, 9 Feb. 1994, No. 3-442/139, on the Role of the European Parliament in the Appointment of Judges to the Court of Justice of the European Communities.

Resolution on the European Parliament's Position Concerning the Reform of The Treaties and the Achievement of European Union, 1982, *Official Journal of the European Communities*, Commission of the European Communities, Series C, Volume 238, page 25 [OJ (C 238) 25], 6 July 1982.

Resolution on the General Outline for a Draft Revision of the Treaties, 1997, OJ (C 33) 66. (B4-0040/97), 16 January 1997.

Written Declaration on the Appointment of Women Judges to the Court of First Instance, 1989 OJ (C 120) 304. (Doc 25/88), 13 April 1989.

Commission of the European Communities, 'Written Question No. 1750/85 by Dieter Rogalla to the Commission: Appointment of Judges and Advocates-General', 1986, OJ (C 99) 23 14 October 1985.

Commission of the European Communities, 'Written Question No. 1751/85 by Dieter Rogalla to the Council: Appointment of Judges and Advocates General', 1986, OJ (C 32) 31, 14 October 1985.

Commission of the European Communities, 'Written Question No. 2529/95 by Jaak Vandemeulebroucke to the Council: Appointment of a Belgian Judge to the Court of Justice', 1996, OJ (C 56) 24, 13 September 1995.

European Parliament, *Rules of Procedure, June, 1994* (Strasbourg: European Parliament, 1993).

'Question No. 59 by Mr. Sieglershmidt (H-138/80) on Participation by the European Parliament in the Selection of Members of the Court of Justice', *Official Journal of the European Communities, Annex: Debates of the European Parliament* I-256 (21 May 1980), 175.

'Question No. 60 by Mr. Glinne (H-139/80) on Participation by the European Parliament in the Selection of Members of the Court of Justice', *Official Journal of the European Communities, Annex: Debates of the European Parliament* I-256 (21 May 1980), 175.

'Question No. 66 by Mr. Sieglershmidt (H-203/80) on Involvement of the European Parliament in the Appointment of Members of the Court of Justice of the European Communities', *Official Journal of the European Communities, Annex: Debates of the European Parliament* I-256 (19 June 1980), 184.

Books, Articles and Chapters Cited

H.J. Abraham, *Justices and Presidents: A Political History of Appointments to the Supreme Court*, 3rd edn (Oxford: Oxford University Press, 1992).

H.J. Abraham, *The Judicial Process*, 6th edn (New York: Oxford University Press, 1993).

L. Abu-Lughod, *Writing Against Culture* (Berkeley, CA: University of California Press, 1994).

A. Adonis and R. Rice, 'In the Hot Seat of Judgment: The European Court is coming Under Fire, Accused of Pushing a Political Agenda', *Financial Times*, April 3, 1995, 17.

Agence Europe 'EC: News of the Week', December 7, 1993, 1.

Agence France Presse, 'Belgium's Ex-Justice Minister Accused in Dassault Bribe Case', April 1, 1997, 1.

A. Agh, 'The Permanent Constitutional Crisis in the Democratic Transition: The Case of Hungary', in J.J. Hesse and N. Johnson (eds), *Constitutional Policy and Change in Europe* (Oxford: Oxford University Press, 1995), 296–326.

G. Ajani, 'The Rise and Fall of the Law-Based State in the Experience of Russian Legal Scholarship: Foreign Patterns and Domestic Style', in D.D. Barry (ed.), *Toward the 'Rule of Law' in Russia? Political and Legal Reform in the Transition Period* (Armonk, NY: M.E. Sharpe, 1992), 3–21.

L. Alexander, 'Banning Hate Speech and the Sticks and Stones Defense', *Constitutional Commentary* 13 (1996), 71.

G.A. Almond, *The American People and Foreign Policy* (New York: Harcourt, Brace, 1950).

K. Alter, 'The Rule of Law in Europe: Theories of Legal Integration and Judicial Politics in Germany', presented at the ECSA World Conference, Copenhagen, May 1994.

M. Anwar, 'The Context of Leadership: Migration, Settlement and Racial Discrimination', in P. Werbner and M. Anwar (eds), *Black and Ethnic Leadership in Britain: The Cultural Dimensions of Political Action* (New York: Routledge, 1991), 1–13.

A. Arato, 'Elections, Coalitions and Constitutionalism in Hungary', *East European Constitutional Review* 3 (1994), 26–32.

A. Arato, 'Constitution-Making Endgame in Hungary', *East European Constitutional Review* 5 (1996), 31–9.

A. Arnull, 'Reflections on Judicial Attitudes at the European Court', *International and Comparative Law Quarterly* 34 (1985), 168–77.

P. Atiyah and R.S. Summers, *Form and Substance in Anglo-American Law* (New York: Oxford University Press, 1987).

M.M. Atkinson and W.D. Coleman, 'Strong States and Weak States: Sectoral Policy Networks in Advanced Capitalist Economies', *British Journal of Political Science*, 19 (1989), 47–67.

P. Avril and J. Gicquel, *Le conseil constitutionnel* (Paris: Montchrestien, 1992).

G. Babel, *Probleme der abstrakten Normenkontrolle* (Berlin: Duncker & Humblot, 1965).

A. Babington, *The Rule of Law in Britain from the Roman Occupation to the Present Day: The Only Liberty* (London: Barry Rose, 1978).

R. Bacon, 'Interview: A Judgment on the European Court', *International Corporate Law* (November 1993), sec. 30, 29–32.

F.C. Barghoorn, *Detente and the Democratic Movement in the USSR* (New York: Free Press, 1976).

P.C. Bartholomew, *The Irish Judiciary* (Notre Dame: University of Notre Dame Press, 1971).

L. Baum, 'Review Article: Research on the English Judicial Process', *British Journal of Political Science* 7 (1977), 511–27.

L. Baum, *The Puzzle of Judicial Behavior* (Ann Arbor: University of Michigan Press, 1997).

A.F. Bayefsky, *International Human Rights Law: Use in Canadian Charter of Rights and Freedoms Litigation* (Toronto: Butterworth, 1992).

R.N. Bellah, R. Madsen, W.M. Sullivan, A. Swidler and S.M. Tipton. *Habits of the Heart* (New York: Harper & Row, 1985).

R. Berger, 'Standing to Sue in Public Actions: Is it a Constitutional Requirement?', *Yale Law Journal*, 78 (1969), 816–40.

L.C. Berkson, 'Judicial Selection in the United States: A Special Report.' *Judicature* 64.4 (1980), 176–193.

H.J. Berman, 'The Rule of Law and the Law-Based State (*Rechtsstaat*) (With Special Reference to Developments in the Soviet Union)', *Harriman Institute Forum*, 4, 5 (May 1991), 1–12.

K.A. Bettermann, *'Richterliche Normenkontrolle als negative Gesetzgebung?' Deutsches Verwaltungsblatt*, (1982), 91–5.

J. Bhabha and S.Shutter, *Women's Movement: Women Under Immigration, Nationality And Refugee Law* (Staffordshire, England: Trentham Books, 1994).

A.M. Bickel, *The Least Dangerous Branch*, 2nd edn (New Haven, CT, and London: Yale University Press, 1986).

Birmingham Post, 'Banned couple plan reunion', 17 December 1993.

M.M. Bledsoe, 'The Advisory Opinion in North Carolina: 1947 to 1991', *North Carolina Law Review*, 70 (1992), 1853–98 (student comment).

L. Blom-Cooper, 'Justinian; Major Reshuffle on the Bench', *Financial Times*, 30 September 1991, sec. I, 36.

J.B. Board, Jr, 'Legal Culture and the Environmental Protection Issue: The Swedish Experience', *Albany Law Review*, 37 (1973), 603–31.

E.L. Bonk, *'Ob Odnoi Probleme Sotsiologicheskikh Issledovanii Obshchestvennogo Mneniia O Prave'*, *Sovetskoe Gosudarstvo i Pravo* #8 (1986), 120–3.

K. Borchardt, *The ABC of Community Law,* 3rd edn (Luxembourg: Office for Official Publications of the European Communities, 1991).

A. Borovoy and K. Mahoney, 'Language as Violence v. Freedom of Expression: Canadian and American Perspectives on Group Defamation', *Buffalo Law Review* 37 (1988/89), 337–73.

G.W. Breslauer, *Khrushchev and Brezhnev as Leaders: Building Authority in Soviet Politics* (London: Allen & Unwin, 1982).

R. Brickman, S. Jasanoff and T. Ilgen. *Controlling Chemicals: The Politics of Regulation in Europe and the United States* (Ithaca, NY, and London: Cornell University Press, 1985).

J. Bridge, 'American Analogues in the Law of the European Communities', *Anglo-American Law Review* April–June (1982), 130–54.

L. Bridges, G. Meszaros and M. Sunkin, *Judicial Review in Perspective* (London: The Public Law Project, 1996).

L. Brilmayer, 'The Jurisprudence of Article III: Perspectives on the "Case or Controversy" Requirement', *Harvard Law Review* 93 (1979), 297–321.

L. Brilmayer, 'A Reply', *Harvard Law Review* 93 (1980), 1727–33.

L.N. Brown, *The Court of Justice of the European Communities*, 3rd edn (London: Sweet & Maxwell, 1989).

L.N. Brown, and J. S. Bell, *French Administrative Law*, 4th edn (Oxford, UK: Clarendon Press, 1993).

L.N. Brown, and T. Kennedy, *The Court of Justice of the European Communities*, 4th edn (London: Sweet & Maxwell, 1994).

I. Brownlie (ed.), *Basic Documents on Human Rights*, 2nd edn (New York: Clarendon Press, 1981).

W. Rogers Brubaker, 'Introduction' in W. Rogers Brubaker (ed.) *Immigration and the Politics of Citizenship in Europe and North America* (Lanham, MD: University Press of America, 1989).

G. Brunner, '*Die Verfassungsentwicklung in Ungarn seit der Verfassungsrevision von 1972*', *Das Jahrbuch des Öffentlichen Rechts der Gegenwart* 30 (1981), 279–344.

G. Brunner, 'Development of a Constitutional Judiciary in Eastern Europe', *Review of Central and East European Law* 18 (1992), 535–53.

G. Brunner, '*Vier Jahre ungarische Verfassungsgerichts-barkeit*', in G. Brunner and L. Sólyom (eds), *Verfassungsgerichtsbarkeit in Ungarn: Analysen und Entscheidungssammlung, 1990–1993* (Baden-Baden: Nomos Verlagsgesellschaft, 1995), 13–58.

G. Brunner and L. Sólyom, (eds), *Verfassungsgerichtsbarkeit in Ungarn: Analysen und Entscheidungssammlung, 1990–1993* (Baden-Baden: Nomos Verlagsgesellschaft, 1995).

A. Burley, 'Democracy and Judicial Review in the European Community', *University of Chicago Legal Forum* (1992), 81–91.

A. Burley and W. Mattli, 'Europe Before the Court: A Political Theory of Legal Integration', *International Organization* 47, 1 (1993), 41–76.

W.G. Buss, 'School Newspapers, Public Forum, and the First Amendment', *Iowa Law Review* 74 (1989), 505–43.

M. Byron, *Post-War Caribbean Migration to Britain: The Unfinished Cycle* (Aldershot, England: Avebury, 1994).

A. Bzdera, 'The Court of Justice of the European Community and the Politics of Institutional Reform', *West European Politics* 15, 3 (1992), 123–36.

M. Cain and A. Hunt. *Marx and Engels on Law* (London, New York and San Francisco: Academic Press, 1979).

G.A. Caldeira, 'Neither the Purse Nor the Sword: The Dynamics of Public Confidence in the United States Supreme Court', *American Political Science Review* 80, 4 (1986), 1209–26.

G.A. Caldeira, 'Public Opinion and the U.S. Supreme Court: FDR's Court-Packing Plan', *American Political Science Review* 81 (1987), 1139–52.

G.A. Caldeira and J.L. Gibson, 'The Legitimacy of the Court of Justice in the European Community: Models of Institutional Support', *American Political Science Review* 89 (1995), 356–76.

P.F. Calogero, Jr, 'Advisory Opinions: A Wise Change for Louisiana and Its Judiciary?' *Loyola Law Review* 38 (1992), 329–86.

J.M. Calvo, 'Spouse-Based Immigration laws: the legacy of coverture', in A.K. Wing (ed.), *Critical Race Feminism: A Reader* (New York: New York University Press, 1997), 380–6.

D.T. Campbell, '"Degrees of Freedom" and the Case Study', *Comparative Political Studies*, 8, 2 (July 1975), 178–93.

M. Cappelletti, 'Governmental and Private Advocates for the Public Interest in Civil Litigation: A Comparative Study', *Michigan Law Review*, 73 (1975), 793–884.

M. Cappelletti, 'The Mighty Problem of Judicial Review and the Contribution of Comparative Analysis', *Legal Issues of European Integration* 2 (1979), 1–29.

M. Cappelletti, 'Who Watches the Watchmen? A Comparative Study on Judicial Responsibility', in S. Shetreet and J. Deschenes (eds), *Judicial Independence: The Contemporary Debate* (Dordrecht: Martinus Nijhoff, 1985), 393–402.

M. Cappelletti, 'Is the European Court of Justice "Running Wild"?' *European Law Review* 12, 1 (1987), 3–17.

M. Cappelletti, 'The Law-Making Power of the Judges and Its Limits', in M. Cappelletti (ed.), *The Judicial Process in Comparative Perspective* (Oxford: Clarendon Press, 1989), 3–56.

R.A. Carp and R. Stidham, *Judicial Process in America*, 3rd edn (Washington, DC: Congressional Quarterly Press, 1996), 229–90.

S.L. Carter, 'The Morgan "Power" and the Forced Reconsideration of Constitutional Decisions', *The University of Chicago Law Review* 53 (1986), 819–63.

M.E. Cartier, '*La Cour de cassation et l'application de la déclaration des droits de 1789*', *La Cour de cassation et la Constitution de la République* (Aix-en-Provence: Presses universitaire d'Aix-en-Provence, 1995), 153–72.

J. Carvel, 'Europe's Shadowy Arbiters of Power', *The Guardian*, 28 June 1992, sec. F, 27.

G. Casper, 'Changing Concepts of Constitutionalism: 18th to 20th Century', *Supreme Court Review* (1989), 311–32.

A. Cawson, 'Conclusion: some implications for state theory', in A. Cawson (ed), *Organized Interests and the State* (London: Sage, 1985), 221–6.

Centre for Human Rights (Geneva), *Human Rights: Status of International Instruments* (New York: United Nations, 1987).

B.C. Chambers, 'Business and the Law: New Faces on the Bench – European Court', *Financial Times*, 11 October 1994, 13.

H.W. Chase, *Federal Judges: The Appointing Process* (Minneapolis, MN: University of Minnesota Press, 1972).

J. Clifford, *The Predicament of Culture* (Cambridge, MA: Harvard University Press, 1988).

R.N. Clinton, 'A Mandatory View of Federal Court Jurisdiction: A Guided Quest for the Original Understanding of Article III', *University of Pennsylvania Law Review* 132 (1984), 741–866.

S. Coliver, *Striking a Balance: Hate Speech, Freedom of Expression and Non-Discrimination* (London: University of Essex, 1992).

Comment, 'The Law Clerk's Duty of Confidentiality', *University of Pennsylvania Law Review* 129 (May 1981), 1230–66.

E. Comisso, 'Legacies of the Past or New Institutions? The Struggle over Restitution in Hungary', *Comparative Political Studies* 28 (1995), 200–38.

M. Constable, 'Sovereignty and Governmentality in Modern American Immigration Law', *Studies in Law, Politics and Society* 13 (1993), 249–71.

L. Constantinesco, *Rechtsvergleichung* [Comparative Law], vol. 3 (Cologne: B. Heymanns, 1983).

B.B. Cook, 'Women Judges: The End of Tokenism', in W.L. Hepperle and L. Crites, eds., *Women in the Courts* (Williamsburg, VA: National Center for State Courts, 1978), 84–105.

B.B. Cook, L.F. Goldstein, K. O'Connor and S.M. Talarico, *Women in the Judicial Process* (Washington, DC: American Political Science Association, 1988).

P. Craig, *Public Law and Democracy in the United Kingdom and the United States of America* (Oxford: Oxford University Press, 1990).

D.P. Currie, *The Constitution of the Federal Republic of Germany* (Chicago: The University of Chicago Press, 1994).

R. Dahrendorf, 'A Confusion of Powers: Politics and the Rule of Law', *The Modern Law Review*, 40, 1 (January 1977), 1–15.

M.R. Damaška, *The Faces of Justice and State Authority* (New Haven, CT: Yale University Press, 1986).

M. D'Amico, 'Juge constitutionnel, juges du fond et justiciables dans l'évolution de la justice constitutionnelle italienne', *Annuaire international de justice constitutionnelle: 1989* (Paris/Aix-en-Provence: Economica/Presses Universitaires d'Aix-en-Provence, 1990), 79–96.

H. Däubler-Gmelin, Interview by author, Bonn, Germany (5 December 1993).

J.P. Dawson, *The Oracles of the Law* (Ann Arbor, MI: University of Michigan Law School, 1968), 375–6.

J. Dearlove, 'Bringing the Constitution Back In: Political Science and the State', *Political Studies* 37 (1989), 521–39.

J. Dewey, *The Public and its Problems* (Chicago: Swallow Press, 1954 [1927]).

R. Dhavan, 'So why are there so few cases? Anti-discrimination and race relations law and policy in the United Kingdom', Paper presented at the annual meeting of the Law and Society Association, 1989.

T. Dickson, 'EC Squabble "Disrupting Court Timetable"', *Financial Times*, 13 September 1988a, sec. I, 2.

T. Dickson, 'Italy Yields to Spain in Squabble Over Euro Court Judges', *Financial Times*, 27 September 1988b, sec. I, 2.

T. Dickson, 'Law Lord of Luxembourg: The Monday Interview', *Financial Times*, 3 October 1988c, sec. I, 52.

G. Drewry, 'British Law Journals as a Resource for Political Studies', *Political Studies* 39 (1991), 560–7.

A. Dummett, 'Immigration and Nationality', in C. McCrudden and G. Chambers (eds), *Individual Rights and the Law in Britain* (New York: Clarendon Press, 1994), 137–58.

R. Dworkin, 'Liberty and Pornography', *New York Review of Books*, 15 August 1991, 14.

C. Dyer, and J. Carvel, 'Euro-court punches hole in migrant law', *The Guardian*, 7 August 1992, 2.

K. Dyson, 'Theories of Regulation and the Case of Germany: A Model of Regulatory Change', in K. Dyson (ed.), *The Politics of German Regulation* (Aldershot, England: Dartmouth, 1992), 1–28.

H. Eckstein, 'Case Study and Theory in Political Science', in F.I. Greenstein and N.W. Polsby (eds), *Handbook of Political Science*, vol. 7: *Strategies of Inquiry* (Reading, MA: Addison-Wesley, 1975), 79–137.

The Economist, 'Where the Buck Stops', 6 May 1989, UK edn, 58.

The Economist 'European Parliament: Heal Thyself', 13 April 1991, 48–50.

The Economist 'The Democratic Dream', 21 May 1994, UK edn, 21–4.

The Economist, 'European Court of Justice: Biased Referee?' 17 May 1997, 59–60.

J.H. Ely, 'Flag Desecration: A Case Study', *Harvard Law Review* 88 (1975), 1482–1505.

B. Emecheta, *The Family* (New York: George Braziller, 1989).

'EC: Mr. Goppel Criticizes the EP Report on the Court of Justice', *Reuter Textline Agence Europe*, 5 October 1993, 1.

'EC: Court of Justice: Criticism of the Court's Growing Role', *Reuter Textline Agence Europe*, 9 December 1993, 1.

'Euro Court Makes Surprise Choice as New President', *Reuter European Community Report* 7 October 1994, BC Cycle edn, 29.

W. Ewald, 'Comparative Jurisprudence (I), What Was It Like to Try a Rat?', *University of Pennsylvania Law Review*, 143 (1995), 1889–2149.

L. Favoreu, 'Europe Occidentale', in L. Favoreu and J.-A. Jolowicz (eds), *Le Contrôle Juridictionnel des Lois* (Aix-en-Provence: Presses Universitaires d'Aix-Marseille and Paris: Economica, 1984), 17–68.

L. Favoreu, 'American and European Models of Constitutional Justice', in D.S. Clark (ed.), *Comparative and Private International Law* (Berlin: Duncker & Humblot, 1990), 105–20.

L. Favoreu and T. Renoux, '*Rapport général introductif*', *La Cour de Cassation et la Constitution de la République* (Aix-en-Provence: Presses Universitaires d'Aix-en-Provence, 1995), 15–34.

W. Feld, 'The Judges of the Court of Justice of the European Communities', *Villanova Law Review* 9l (Fall 1963), 37–58.

R. Fernhout, 'The United States of Europe Have Commenced: But For Whom?' *Netherlands Quarterly of Human Rights* 11, 3 (1993), 249–65.

M. Fineman, *The Neutered Mother* (New York: Routledge, 1995).

L. Fisher, *Constitutional Dialogues: Interpretation as Political Process* (Princeton, NJ: Princeton University Press, 1988).

F. Frankfurter, 'Advisory Opinions', in E.R.A. Seligman and A. Johnson, eds., *Encyclopaedia of the Social Sciences*, Vol. 1 (New York: Macmillan, 1930), 475–8.

N. Fraser and L. Gordon, 'A Genealogy of *Dependency*: Tracing a Keyword of the U.S. Welfare State', *Signs* 19, 2 (1994), 309–36.

G.P. Freeman, 'Commentary: Britain, the deviant case', in W.A. Cornelius, P.L. Martin and J.F. Hollifield (eds), *Controlling Immigration* (Stanford, CA: Stanford University Press, 1994), 297–302.

D.A.C. Freestone, and J.S. Davidson, 'The Court of Justice', in *The Institutional Framework of the European Communities* (New York: Croom Helm, 1988), 133–78.

L.M. Friedman, *The Legal System: A Social Science Perspective* (New York: Russell Sage Foundation, 1975).

S.W. Gard, 'Fighting Words as Free Speech', *Washington University Law Quarterly* 58 (1980), 531, 534–5.

G. Garrett, 'The Politics of Legal Integration in the European Union', *International Organization* 49 (1995), 171–81.

H.L. Gates, Jr, 'War of Words: Critical Race Theory and the First Amendment', in H.L. Gates *et al.* (eds), *Speaking of Race, Speaking of Sex* (New York: New York University Press, 1994), 17–58.

A.L. George, 'Case Studies and Theory Development: The Method of Structured, Focused Comparison', in P.G. Lauren (ed.), *Diplomacy: New Approaches in History, Theory and Policy* (New York: Free Press, 1979), 43–68.

A.L. George and T.J. McKeown, 'Case Studies and Theories of Organizational Decision Making', *Advances in Information Processing in Organizations*, 2 (1985), 21–58.

J.L. Gibson and G.A. Caldeira, 'The Legitimacy of Transnational Legal Institutions: Compliance, Support, and the European Court of Justice', *American Journal of Political Science* 39 (1995), 459–89.

J.L. Gibson and G.A. Caldeira, 'The Legal Cultures of Europe', *Law & Society Review* 30, 1 (1996), 55–85.

J. Gicquel, *Droit constitutionnel et institutions politiques*, 12th edn (Paris: Montchrestien, 1993).

P. Gilroy, *'There Ain't No Black in the Union Jack': The Cultural Politics of Race and Nation* (Chicago: University of Chicago Press, 1991).

P. Gilroy, *Small Acts* (London: Verso Press, 1994).

A. Giorgis, E. Grosso and J. Luther, 'A propos de quelques nouveautés dans la jurisprudence de la Cour constitutionnelle italienne', *Annuaire international de justice constitutionnelle: 1993* (Paris/Aix-en-Provence: Economica/Presses Universitaires d'Aix-en-Provence, 1995), 531–43.

M.A. Glendon, *Rights Talk: The Impoverishment of Political Discourse* (New York: Macmillan, 1991).

S. Goldman, 'Should There Be Affirmative Action for the Judiciary?' *Judicature* 62#10 (May 1978), 488–94.

S. Goldman, 'Bush's Judicial Legacy: The Final Imprint', *Judicature* 76 (1993), 282–98.

S. Goldman, *Picking Federal Judges: Lower Court Selection from Roosevelt through Reagan* (New Haven, CT: Yale University Press, 1997).

S. Goldman and M.D. Saronson, 'Clinton's Nontraditional Judges: Creating a More Representative Bench', *Judicature* 78, 2 (1994), 68–73.

J. Goldsworthy, 'The Constitutional Protection of Rights in Australia', in G. Craven (ed.), *Australian Federation:Toward the Second Century* (Carleton, Victoria: Melbourne University Press, 1992), 151–76.

H. Goulbourne, *Ethnicity and Nationalism in Post-Imperial Britain* (Cambridge: Cambridge University Press, 1991).

B.L. Graham, 'Judicial Recruitment and Racial Diversity on State Courts: An Overview', *Judicature* 74, 1 (June–July 1990), 28–34.

L. Grant, 'Trapped in the Pages of a Catch 22 Rule Book', *The Guardian*, 14 February 1995, Society section, 2–3.

D. Greenberg, S.N. Katz, M.B. Oliviero and C. Wheatley (eds), *Constitutionalism and Democracy: Transitions in the Contemporary World* (NY: Oxford University Press, 1993).

K.T. Greenawalt, 'Criminal Coercion and Freedom of Speech', *Northwestern Law Review* 78 (1983), 108.

K.T. Greenawalt, *Fighting Words* (Princeton, NJ: Princeton University Press, 1995).

I. Griazin, *'Pravovoe Gosudarstvo* [The Law-Governed State]', *Novyi Mir* #8 (1988), 266–71.

J.A.G. Griffith, *The Politics of the Judiciary* (London: Fontana, 1981).

J.B. Grossman, *Lawyers and Judges: The ABA and the Politics of Judicial Selection* (New York: Wiley, 1965).

G. Gunther, *Constitutional Law*, 12th edn (Westbury, NY: The Foundation Press, 1991).

T. Gustafson, *Reform in Soviet Politics: Lessons of Recent Policies on Land and Water* (Cambridge: Cambridge University Press, 1981).

C. Gusy, *Parlamentarischer Gesetzgeber und Bundesverfassungsgericht* (Berlin, Germany: Duncker & Humblot, 1985).

C. Gusy, *Verfassungsbeschwerde: Voraussetzungen und Verfahren* (Heidelberg: Müller, 1988).

P.A. Hall, *Governing the Economy: The Politics of State Intervention in Britain and France* (Cambridge Polity Press, 1986).

W. Hallstein. *Europe in the Making* (New York: Norton, 1972), 30–79.

G. Halmai, *'Einleitung zur ungarnischen Verfassungs-revision'*, *Jahrbuch des Offentlichen Rechts der Gegenwart* 39 (1990), 253–83.

T.C. Hartley, *The Foundations of European Community Law: An Introduction to the Constitutional and Administrative Law of the European Community*, 2nd edn (Oxford: Oxford University Press, 1988).

T.C. Hartley, *The Foundations of European Community Law*, 3rd edn (Oxford: Clarendon Press, 1994).

H. Hausmaninger, 'From the Soviet Committee of Constitutional Supervision to the Russian Constitutional Court', *Cornell International Law Journal*, 25, 2 (Spring 1992), 305–37.

J.N. Hazard, 'Is Russian Case Law Becoming Significant As a Source of Law?', *Parker School Journal of East European Law*, 1, 1 (1994a), 23–46.

J.N. Hazard, 'Russian Judicial Precedent Revisited', *Parker School Journal of East European Law*, 1, 4 (1994b), 471–7.

S. Helm, 'Judge Accused of Cover-Up in Cools Murder Case', *The Independent*, 13 September 1996a, 11.

S. Helm, 'Britannia Faces Her Judges', *The Independent*, 28 October 1996b, 14.

J. Henderson, 'Jury Trial, Russian Style', *King's College Law Journal*, 5 (1994–5), 63–76.

K. Hendley, 'The Spillover Effects of Privatization On Russian Legal Culture', *Transnational Law and Contemporary Problems*, 5, 1 (Spring 1995), 39–64.

K. Hendley, 'Remaking an Institution: The Transition in Russia from State *Arbitrazh* to *Arbitrazh* Courts', *American Journal of Public Law*, forthcoming.

A.H. Hermann, 'Commission is Criticized For Predatory Pricing Decision', *Financial Times*, 18 May 1989, sec. I, 43.

W. Heyde, '§ 97: *Gutachten-Verfahren*', in D. C. Umbach and T. Clemens (eds), *Bundesverfassungsgerichtsgesetz* (Heidelberg: C.F. Müller Juristischer Verlag, 1992), 1408–9.

D. Hoffman, *Our Elusive Constitution* (Albany, NY: State University of New York Press, 1997).

P.W. Hogg, *Constitutional Law of Canada*, 3d edn (Scarborough, Ontario: Carswell, 1992).

K.M. Holland, 'Introduction', in K.M. Holland (ed.), *Judicial Activism in Comparative Perspective* (New York: St Martin's Press, 1991), 1–11.

S. Holmes, 'Back to the Drawing Board: An Argument for Constitutional Postponement in Eastern Europe', *East European Constitutional Review* 2 (1993), 21–5.

S. Holmes, *Passions and Constraints: On the Theory of Liberal Democracy* (Chicago: The University of Chicago Press, 1995).

Home Office, *Home Office Statistical Bulletin*, Issue 9/95 (London: HMSO, 12 May 1995).

P. Hooley, 'Britain Will Fight EC On Migrant Marriages', *Daily Express* 9 July 1992.

H. Hovenkamp, *Enterprise and American Law 1836–1937* (Cambridge, MA: Harvard University Press, 1991).

E. Huskey, 'A Framework for the Analysis of Soviet Law', *The Russian Review*, 50, 1 (January 1991), 53–70.

R. Hussein and D. Seddon, 'Recourse to Public Funds and Indirect Reliance', *Immigration and Nationality Law and Practice* 10(2) (1996), 50–53.

A.C. Hutchinson and P. Monahan (eds), *The Rule of Law: Ideal or Ideology* (Toronto: Carswell, 1987).

J.M. Ihenacho, 'The Effect of the Introduction of DNA Testing on Immigration Control Procedures: Case Studies of Bangladeshi Families', Research Paper in Ethnic Relations No. 16 (University of Warwick: Centre for Research in Ethnic Relations, 1991).

P.R. Ireland, 'Fragmented Social Policy: Migration', in S. Leibfried and P. Pierson (eds), *Fragmented Social Policy: The EC Social Dimension in Comparative Perspective* (Washington, DC: Brookings Institution, 1995), 231–66.

J. Isensee and P. Kirchhof (eds), *Handbuch des Staatsrechts*, Vol. 2 (Heidelberg: C.F. Müller Juristischer Verlag, 1987).

D.D. Jackson, *Judges* (New York: Atheneum, 1974).

236   *Books, Articles and Chapters Cited*

D.W. Jackson, 'Judging Human Rights: The Formative Years of the European Court of Human Rights: 1959–89', *Windsor Yearbook of Access to Justice* 13 (1993), 217–36.

H. Jacob, 'Introduction', in H. Jacob *et al.* (eds), *Courts, Law and Politics in Comparative Perspective* (New Haven, CT: Yale University Press, 1996), 1–15.

H. Jacob, E. Blankenburg, H.M. Kritzer, D.M. Provine and J. Sanders (eds), *Courts, Law and Politics in Comparative Perspective* (New Haven, CT: Yale University Press, 1996).

F.G. Jacobs, 'The Member States, the Judges and the Procedure', *La Cour de Justice des Communautes Européennes et les États Membres* (Bruxelles: Éditions De L'Universite de Bruxelles, 1981).

R. Jervis, 'Models and Cases in the Study of International Conflict', *Journal of International Affairs* 44 (Spring/Summer 1990), 81–101.

N. Johnson, 'Law as the Articulation of the State in Western Germany: A German tradition seen from a British perspective', *West European Politics*, 1 (1978), 177–92.

N. Johnson, 'Constitutionalism: Procedural Limits and Political Ends', in J.J. Hesse and N. Johnson (eds), *Constitutional Policy and Change in Europe* (Oxford: Oxford University Press, 1995), 49–63.

C. Joppke, 'Asylum and State Sovereignty', *Comparative Political Studies*, 30, 3 (1997), 291–330.

C. Joppke, 'Why Liberal States Accept Unwanted Immigration', *World Politics* (forthcoming, January 1998).

Journal of the American Judicature Society, 'Choosing Judges: Election, Selection and Retention', *Judicature* 77, 6 (1994), 288–337.

D. Kairys, 'Introduction', in D. Kairys (ed.), *The Politics of Law: A Progressive Critique*, rev. edn (New York: Pantheon, 1990), 1–9.

D. Kaminskaya, *Final Judgement: My Life as a Soviet Defense Attorney* (New York: Simon & Schuster, 1982).

K.L. Karst, and H.W. Horowitz, 'The *Bakke* Opinions and Equal Protection Doctrine', *Harvard Civil Rights-Civil Liberties Law Review* 14 (1979), 7–87.

I. Katznelson, and K. Prewitt, 'Constitutionalism, Class, and the Limits of Choice in U.S. Foreign Policy', in R.R. Fagen (ed.), *Capitalism and the State in U.S.–Latin American Relations* (Stanford, CA: Stanford University Press, 1979), 25–40.

P. Katzenstein, *Policy and Politics in West Germany* (Philadelphia: Temple University Press, 1987).

T. Kavanagh, 'Fake Migrant Blow', *The Sun*, 8 July 1992, 1.

J.T.S. Keeler, 'Comment on Wilson', *American Political Science Review*, 79 (1985), 819–22.

J. Kelly, *The Irish Constitution*, 2nd edn (Dublin: Jurist 1984).

H. Kelsen, 'La garantie juridictionnelle de la constitution', *Revue du droit public* 44 (1928), 197–257.

T. Kennedy, 'The Essential Minimum: The Establishment of the Court of First Instance', *European Law Review* 14, 1 (1989), 7–27.

T. Kennedy, 'Thirteen Russians! The Composition of the European Court of Justice', in A.I.L. Campbell and M. Voyatzi (eds), *Legal Reasoning and*

Judicial Interpretation of European Law: Essays in Honour of Lord Mackenzie-Stuart (London: Trenton Publishing, 1996).

S.J. Kenney, *For Whose Protection?* (Ann Arbor, MI: University of Michigan Press, 1992).

S.J. Kenney, 'The Role of *Référendaires* at the Court of Justice of the European Communities', (International Political Science Association Research Committee on Comparative Judicial Studies, Florence, August 1994).

K. Khan, 'A Ray of Hope for Divided Families', *Q news*, 17 July 1992, 4.

B. Kilroy, 'Member State Control or Judicial Independence: The Integrative Role of the European Court of Justice, 1958–1994', (Annual Meeting of the American Political Science Association, Chicago, 31 August 1995).

S. Klein Schonnefeld, 'Germany', in B. Rolston and A. Eggert (eds), *Abortion in the New Europe: A Comparative Handbook* (Westport, CT: Greenwood Press, 1994).

E. Klingsberg, 'Hungary: Safeguarding the Transition', *East European Constitutional Review* 5 (1993), 44–7.

E. Klingsberg, 'Contextualizing the Calculus of Consent: Judicial Review of Legislative Wealth Transfers in a Transition to Democracy and Beyond', *Cornell International Law Journal* 27 (1994), 303–42.

U. Klug, *'Die rechtspolitische Bilanz der Freien-Demokraten'*, *Zeitschrift fur Rechtspolitik* 9 (1976), 218–21.

D.P. Kommers, 'German Constitutionalism: A Prolegomenon', *Emory Law Journal* 40 (1991), 837–73.

D.P. Kommers, *The Constitutional Jurisprudence of the Federal Republic of Germany* (Durham, NC: Duke University Press, 1989), 19–21, 262–3, 294–303, 370–4, 430.

D.P. Kommers, *The Constitutional Jurisprudence of the Federal Republic of Germany*, 2nd edn (Durham, NC: Duke University Press, 1997).

D.P. Kommers, 'The Federal Constitutional Court in the German Political System', *Comparative Political Studies*, 26 (1994), 470–91.

D.P. Kommers and W.J. Thompson, 'Fundamentals in the Liberal Constitutional Tradition', in J.J Hesse and N. Johnson (eds), *Constitutional Policy and Change in Europe* (Oxford: Oxford University Press, 1995).

T. Koopmans, 'Europe and Its Lawyers in 1984', *Common Market Law Review* 22 (1985a), 9–18.

T. Koopmans, 'The Judicial System Envisaged in the Draft Treaty', in R. Bieber, J. Jacque and J.H. Weiler (eds), *An Ever-Closer Union: A Critical Analysis of the Draft Treaty Establishing the European Union* (Luxembourg: Office for Official Publications of the European Communities, 1985b), 57–72.

T. Koopmans, 'The Role of Law in the Next Stage of European Integration', *International and Comparative Law Quarterly*, 35 (1986), 925–31

A. Korkeakivi, 'Russia On the Rights Track: Human Rights in the New Constitution', *Parker School Journal of East European Law*, 1, 2 (1994a), 233–53.

A. Korkeakivi, 'The Russian Constitutional Court and Human Rights', *Parker School Journal of East European Law*, 1, 5–6 (1994b), 591–617.

K. Kress, 'Coherence', in D. Patterson (ed.), *A Companion to the Philosophy of Law and Legal Theory* (Oxford: Blackwell 1996), 533–52.

238   *Books, Articles and Chapters Cited*

S. Krislov, C. Ehlermann and J. Weiler, 'The Political Organs and the Decision-Making Process in the United States and the European Community', in M. Cappelletti, M. Seccombe and J. Weiler (eds), *Integration Through Law* (New York: Walter de Gruyter, 1986), 3–110.

M. Krygier, 'Marxism and the Rule of Law: Reflections After the Collapse of Communism', *Law and Social Inquiry*, 15, 4 (Fall 1990), 633–63.

Kulli, 'Leaving Home', in Southall Black Sisters (eds), *Against the Grain: A Celebration of Survival and Struggle* (Southall, Middlesex: Southall Black Sisters,1990), 77–8.

H. Kureishi, *The Buddha of Suburbia* (New York: Macmillan Press, 1990).

V. Lamm (eds), *Parliamentarism and Government in a One-Party System*, trans. M. Kocsis and S. Simon (Budapest: Akademiai Kiady, 1988).

C. Landfried, *Bundesverfassungsgericht und Gesetz-geber: Wirkungen der Verfassungsrechtsprechung auf parlament-arische Willensbildung und soziale Realität* (Baden-Baden: Nomos Verlagsgesellschaft, 1984).

C. Landfried, 'Judicial Policymaking in Germany: The Federal Constitutional Court', *West European Politics* 15 (1992), 50–67.

C.R. Lawrence, 'If He Hollers Let Him Go: Regulating Racist Speech on Campus', *Duke Law Journal* (1990), 431–83.

The Lawyer 'Howard Rebuked for EU Remarks', 9, 11 (14 March 1995), 1–2.

Z. Layton-Henry, *The Politics of Immigration* (Oxford: Blackwell, 1992).

L. Lederer, and R. Delgado (eds), *The Price We Pay* (Collection of essays presented at 1993 conference at University of Chicago Law School, 1995).

G. Lehmbruch, 'The Institutional Framework of German Regulation', in K. Dyson (ed.), *The Politics of German Regulation* (Aldershot, Brookfield, Hong Kong, Singapore, Sydney: Dartmouth, 1992), 29–52.

S. Leibfried and P. Pierson (eds), *Fragmented Social Policy: The EC Social Dimension in Comparative Perspective* (Washington, DC: Brookings Institution, 1995).

K. Lenaerts, 'Constitutionalism and the Many Faces of Federalism', *American Journal of Comparative Law* 38 (1990), 205–63.

L.W. Levy, *Emergence of a Free Press* (New York: Oxford University Press, 1985).

C.A. Linden, *Khrushchev and the Soviet Leadership, 1957–1964* (Baltimore, MD: Johns Hopkins University Press, 1966).

S.M. Lipset, *Continental Divide: The Values and Institutions of the United States and Canada* (Rutledge New York: Routledge, 1990).

M. Lodge, *Soviet Elite Attitudes Since Stalin* (Columbus, OH: Merrill, 1969).

M. Loughlin, *Public Law and Political Theory* (Oxford: Oxford University Press, 1992).

A. Maass, *Area and Power* (Glencoe, IL: Free Press, 1959).

C. Macdonald, 'Scots Judge in Joint Ruling', *The Glasgow Herald*, 13 November 1996, 8.

L. Mackenzie Stuart, 'The Court of Justice: A Personal View', in S.J. Bates, W. Finnie, J.A. Usher and H. Wildberg (eds), *European Governmental Studies* (London: Sweet & Maxwell, 1983), 118–27.

C.A. MacKinnon, 'Pornography, Civil Rights, and Speech', *Harvard Civil Rights-Civil Liberties Law Review* 20 (1985), 1–70.

W. Maihofer, Interview by author. Berlingen am Bodensee, 17 December 1993.

G.F. Mancini, 'The Making of a Constitution for Europe', *Common Market Law Review* 26 (1989), 595–614.

I. Markovits, 'Playing the Opposites Game: On Mirjan Damaska's *The Faces of Justice and State Authority*', *Stanford Law Review* 41 (1989), 1313–41.

T.R. Marshall, *Public Opinion and the Supreme Court* (Boston, MA: Unwin Hyman, 1989).

M.J. Matsuda, C.R. Lawrence III, R. Delgado, and K. Williams Crenshaw, *Words That Wound: Critical Race Theory, Assaultive Speech, and the First Amendment* (Boulder, CO: Westview 1993).

T. Maunz, B. Schmidt-Bleibtreu, F. Klein, G. Ulsamer, H. Bethge and K. Winter, *Bundesverfassungsgerichtsgesetz: Kommentar* (Munich: C.H. Beck'sche Verlagsbuchhandlung, 1993).

M.D. McCubbins, R.G. Noll and B.R. Weingast, 'Positive and Normative Models of Procedural Rights: An Integrative Approach to Administrative Procedures', *Journal of Law, Economics, and Organization* 6 (1990), 307–32.

H.W. McGee, 'Counsel for the Accused: Metamorphosis in Spanish Constitutional Rights', *Columbia Journal of Transnational Law* 25 (1987), 253–99.

B. McKain, 'Vision of a Just Europe', *The Glasgow Herald*, 22 February 1993, 11.

G. Meade, 'Shy Judge is Keen on Europe', *Press Association Newsfile*, 13 November 1996, sec. Home News.

A. Meiklejohn, *Free Speech and its Relation to Self-Government* (New York: Harper Collins, 1948).

J.H. Merryman, *Civil Law Tradition*, 2d edn (Stanford, CA: Stanford University Press, 1985).

J.H. Merryman, D.S. Clark and J.O. Haley, *The Civil Law Tradition: Europe, Latin America and East Asia* (Charlottesville, VA: Michie, 1994).

J.H. Merryman and V. Vigoriti, 'When Courts Collide: Constitution and Cassation in Italy', *American Journal of Comparative Law* 15 (1967), 665–86.

J. Mertens de Wilmars, 'Souvenirs Externes Sur Les Débuts de la Cour', *XXXV Anni, 1952–1987* (Luxembourg: Court of Justice of the European Communities, 1988), 47–51.

A. Messina, *Race and Party Competition in Britain* (Oxford: Oxford University Press, 1989).

F.I. Michelman, 'Conceptions of Democracy in American Constitutional Argument', *Tennessee Law Review* 56 (1989), 291.

I.B. Mikhailovskaia, 'Constitutional Rights in Russian Public Opinion', *East European Constitutional Review*, 4, 1 (Winter 1995), 70–6.

L. Milbrath and M.L. Goel, *Political Participation*, 2nd edn (Chicago: Rand McNally, 1977).

D. Millward, 'Civil Servant 'set up weddings for illegal migrants'', *The Daily Telegraph*, 7 July 1995.

T. Modood, S. Beison and S. Virdee, *Changing Ethnic Identities* (London: Policy Studies Institute, 1994).

H. Monaghan, 'The Who and When', *Yale Law Journal* 82 (1973), 1363–97.

F.L. Morton, 'Judicial Review in France: A Comparative Analysis', *American Journal of Comparative Law* 36 (1988), 89–110.

K. Morvai, 'Retroactive Justice based on International Law: A Recent Decision by the Hungarian Constitutional Court', *East European Constitutional Review* 2 (1994), 32–4.

W.F. Murphy, and J. Tanenhaus, *Comparative Constitutional Law: Cases and Commentaries* (New York: St, Martin's Press, 1977).

A. Neier, *Defending My Enemy: American Nazis, the Skokie Case, and the Risks of Freedom* (New York: Dutton, 1979).

J.P. Nettl, 'The State as a Conceptual Variable', *World Politics* 20 (1968), 559–92.

F. Neumann, *The Rule of Law: Political Theory and the Legal System in Modern Society* (Dover, NH: Berg, 1986).

New York Times Magazine (December 3, 1995).

Note, 'Advisory Opinions on the Constitutionality of Statutes', *Harvard Law Review*, 69 (1956), 1302–13.

R.C. North *et al.* (eds), *Content Analysis: A Handbook with Applications for the Study of International Crisis* (Evanston, IL: Northwestern University Press, 1963).

J.E. Nowak and R.D. Rotunda, *Constitutional Law*, 5th edn (St. Paul, MN.: West, 1995).

M-C. Panthoreau, 'L'article 2 de la Constitution italienne et la concrétisation de droits non-écrits', *Annuaire internationale de justice constitutionnelle: 1989* (Paris/Aix-en-Provence: Economica/Presses Universitaires d'Aix-en-Provence, 1990), 97–136.

Parliamentary Debates (House of Commons) (London: Her Majesty's Stationery Office 30 June 1992), Col. 523w.

C. Pateman, *The Sexual Contract* (Palo Alto, CA: Stanford University Press, 1988).

Q. Peel, 'Luxembourg 5; Referee in Institutional Warfare', *Financial Times*, 19 November 1986, sec. V.

B. Perry, *A 'Representative' Supreme Court? The Impact of Race, Religion and Gender on Appointments* (New York: Greenwood Press, 1991).

R. Peston, 'Major Condemns EU Court Ruling on 48-Hour Work Week: Eurosceptic Doubts Over Government Plan to Limit Brussels' Power', *Financial Times*, 13 March 1996, 1.

A. Pizzorusso, 'Constitutional Review and Legislation in Italy', in C. Landfried (ed.), *Constitutional Review and Legislation* (Baden-Baden: Nomos, 1989), 109–26.

S.I. Pogany, 'Constitutional Reform in Central and Eastern Europe: Hungary's Transition to Democracy', *International and Comparative Law Quarterly* 42 (1993), 332–55.

R.C. Post, 'Managing Delibeation: The Quandary of Democratic Dialogue', *Ethics* 103 (1993), 654–78.

B. Poullain, 'Table Ronde', *La Cour de Cassation et la Constitution de la République* (Aix-en-Provence: Presses Universitaires d'Aix-en-Provence, 1995), 279–80.

U.K. Preuss, 'Patterns of Constitutional Evolution and Change in Eastern Europe', in J.J. Hesse and N. Johnson (eds), *Constitutional Policy and Change in Europe* (Oxford: Oxford University Press, 1995), 95–126.

J.K. Puar, 'Resituating Discourses of 'Whiteness' and 'Asianness' in Northern England: Second Generation Sikh Women and Constructions of Identity', *Socialist Review*, 94, 1–2 (1995), 21–54.

J. Quigley, 'The Soviet Union as a State under the Rule of Law: An Overview', *Cornell International Law Journal* 23 (1990), 205–25.

P.E. Quint, 'Free Speech and Private Law in German Constitutional Theory', *Maryland Law Review*, 48 (1989), 261–349.

D. Rabban, 'The Ahistorical Historian: Leonard Levy on Freedom of Expression in Early American History (1985), 795–856,' *Stanford Law Review* 37.

A. Rakhmilovich, 'The Constitutional Court of the Russian Federation: Recent Cases On Protecting the Freedom of Thought and Speech and Related Matters', *Review of Central and East European Law*, 22, 2 (1996), 129–34.

J.M. Ramseyer, 'The Puzzling (In)dependence of Courts: A Comparative Approach', *Journal of Legal Studies* 23 (1994), 721–52.

H. Rasmussen, *On Law and Policy in the European Court of Justice: A Comparative Study in Judicial Policymaking* (Boston, MA: Martinus Nijhoff, 1986).

H. Rasmussen, 'Between Self-Restraint and Activism: A Judicial Policy for the European Court', *European Law Review* 13 (1988), 28–38.

P. Reddaway, *Uncensored Russia: The Human Rights Movement in the Soviet Union* (New York: American Heritage Press, 1972).

C.A. Reich, 'The New Property', *Yale Law Journal* 73 (1964), 733–87.

W.M. Reisinger, A.H. Miller and V.L. Hesli, 'Russians' Views of the Law', *Journal of Communist Studies and Transition Politics*, 13, 3 (September 1997), 24–55.

J.C. Reitz, 'Constitutionalism and the Rule of Law: Theoretical Perspectives', in R.D. Grey (ed.), *Democratic Theory and Post-Communist Change* (New York: Prentice-Hall, 1996a), 111–43.

J.C. Reitz, 'Progress in Building Institutions for the Rule of Law', in R.D. Grey (ed.), *Democratic Theory and Post-Communist Change* (New York: Prentice-Hall, 1996b), 144–80.

D. Remnick, 'Letter from Moscow: The Tycoon and the Kremlin', *New Yorker*, 20 and 27 February 1995, 118–39.

T.S. Renoux and M. de Villiers, *Code Constitutionnel* (Paris: Libraire de la Cour de Cassation, 1994).

R. Rice, 'Four New Judges Appointed to European Court of Justice', *Financial Times*, 7 October 1994, 20.

R. Rice, 'Judges Fight Their Corner – The European Court of Justice is Under Fire', *Financial Times*, 22 August 1995, 10.

A. Rinken, *'Vorbemerkung zu Artikel 93 u. 94'*, in *Kommentar zum Grundgesetz fur die Bundesrepublik Deutschland [Reihe Alternativkommentare]*, Vol. 2 (Neuwied and Darmstadt: Hermann Luchterhand Verlag, 1984), 986–1035.

M.J. Roe, 'A Political Theory of American Corporate Finance', *Columbia Law Review* 91 (1991), 10–67.

C. Rossiter (ed.), *The Federalist Papers* (New York: New American Library, 1961).

D. Rousseau, *Droit du contentieux constitutionnel*, 3rd edn (Paris: Montchrestien, 1993).

D. Rousseau, *La justice constitutionnelle en Europe*, 2nd edn (Paris: Montchrestien, 1996).

J. Rubenstein, 'Dissent', in J. Cracraft (ed.), *The Soviet Union Today: An Interpretive Guide*, second revised and expanded edn (Chicago: University of Chicago Press, 1988), 64–76.

B.A. Ruble, *Money Sings: The Changing Politics of Urban Space in Post-Soviet Yaroslavl* (New York: Cambridge University Press, 1995).

B. Rudden, *Basic Community Cases* (Oxford: Clarendon, 1987).

O.G. Rumyantsev, 'The Present and Future of Russian Constitutional Order', *The Harriman Review*, 8, 2 (July 1995), 21–35.

W. Safran, *The French Polity*, 4th edn (New York: Longman Group, 1995).

G. Sahgal and N. Yuval-Davis, *Refusing Holy Orders: Women and Fundamentalism in Britain* (London: Virago Press, 1993).

A. Sajo, 'National Reports: Hungary', in K. Rokumoto (ed.), *The Social Role of the Legal Profession: Proceedings of the International Colloqium of the International Association of Legal Science* (Tokyo: International Center for Comparative Law and Politics, 1993), 131–50.

A. Sajo, 'Reading the Invisible Constitution: Judicial Review in Hungary', *Oxford Journal of Legal Studies* 15 (1995), 253–67.

A. Sajo, 'How the Rule of Law Killed Welfare Reform', *East European Constitutional Review* 5 (1996), 31–41.

R.H. Salisbury, 'Why No Corporatism in America?', in P.C. Schmitter and G. Lehmbruch, *Trends Toward Corporatist Intermediation* (Beverly Hills and London: Sage Publications, 1979), 213–30.

L. Salyer, *Laws as Harsh as Tigers* (Chapel Hill, NC: University of North Carolina Press, 1995).

T. Sandalow and E. Stein (eds), *Courts and Free Markets: Perspectives from the United States and Europe* (Oxford: Clarendon Press, 1982).

T. Scanlon, 'A Theory of Free Expression', *Philosophy and Public Affairs*, 1 (1972), 204–26.

R. Scannell, 'Recent Developments in Immigration Law', *Legal Action* (November 1990), 18–19.

R. Scannell, 'Recent Developments in Immigration Law', *Legal Action* (February 1992), 19–20.

F. Schauer, *Free Speech: A Philosophical Enquiry* (Cambridge: Cambridge University Press, 1982).

F. Schauer, 'Rules and the Rule of Law', *Harvard Journal of Law and Public Policy*, 14, 3 (1991), 645–94.

S.A. Scheingold, *The Rule of Law in European Integration: The Path of the Schuman Plan* (New Haven, CT: Yale University Press, 1965).

J.R. Schmidhauser, *Judges and Justices: The Federal Appellate Judiciary* (Boston, MA: Little, Brown, 1979).

J.R. Schmidhauser (ed.), *Comparative Judicial Systems: Challenging Frontiers in Conceptual and Empirical Analysis* (London: Butterworths, 1987).

F. Schockweiler, 'L'Indépendance et la Legitimate du Juge Dans L'Ordre Juridique Communautaire', *Revista Di Diritto Europea* 33 (1993), 671–80.

H. Schwartz, 'In Defense of Aiming High', *East European Constitutional Review* 1 (1992a), 25–8.

H. Schwartz, 'The New East European Constitutional Courts', *Michigan Journal of International Law* 13 (1992b), 741–85.

F. Sejersted, 'Democracy and the Rule of Law: Some Historical Experiences of Contradictions in the Striving for Good Government', in J. Elster and R. Slagstad (eds), *Constitutionalism and Democracy* (New York: Cambridge University Press, 1988), 131–52.

Seventh Conference of European Constitutional Courts, *Annuaire internationale de justice constitutionnelle: 1990* (Paris/Aix-en-Provence: Economica/Presses Universitaires d'Aix-en-Provence, 1991), 15–226.

I. Shapiro (ed.), *The Rule of Law*, Nomos XXXVI (New York: New York University Press, 1994).

M. Shapiro, 'Comparative Law and Comparative Politics', *Southern California Law Review*, 53, 2 (1980), 537–42.

M. Shapiro, *Courts: A Comparative and Political Analysis* (Chicago: University of Chicago Press, 1981).

M. Shapiro, 'Review of Rasmussen's "On Law and Policy in the European Court of Justice: A Comparative Study in Judicial Policymaking"', *American Journal of International Law* 81 (1987), 1007–11.

M. Shapiro, *Who Guards the Guardians?* (Athens, GA: University of Georgia Press, 1988).

M. Shapiro 'The European Court of Justice', in Alberta Spragia (ed.), *Europolitics* (Washington, DC: The Brookings Institute, 1990), 123–56.

M. Shapiro, 'The United States', in C.N. Tate and T. Vallinder (eds), *The Global Expansion of Judicial Power* (New York: New York University Press, 1995), 43–66.

M. Shapiro and A. Stone (eds), 'Special Issue: The New Constitutional Politics of Europe', *Comparative Political Studies* 26, 4 (January 1994), 397–561.

R. Sharlet, 'Pushikanis and the Withering Away of the Law in the USSR', in S. Fitzpatrick (ed.), *Cultural Revolution in Russia, 1928–1931* (Bloomington, IN: Indiana University Press, 1978), 169–88.

R. Sharlet, 'Soviet Legal Reform in Historical Context', *Columbia Journal of International Law*, 28 (1990), 5–17.

R. Sharlet, 'The New Russian Constitution and Its Political Impact', *Problems of Post-Communism*, 42, 1 (January–February 1995), 3–7.

L.I. Shelley, 'Legal Consciousness and the *Pravovoe Gosudarstvo*', in D.D. Barry (ed.), *Toward the 'Rule of Law' in Russia? Political and Legal Reform in the Transition Period* (Armonk, NY: M.E. Sharpe, 1992), 63–76.

M. Simmons, 'A Love so Dear and Yet so Far', *The Guardian*, 17 May 1995, 2–3.

T. Skocpol, 'Bringing the State Back In: Strategies of Analysis in Current Research', in Peter B. Evans *et al.* (eds), *Bringing the State Back In* (Cambridge, New York, New Rochelle, Melbourne, Sydney: Cambridge University Press, 1985), 3–37.

E.E. Slotnick, 'Federal Judicial Recruitment and Selection Research: A Review Essay', *Judicature* 71, 6 (1988), 317–24.

E.E. Slotnick (ed.), *Judicial Politics: Readings from Judicature* (Chicago: American Judicature Society, 1992).

G. Smith, *The European Court of Justice: Judges or Policy Makers?* (London: Bruges Group, 1990).

G.B. Smith, *The Soviet Procuracy and the Supervision of Administration* (Alphen aan den Rijn, Netherlands: Sijthoff & Noordhoff, 1978).

G.B. Smith, *Reforming the Russian Legal System* (New York: Cambridge University Press, 1996).

T. Smith, 'The Violation of Basic Rights in the Russian Federation', *East European Constitutional Review* 3, 3–4 (Summer–Fall 1994), 42–7.

P. Smyth, 'Cathedral Where Sins of EU States are Heard', *Irish Times* city edn, 20 May 1995, 8.

A. Sobchak, 'Democracy Seems to Be a Reality Now, If Not in Every Respect', *International Affairs (Moscow)*, #2 (1995), 6–10.

H. Söhn, 'Die Abstrakte Normenkontrolle', in Christian Starck (ed.), *Bundesverfassungsgericht und Grundgesetz*, Vol. 1 (Tubingen: J.C.B. Mohr (Paul Siebeck), 1976), 293–322.

W. Sokolewicz, 'The Relevance of Western Models for Constitution-Building in Poland', in J.J. Hesse and N. Johnson (eds), *Constitutional Policy and Change in Europe* (Oxford: Oxford University Press, 1995), 243–77.

P.H. Solomon, Jr, 'Soviet Criminal Justice and the Great Terror', *Slavic Review* 46, 3/4 (Fall/Winter 1987), 391–413.

P.H. Solomon, Jr, 'Legality in Soviet Political Culture: A Perspective On Gorbachev's Reforms', in N. Lampert and G.T. Rittersporn (eds), *Stalinism: Its Nature and Aftermath* (Armonk, NY: M.E. Sharpe, 1992), 260–87.

P.H. Solomon, Jr, 'The Limits of Legal Order in Post-Soviet Russia', *Post-Soviet Affairs* 11, 2 (1995), 89–114.

L. Solyom, '*Zum Geleit zu den Entscheidungen des Verfassungsgerichts der Republik Ungarn*', in G. Brunner und L. Sólyom (eds), *Verfassungs-gerichts-barkeit in Ungarn: Analysen und Entscheidungssammlung, 1990–1993* (Baden-Baden: Nomos Verlagsgesellschaft, 1995), 59–116.

Southall Black Sisters (eds), *Against the Grain: A Celebration of Survival and Struggle* (Southall, Middlesex: Southall Black Sisters, 1990).

E. Stein, 'Lawyers, Judges and the Making of a "Transnational Constitution"', *American Journal of International Law* 75 (1986), 1–27.

S. Sterett, *Creating Constitutionalism* (Ann Arbor, MI: University of Michigan Press, 1997).

S. Sterett, 'Judicial Review in Britain', *Comparative Political Studies*, 26, 4 (January 1994), 421–42.

K. Stern, 'Zweitbearbeitung Art. 93', in R. Dolzer (ed.), *Kommentar zum Bonner Grundgesetz* (Looseleaf Collection), Vol. 8 (Heidelberg, C.F. Müller Juristischer Verlag, 1982), 3–350.

R. Stewart, 'The Reformation of American Administrative Law', *Harvard Law Review* 88 (1975), 1667–1813.

A. Stone, 'Legal Constraints to Policy-Making: The *Conseil Constitutionnel* and the *Conseil d'État*', in P. Godt (ed.), *Policy-Making in France, From De Gaulle to Mitterrand* (London: Pinter; New York: Columbia University Press, 1989), 28–41.

A. Stone, 'The Birth and Development of Abstract Review in Western Europe: Constitutional Courts and Policy-Making in Western Europe', *Policy Studies Journal* 19 (1990), 81–95.

A.S. Stone, *The Birth of Judicial Politics in France: The Constitutional Council in Comparative Perspective* (New York: Oxford University Press, 1992).

A.S. Stone, 'Judging Socialist Reform: The Politics of Coordinate Construction in France and Germany', *Comparative Political Studies* 26 (1994a), 397–420.

A.S. Stone, 'Constructing a Supranational Constitution: The Reception and Enforcement of European Community Law By National Courts', National Science Foundation Grant Proposal (unpublished, 1994b).

A.S. Stone, 'Governing with Judges: The New Constitutionalism', in J. Hayward and E.C. Page (eds), *Governing the New Europe* (Oxford: Polity, 1995), 286–314.

A.S. Stone, 'Constitutional Dialogues in the European Community', in A.M. Slaughter, J. Weiler, and A.S. Stone (eds), *The European Court and the National Courts – Doctrine and Jurisprudence: Legal Change and Social Context* (Evanston, IL: Northwestern University Press, forthcoming 1998).

A.S. Stone and T. Brunell, 'Constructing a Supranational Constitution: Dispute Resolution and Governance in the European Community', *American Political Science Review* forthcoming (March 1998).

H.P. Stumpf, *American Judicial Politics* (San Diego, CA: Harcourt, Bruce, Jovanovich, 1988).

G. Stone, 'Restrictions of Speech Because of its Content: The Peculiar Case of Subject-Matter Restrictions', *University of Chicago Law Review*, 46 (1978), 81–115.

G. Stone, 'Content Regulation and the First Amendment', *William & Mary Law Review*, 25 (1983), 189–252.

I.P. Stotzky (ed.), *Transition to Democracy in Latin America: The Role of the Judiciary* (Boulder, CO: Westview Press, 1993).

H.P. Stumpf, *American Judicial Politics* (San Diego, CA: Harcourt, Brace, Jovanovich, 1988).

S. Stuth, '§76 Zulässigkeit des Antrags', in D. C. Umbach and T. Clemens (eds), *Bundesverfassungsgerichtsgesetz* (Heidelberg: C.F. Müller Juristischer Verlag, 1992), 982–91.

C. Summers, 'Comparisons in Labor Law: Sweden and the United States', *Industrial Relations Law Journal* 7 (1985), 1–27.

M. Sunkin, L. Bridges and G. Meszaros, *Judicial Review in Perspective: An Investigation of Trends in the Use and Operation of the Judicial Review Procedure in England and Wales* (London: The Public Law Project, 1993).

C. Sunstein, 'Something Old, Something New: Rights, Aspirations and State Action', *East European Constitutional Review* 1 (1992), 18–21.

C. Sunstein, 'Against Positive Rights: Why social and economic rights don't belong in the new constitutions', *East European Constitutional Review* 2 (1993a), 35–8.

C. Sunstein, *The Partial Constitution* (Cambridge, MA: Harvard University Press, 1993b).

C.N. Tate, 'Judicial Institutions in Cross-National Perspective: Toward Integrating Courts into the Comparative Study of Politics' in J. Schmidhauser, *Comparative Judicial Systems* (Boston, MA: Butterworths, 1987), 7–33.

C.N. Tate, and T. Vallinder (eds), *The Global Expansion of Judicial Power* (New York: New York University Press, 1995).

M. Tatu, *Power in the Kremlin: From Khrushchev to Kosygin* (New York: Viking, 1968).

J. Teagarden, 'Say It Simple', *Victor* 40-0138 (1942).

H. Teune, 'Comparing Countries: Lessons Learned', in E. Oyen (ed.), *Comparative Methodology: Theory and Practice in International Social Research* (Newbury Park, CA: Sage, 1990), 38–62.

S.C. Thaman, 'Trial By Jury and the Constitutional Rights of the Accused in Russia', *East European Constitutional Review*, 4, 1 (Winter 1995), 77–80.

R.L. Tokes (ed.), *Dissent in the USSR: Politics, Ideology and People* (Baltimore, MD: Johns Hopkins University Press, 1975).

L. H. Tribe, *American Constitutional Law*, 2nd edn (Mineola, NY: Foundation Press, 1988).

J. Tully, *Strange Multiplicity: Constitutionalism in an Age of Diversity* (New York: Cambridge University Press, 1995).

University of Chicago Legal Forum, *Europe and America in 1992 and Beyond: Common Problems … Common Solutions?* (Chicago: University of Chicago Press, 1992).

UPI, 'International Section', *United Press International* (December 3, 1983), AM Cycle edn: 1.

A. Van Hamme, 'The European Court of Justice', in L. Hurwitz and C. Lequesne (eds), *The State of the European Community* (Boulder, Co: Lynne Rienner, 1991), 45–63.

N.T. Vedernikov and O.N. Vedernikova, 'Problems of Constitutional Jurisprudence and the Formulation of a "Rule of Law" State in Russia', *Saint Louis University Law Journal* 38 (Summer 1994), 907–13.

M.L. Volcansek, *Judicial Politics in Europe* (New York: Peter Lang, 1986).

M.L. Volcansek, 'Judges, Courts and Policy-Making in Western Europe', *West European Politics* 15, 3 (1992a), 1–8.

M.L. Volcansek, 'The European Court of Justice: Supranational Policy-Making', *West European Politics* 15, 3 (1992b), 109–21.

M.L. Volcansek, 'Judicial Creativity: The European Court of Justice and a Bill of Rights for the Community', Annual Meeting of the Comparative Judicial Politics Research Group of the International Political Science Association, Santa Fe, August 1993.

M.L. Volcansek, and J.L. Lafon, *Judicial Selection: The Cross-Evolution of French and American Practices* (New York: Greenwood Press, 1988).

S. Walker, *Hate Speech: The History of an American Controversy* (Lincoln, NE: University of Nebraska Press, 1994).

S. Walters, 'Crackdown on Migrant Marriages', *The Sun*, 2 August 1995.

A. Weber, 'Le contrôle juridictionnel de la constitutionnalité des lois dans les pays d'Europe Occidentale', *Annuaire internationale de justice constitutionnelle: 1985* (Paris/Aix-en-Provence: Economica/Presses Universitaires d'Aix-en-Provence, 1986), 39–76.

M. Weber, *Max Weber on Law in Economy and Society* (Cambridge, MA: Harvard University Press, 1954) [M. Rheinstein (ed.), E. Shils and M. Rheinstein, translators from M. Weber, *Wirtschaft und Gesellschaft*, 2nd edn (Tubingen: Mohr, 1925)].

M. Weber, *Economy and Society: An Outline of Interpretive Sociology*, 2 vols, ed. by Guenther Roth and Claus Wittich (Berkeley, CA: University of California Press, 1979).

R.P. Weber, *Basic Content Analysis*, 2nd edn (Beverly Hills, CA: Sage, 1990).

J.H.H. Weiler, 'Eurocracy and Distrust: Some Questions Concerning the Role of the European Court of Justice in the Protection of Fundamental Human Rights Within the Legal Order of the European Communities', *Washington Law Review* 61 (1986), 1103–42.

J.H.H. Weiler, 'A Quiet Revolution: The European Court of Justice and Its Interlocutors', *Comparative Political Studies* 26 (1994), 510–34.

J.H.H. Weiler and N.J.S. Lockhart, '"Taking Rights Seriously" Seriously: The European Court and its Fundamental Rights Jurisprudence – Part 1', *Common Market Law Review* 32 (1995), 51–94.

J. Weinstein, 'A Constitutional Roundup to the Regulation of Campus Hate Speech', *Wayne Law Review*, 38 (1991), 163–247.

M. Westlake, *A Modern Guide to the European Parliament* (London: Pinter, 1994).

S. Wilks and M. Wright, 'The Comparative Context of Japanese Political Economy', in S. Wilks and M. Wright (eds), *The Promotion and Regulation of Industry in Japan* (New York: St Martin's Press, 1991), 11–31.

J.P. Willerton, *Patronage and Politics in the USSR* (New York: Cambridge University Press, 1992).

D. Wilsford, *Doctors and the State – The Politics of Health Care in France and the United States* (Durham, NC, and London: Duke University Press, 1991).

F.L. Wilson, 'French Interest Group Politics: Pluralist or Neocorporatist?', *American Political Science Review* 77 (1983), 895–910.

F.L. Wilson, 'Reply to Keeler', *American Political Science Review*, 79 (1985), 822–3.

Wolverhampton Express and Star, 'Immigration 'vendetta' claim by wife', 31 July 1992.

Wolverhampton Express and Star, 'Immigrant wins court test case', 11 December 1993.

Wolverhampton Express and Star, 'Wife fights UK ban on her husband', 10 May 1994a.

Wolverhampton Express and Star, 'Wanted: two happy endings', 31 December 1994b.

B. Woodward and S. Armstrong, *The Brethren: Inside the Supreme Court* (New York: Avon, 1981).

H. Woolf, *Protection of the Public: A New Challenge* (London: Stevens & Sons, 1990).

R.S. Wortman, *The Development of a Russian Legal Consciousness* (Chicago: University of Chicago Press, 1976).

K. Yamamura and Y. Yasuba (eds), *The Political Economy of Japan: The Domestic Transformation*, vol. 1 (Stanford, CA: Stanford University Press, 1987).

G. Zagrebelsky, 'La doctrine du droit vivant', *Annuaire international de justice constitutionnelle: 1986* (Paris/Aix-en-Provence: Economica/Presses Universitaires d'Aix-en-Provence, 1987), 55–77.

J. Zysman, *Governments, Markets, and Growth* (Ithaca, NY: Cornell University Press, 1983).

Index

a posteriori review   81
a priori review   65, 87
absence of women on ECJ   143, 144, 169
abstract review   5, 10–12, 23–4, 28, 30, 32, 45, 52, 56, 58, 62–88, 199, 202, 211
advisory opinions   9, 10, 66, 82
advokaty   178
affirmative action   101
Alber, MEP, AG of ECJ   165
American judicial review   9
auto-limitation   48
autonomy of state   77

Bahlman, Kai, Judge at ECJ   152
Bosco, Giancito, Judge at ECJ   154, 158
Brilmayer, Lea   81
British judges   158

Canadian Charter   98, 100, 103, 105, 113
Capotorti, Francesco, AG at ECJ   154, 157
Cappelletti, Mauro   69
cases and controversies   66
Chloros, Alexandros, Judge at ECJ   154, 159
combined proportional and single district electoral system   51
common law and civil law   177, 181, 187, 207
common law constitutional judges   213
comparative law   2, 73–4, 120, 193–4
concepts of the state   74
concrete review   11, 13–14, 24, 29, 30, 32, 37, 54, 56, 64, 68, 71, 79–81, 83, 85–6
constitutional
    case law   19

complaint   11, 14, 24, 29, 30, 32–6, 55–8, 87
courts   8, 10, 11, 14–15, 18, 20, 22–4, 27, 31, 33–4, 36, 40, 71, 82–3, 196, 201, 211
decisionmaking   19–21, 24–7, 31–2, 40
dialogue   4–7, 8–41, 43
judges   10, 21, 23, 26–7, 29, 35–36, 40
review   xvii, 9–10, 19, 31, 32, 67, 79, 120 (*see also* judicial review)
rights   10, 15–18, 20–1, 27, 29, 33
structure   96
system   95, 101, 113–14
constitutionalism   119–20
constitutionalization   32–3, 35, 37
content analysis   7, 173, 182–3, 190
Convention on the Elimination of All Forms of Racial Discrimination (CERD) 99–100, 109–10
corporatism   72, 76–8, 80, 87
Cosmas, Georgios, AG at ECJ   153, 159
Council of Europe   165–66
court cases
    Canada: *Regina* v. *Keegstra* (1990) 90, 93, 95–6, 99–104, 113–14; *Regina* v. *Oakes* (1986)   92, 98, 108
    European Court of Human Rights (ECHR): *Jersild* v. *Denmark* (1994)   109–10, 113–14
    Federal Republic of Germany: First Abortion Case (1975) 28, 47, 52; Láth Free Speech Case   33–5; Numerus Clausus I (1972)   46; Party Finance Cases   50; Second Abortion Case (1993)   28–9;

court cases (*Cont.*)
  University Governance Case
    (1973) 30–1
  Great Britain: *Abdulaziz, Cabales
    and Balkandali* v. *United
    Kingdom* (1995) 126–7; *R* v.
    *Immigration Appeal Tribunal
    ex p. Amin (1992)* 131, 133;
    R. v. *Immigration Appeal
    Tribunal ex p. Begum* (1995)
    138; *R.* v. *Immigration Appeal
    Tribunal ex p. Iqbal* (1993)
    125, 128, 129, 131; *R.* v.
    *Immigration Appeal Tribunal,
    ex p. Kumar* (1986) 128; *R.*
    v. *Immigration Appeal
    Tribunal ex p. Singh* (1990)
    129
  Hungary: Compensation Cases
    (1990, 1991) 49, 52; Paternity
    Case (1991) 55; Retroactive
    Justice Case (1993) 49;
    Welfare Case (1995) 52
  Italy: Pension Cases 29–30;
    Right to Counsel 36–7
  Spain: Free Speech Cases 35–6
  United States: *Brandenburg* v.
    Ohio (1969) 92; *Marburg* v.
    Madison (1803) 66, 211,
    213; *RAV* v. *City of St. Paul,
    Minnesota* (1992) 90, 94, 96,
    101, 102, 113; *Watts* v. *United
    States* (1969) 96, 108
courts, definition of 82
courts, ideal prototype of 169–70
courts and politics xiii, 1, 2
critical legal studies 2
cultural stereotypes 125
culture 120

Da Cruz Vilaça, José, AG at ECJ
    154, 160
Damaöka, Mirjan 63
Däubler-Gmelin, Herta 50
Delvaux, Louis, Judge at ECJ 156
Diez de Valesco Vellejo, Manuel,
    Judge at ECJ 152, 160
discourse of European law,
    transformation in xiv–xv

division of powers hypothesis
    196–7, 200–5, 210
doctrinal scholarship (*la Doctrine*)
    xii
Donner, Andreas, President of ECJ
    154, 155, 170
Due, Ole, President of ECJ 155,
    158, 160
Dutheillet de Lamonthe, Alain,
    Judge at ECJ 154, 170

economic and social rights 42, 44,
    46
Edward, David, Judge at ECJ 158,
    171
Elmer, Michael, AG at ECJ 153
European
  Coal and Steel Community 145,
    151
  Community/European Union:
    constitution 145, 165;
    Council of Ministers 144;
    Court of First Instance 146,
    148, 154, 156, 158, 160;
    democracy deficit 144; 1996
    intergovernmental conference
    163, 166, 167, 171
  Convention on Human Rights
    105, 109, 112, 114–16, 200–2,
    205
  Court of Human Rights 3, 4,
    109, 122, 126, 127, 156, 165,
    166
  Court of Justice 3, 4, 122, 136,
    137, 139, 200, 206, 216, 219;
    advocates general 144, 146,
    147, 151, 153, 157, 165;
    Austria's appointments to
    160; Belgium's appointments
    to 156; c.f. U.S. Supreme
    Court 144–8; *cabinet* 147;
    délibéré 147; Denmark's
    appointments to 158;
    division of powers hypothesis
    196, 197, 200–5, 210; doctrine
    of direct effect 145; doctrine
    of supremacy 145; euro-
    sceptics 168; extra members
    151: Finland's appointments

to 160; France's appointments to 156; and gender 163; Germany's appointments to 157; Greece's appointments to 159; human rights cases 145; Irish appointments to 159; Italy's appointments to 157; judicial independence and 161, 166, 168; judgments 146; *juge-rapporteur* 155, 146; language 147; Luxembourg's appointments to 156; Member State selection procedure for judges 143, 148, 156, 159, 161–4; members, characteristics 151, 154; Netherlands appointments to 156; oral argument 144, 150; Portugal's appointments to 160; President 144, 155; *référendaires* 147, 150, 157, 171; secrecy 144, 149, 163, 169; Spain's appointments to 160; Sweden's appointments to 161, 166; terms 146; turnover 147; UK appointments to 158

Free Trade Area Court 161
Parliament 144, 154, 162–5, 167–8, 171; direct election of 164; and judicial selection 143, 165–76; written questions 165–6
Everling, Ulrich, Judge at ECJ 157

federalism hypothesis 194–8, 200, 203
Feld, Werner 149, 171
Fennelly, Nial, AG at ECJ 153
fighting words 94, 111, 116
First Amendment of the US Constitution 93, 97–8, 100, 104, 116–17
Fourteenth Amendment of the US Constitution 93, 97
freedom of speech 89, 91, 93, 95–100, 102–5, 107–17, 217–18

French
 Constitution 66, 84
 Constitutional Council 11, 12, 15, 22, 24, 25, 27, 37–39, 82, 162
 Council of State (*Conseil d'État*) 84, 148, 154, 157
 ministère publique 84
 President 76, 204
 Prime Minister 76, 204
 Supreme Court (*Cour de Cassation*) 36–7, 156–7

Gand, Joseph, AG at ECJ 170
German
 Basic Law 46, 49, 54
 Bundesrat 50
 Bundestag 45, 47, 48, 50–52
 Constitution 66
 Federal Constitutional Court 11–12, 22, 28, 30, 31, 33, 34, 46–8, 50–2, 54, 56–7, 61, 83, 162, 199, 216
 Federal Supreme Court 54
 federal system 51
 Free Democratic Party 52
 Social Democratic Party 52
Glinne, MEP 165
Grévisse, Fernand, Judge at ECJ 151, 170
Gulmann, Claus, Judge and AG at ECJ 154, 159

Hallstein, President of European Commission 170
Hammes, President of ECJ 155, 170
hate speech 90, 92, 94, 96–8, 102–5, 107–8, 110, 112, 114–15, 120
Hirsch, Martin 50
human rights 18
Hungarian
 Communist Party 44, 53
 Constitution (1949) 43–4, 46, 60
 Constitution (1989) 42–3, 45, 49
 Constitutional Council (communist era) 44, 53
 Constitutional Court 42–50, 52–3, 55, 58–61

Hungarian (*Cont.*)
  judicial review, institutional design
    of 44–7, 55–9
  Parliament (communist and post-
    communist eras) 43–4,
    47–52
  Presidential Council (communist
    era) 44
  unitary system 51

ideology 73, 74, 201
immigration 120–2, 141
  laws 138, 142
  lawyers 131
  officials 125, 128–30, 136
  policy 122, 140
  regulation 127
  representatives 137, 141
  rules 124
  service 134
  tribunals 128, 131
individual rights 202, 206, 209
individualism 90, 101–2, 104–5
institutionalism 73
integation theory xi
interdisciplinary studies 3
international human rights 193
International Court of Justice 156
International Human Rights
    Treaties 99, 101, 104
Italian Constitutional Court 11, 12,
    22, 29–30, 36–7, 65

Jacobs, Francis, AG at ECJ 154,
    158
Jann, Peter, Judge at ECJ 160
Joliet, René, Judge at ECJ 156,
    170
judicial
  activism 1
  independence 161, 168
  opinions 193
  review 3, 7, 121–2, 162, 194–201,
    203–7, 209–11, 214–15,
    217–18 (*see also*
    constitutional review)
  review, factors explaining its
    emergence 193–219
  selection xvi, 143, 151, 161–4

Kakouris, Constantinos, Judge at
    ECJ 159, 170
konkrete Normenkontrolle (concrete
    control of norms) 87
Koopmans, Tijmen, Judge at ECJ
    150
Kutscher, Hans, President of ECJ
    155

La Pergola, Antonio, Judge at ECJ
    154
Lagrange, Maurice, AG at ECJ
    153, 157, 170
law-governed state 173, 181
legal
  community 2, 178, 180–3, 185–6,
    190
  nihilism 180–1, 185–6
  orientations 173, 179–91
Legal Realists 2
Léger, Phillipe, AG at ECJ 170
legislative-reservation clauses 54
legitimacy of courts generally 70,
    181
legitimacy of judicial review xvii, 7,
    69–71, 81–4, 193–219
liberal ideology 74–5
Lipset, Martin 100–4
litigiousness 181

Mackenzie Stuart, Lord Alexander
    John, President of ECJ 155,
    158, 170
Mancini, Federico, Judge and AG at
    ECJ 154–5, 157
marriage
  arranged 124, 129, 133–5, 141
  Asian 121
  cases 122, 138
  English 121
  genuine 133
  primary purpose of 125, 128–31,
    133, 135–6, 138–40
Marshall, John (Chief Justice of US
    Supreme Court) 66, 145
Mayras, Henri, AG at ECJ
    170
mechanisms for the protection of
    human rights 8

Mertens de Wilmars, Jos., President of ECJ 155–7, 159
Moitinho de Almeida, José, Judge at ECJ 160
motion of unconstitutionality (*motion d´irrecevabilité*) 25

national states 119, 120
natural law 87
new institutionalism 5, 63, 71, 74

objective law or right (*objectives Recht*) 83–5
O'Dalaigh, Cearbhall, Judge at ECJ 154, 171
O'Higgins, Aindrias, Judge at ECJ 154
ordinary courts of law (regular judiciary) 5, 53–8
ordinary judges 9, 33, 35–7
Ortega, Medina, MEP 166

Pangalos, President of EU Council 165–6
parens patriae suits 67, 68
paternalism 81, 90, 101–2, 104–5
Pilotti, Massimo, President of ECJ 154–5
pluralism 73
pluralist structure 78
political and civil rights 44
political economy 71–8
  fit with systems of judicial review 78–84
political science/law divide xi–xiv, xv–xvi, 1, 3–4
politicization of courts 64, 85
popular complaint 47, 56–7
positive law 186, 188–9
post-Soviet Russia 172, 182
pravovoe gosudarstvo 173–4, 188–90
public opinion, judicial responsiveness to 161

race discrimination 126
racist hate speech 94, 99, 104, 117
Ragnemalm, Hans, Judge at ECJ 161
Rechtsstaat 188, 196, 207

Reise, Otto, Judge at ECJ 170
representativeness of judges 169
rights 178, 181, 187–89, 191
Rodríguez Iglesias, Gil Carlos, President of ECJ 154–5, 160, 170
Roemer, Karl, AG at ECJ 153–54, 157
Rogalla, Dieter, MEP 165
Rozès, Simone, AG at ECJ 157, 164
Ruiz-Jarabo Colomer, Damasco, AG at ECJ 153
rule of law 173, 175, 179–80, 183–5, 188, 195, 207–9
Russian
  Constitutional Court 176, 204
  judiciary 176
  legal orientations 172–92

Scheingold, Stuart 149
Schockweiler, Fernand, Judge at ECJ 167
Sevon, Leif, Judge at ECJ 160
sex discrimination 126, 127
Shapiro, Martin 70, 82
Sieglerschmidt, MEP 165
Single European Act 164
Slynn, Sir Gordon, Judge and AG at ECJ 151, 154, 158, 167, 171
soft constitutional judicial review 202
Sólyom, László 46, 49, 51, 55
Sørensen, Max, Judge at ECJ 158
Spanish Constitutional Tribunal 11, 12, 22, 35, 36
standing of official parties – US law 67–8
state structure 72–3, 75–8
Stein, Eric 111, 118
Stone Sweet, Alec 70, 82
strict guidelines of interpretation 37–9
strong states 72, 80
subjective law or right (*subjectives Recht*) 83
Supreme Court of Canada 89, 91, 95, 97, 99, 100, 102, 103, 108, 115

Talmud   xii
third legislative chamber   69, 70
Touffait, Adolphe, Judge at ECJ
   154
Trabucchi, Alberto, ECJ   151, 154
transitions toward democracy and
   the rule of law   2
transnational courts   4
Treaty of Paris   157
Treaty of Rome   166
   Article 167   143
   Article 177   146

United States
   Constitution   66, 96, 98, 107
   Supreme Court   1, 10, 68–70, 89,
      91, 97–8, 115, 144, 146–8, 154,
      162–3, 166–7
Universal Declaration of Human
   Rights   99, 109, 117

van Gerven, Walter, AG at ECJ
   156
Vandemeulebroucke, Jaak, MEP
   166
Verfassungsbeschwerden
   (constitutional complaints)   87

Waigel, Theodor   51
Warner, Jean Pierre, Judge at ECJ
   158
Wathelet, Melchior, Judge at ECJ
   156, 166
weak states   72, 80
Westminster first-past-the-post
   electoral system   51

yuriskonsulty   178

Zuleeg, Manfred, Judge at ECJ
   157